I SEE WHAT YOU MEAN

Persuasive Business Communication

D. Joel Whalen

SAGE Publications
International Educational and Professional Publisher
Thousand Oaks London New Delhi

For information address:

SAGE Publications, Inc.
2455 Teller Road
Thousand Oaks, California 91320
E-mail: order@sagepub.com

SAGE Publications Ltd.
6 Bonhill Street
London EC2A 4PU
United Kingdom

SAGE Publications India Pvt. Ltd.
M-32 Market
Greater Kailash I
New Delhi 110 048 India

Printed in the United States of America

Library of Congress Cataloging-in-Publication Data

Whalen, D. Joel.
    I see what you mean: Persuasive business communication / author,
D. Joel Whalen.
        p. cm.
    Includes bibliographical references and index.
    ISBN 0-7619-0030-6 (cloth: alk. paper). — ISBN 0-7619-0031-4 (pbk. :
alk. paper)
    1. Business communication. I. Title.
HF5718.W467 1996
650.1'3—dc20   95-32533

This book is printed on acid-free paper.

        98 99 10 9 8 7 6 5 4

Sage Production Editor: Astrid Virding
Sage Typesetter: Danielle Dillahunt

Over the past 15 years, through classroom teaching and seminars, Joel Whalen has shown thousands of people how to be more successful by being more persuasive. Now, that knowledge is in this book—a happy marriage of science and street-smarts designed to help you get what you want. Read this book and you will hear people say, "I see what you mean."

- Create a high-impact presentation in five minutes
- Increase your credibility
- Customize your message for different audiences
- Boost your memos' and reports' readability
- Manage speech anxiety/stage fright before audiences of five or 5,000; and when telephoning people you hate to call
- Design high-impact slides and overheads
- Persuade angry bosses and customers
- Add an important layer of communications skill to your graduate business training in analysis and planning

"I feel your pain."—a politician

"I hear what you're saying."—a telemarketer

"I see what you mean."—a communicator

List of words/name used in this book that have been copyrighted

Big Ideas	Presenter
Einstein's Time Shift	Question Opening
Emotional Buyer	SA/SF
Hand-off	Sensory Mode
Host	Tell 'em
John-the-Baptist	The Cold Closing
Nichol's Two Things	

Contents

This book has selected the best nuggets of scientific knowledge discovered in the mines of persuasive communication over the past 50 years.

Master practical communication techniques proven to work by thousands of Chicagoland businesspeople.

Enjoy communication effectiveness at meetings, in job interviews, in chats over coffee, and on voice mail.

Create a high-impact presentation in five minutes.

Manage stage fright before audiences of five or 5,000 people; and when phoning people you hate to call.

See how you can manage angry bosses and customers.

Learn simple, straightforward, and practical approaches to tapping into your listener's memory.

Add an important layer of communication skill to your graduate business training in analysis and planning.

Hear people say, "I see what you mean."

Companies across America have turned the communications temperature up. In today's workplace, diverse groups of people find themselves laboring together in teams, given less time and fewer resources. You'll find that this book's communication approaches can relieve the pain and stress caused by TQM, TQA, ISO 9000, and reengineering.

Until now, a treasure house of communication psychology was hidden away in proceedings papers and scientific journals; written in arcane terms, theories, and statistics—unavailable and unreadable to businesspeople.

You see, academic scholars are like miners, digging in deep, dark shafts under the earth, seeking nuggets of knowledge. When we find a bright pebble of an idea we dust it off and excitedly scurry about our tunnels showing each other what we've found. Then, we go back to prospecting in the mine. Unfortunately, all too often the valuable discoveries stay in the academic substrata, rarely reaching the surface—where businesspeople are waiting for ideas they can use. This book gives you those ideas.

Rich, scientific ore from hundreds of journal articles was processed, refined, and translated through the author's 30 years in sales and advertising. The result is a happy marriage of science and street-smarts designed to help you get what you want by being more persuasive.

Read it and when you speak people will say, "I see what you mean."

Acknowledgments

Thanks to my editor, Tina M. Ricca, for straining out errors, tightening, polishing, and helping me make sense.

Robert E. Pitts had the first vision of what effective business communication could be and gave this project early support. I am indebted to faculty at DePaul for supporting Effective Communication (KGSB 499): Ronald Patten, Robert O'Keefe, Joan Junkus, Bruce Newman, Ray Coye, Roger Baran, Dan Koys, Steve Kelly, and my teaching partners, Dave Drehmer and Laura Pincus, and to Ralph Iennarella.

Communication science and persuasion psychology came from early mentors, including Don Nichols, Gary Heald, Barbara Walker, Don Ungurait, Wayne Minick, Ed Wotring, and Ed Forrest. Street savvy came from advertising, broadcasting executives, politicians, and clients—including Senator George Firestone, Senator Bill Grant, Greg Farmer, Geno Milner, Don Keyes, Buzz Kilman, Karen Randolph, Barry Rundle, Chip Young, my brother Bob, Ken Platt, and all the guys I sold cars with at Oakland Toyota "South Florida's Volume Leader—We Will Not be Undersold." Ken Thulin taught me that Volkswagen Beetles are air cooled—I like knowing that.

Special thanks to the Kellstadt Fellows (Kell Fells): dedicated teachers, fearless test pilots, and superb communicators all—they make Effective Communication work.

Kell Fells 1994-1995

Tina M. Ricca, Head Kell Fell

Paula Koch, Administrator

Ed Adams

Joe Armstrong

Inga Briedis

Jennifer Cole

Mary Ann Cross

Patrice Crubaugh

Harold Fischer

Mike Foster

Mark Greshmen

Amanda Hull

Monica Jones

Kate O'Brien

Margaret O'Brien

Gary Rabishaw

Mike Reynolds

Carla Rydberg

Bill Sullivan

Ron Watt

Ruth White

Chip Young

Mark Zaugra

And to the students in Effective Communication and Persuasive Business Communication at the Kellstadt Graduate School of Business, DePaul University: They lived this book.

Preface

Today, after managers have performed analyses and designed their plans, they have still more work to do. Business leaders must construct a communications strategy designed to sell their plans.

- To compete effectively for scarce and shrinking resources, managers must have superior persuasive communication skills in packaging their ideas into high-impact messages.
- To communicate, you must learn to think like your listener; you must see your plan through another person's eyes.
- You must work with your fear of speaking, fear of other people, and fear of yourself and break through into a higher, more powerful plane of effective communication with love for yourself, for other people, and for sharing your ideas.

This book is dedicated to helping people who seek to help themselves and others through effective communication.

Diversity Challenges Communication

When you want to advance your ideas through today's new organization, you must convince others to support your plans, to buy in. In the typical corporation, decisions are made by a diverse group of experts. It is not unusual for engineers, financial analysts, marketing people, purchasing managers, and material specialists to be brought together on decision teams. Now, teams are coalitions of people from a variety of technical, social, racial, ethnic, and functional backgrounds.

YOU MUST REENGINEER YOUR
APPROACH TO COMMUNICATION

Other current business phenomena such as *Reengineering, TQA, TQM,* and *ISO 9000* have forced groups of people with disparate backgrounds to work together. The spread of new communication technologies, like e-mail and Collaborative Groupware Software, forces managers to send messages through faceless, voiceless, time-shifting pathways. These business trends have changed the way businesspeople must communicate and have brought rich opportunities to those of us who are facile and trained in communication—and to those people who are willing to take on further training to meet this new communications environment.

GREAT COMMUNICATORS ARE MADE, NOT BORN

People think that driving a car, making love, playing golf, and communicating are things that they can do naturally—they're inborn, no lessons are necessary, we "just do it." In fact, many fine communicators have little or no formal training. Other people, who are poor or barely adequate communicators, have had formal training. The truth is that trained technique is superior to natural inclinations. Lessons do pay off.

Of course, we can't apologize for the poor training a person has received; nor can we expect to awaken a rich, subterranean river of communication talent lying dormant within you. Rather, we've spent the past decade developing a systematic approach to training. The core of that training is in this book.

A UNIQUE APPROACH TO
PERSUASIVE BUSINESS COMMUNICATION

I have taken my academic training—20 years as a professional communicator in broadcasting, advertising, politics, sales, and consulting—and applied it to designing a bold, innovative training program for the students at DePaul University's Kellstadt Graduate School of Business (KGSB).

Course development began in a case analysis class, Decisions in Marketing Management (KGSB 515). In this first step, students were taught communications techniques along with such standard topics as how to manipulate marketing models. Through Constant Process Improvement (and all too much Edisonian trial-and-error experimentation), we developed several methods that dramatically improved the students' performance. Students, faculty, and the administration were enthusiastic about the results.

ONE CLASS CONCENTRATING ON
PERSUASIVE BUSINESS COMMUNICATION

The next logical step was to launch a single course devoted exclusively to training students in persuasive communication. In the spring of 1992, the first group of 40 students took an experimental course called Persuasive Business Communications (MKT 798)—designed to enhance their knowledge and build skills in effective, influential business communication. From the very first class it was clear that we were on to something special in graduate education. The students' response was clear and consistent. These managers by day and MBA candidates at night were fascinated by persuasion psychology and presentation technique. More important, the students told me that they liked a class that taught them ideas and skills that they could put to work the next day. Persuasive Business Communication was giving our students new confidence in dealing with others and a competitive edge at work.

People Finding Success
Through Effective Communication

CASE HISTORIES

Here are stories of how four people who may be just like you (average age, 27-32 years old; business experience, five to seven years) increased their communication power.

• *A 27-year-old man finds that his graduate training in business is not helping him break out of his dull, pension fund management job at the world's largest accounting/consulting firm. He is full of ideas, but the senior managers don't listen to him. After he completes Persuasive Business Communication (KGSB 798) training in message packaging and credibility building, his supervisors start to listen to his marketing ideas with new respect. Opportunities begin to open for him, but he finds that the corporate environment is strangling his entrepreneurial spirit. He is now designing his own company.*

• As she is midway through Persuasive Business Communication (KGSB 798), the Executive Director of a major health foundation has to present complex, federal financial reports to a tough audience. In 10 days she'll stand before her board of directors—who range from Chief Financial Officers of Fortune *100 companies to well-heeled but financially naive benefactors. Using techniques in communicating quantitative data to conceptually brained people (left-brain information to right-brained people), her talk is geared to both types of board members. The "quant-jocks" enjoy the overview supported by precise data-driven insight, and the "data-impaired" members enjoy a new depth of understanding. Her presentation is a smash hit and, through her success, she enjoys a new status with her board and president.*

• An African American accountant with a major Midwestern utility is bored with his job but likes his company. He believes that better meeting facilitation and communication skills will ignite advancement for him. Quickly after completing Persuasive Business Communication (KGSB 798), he seizes the opportunity to chair a cross-departmental briefing session (created at his suggestion). His meeting facilitation receives rave reviews from his supervisor and his supervisor's supervisor. They see this accountant in a new light. His star is on the rise.

• A 31-year-old executive with the world's largest computer manufacturer experiences chronic and debilitating speech anxiety and stage fright. She refuses opportunities to speak before groups within the company or to customer groups—although she knows that career advancement and promotions come out of those meetings. Her technical abilities are high and she has a strong desire to share her ideas with others, but she believes that her speech anxiety is keeping her from faster advancement within the firm. Through Persuasive Business Communication (KGSB 798) she learns how to manage her speech anxiety, how to build open relationships with her audiences, and how to package her ideas in a dynamic and memorable presentation. After the training, her stage fright and speech anxiety dimin-

ish to a manageable level, and by applying the **anxiety** **management and** **presentation techniques** *she has learned that speaking before groups becomes a rewarding and empowering experience for her.*

The success of *Persuasive Business Communication* led to the development of the book you are holding now. This book is designed to support your learning experience and personal growth as an effective communicator.

The Voice in Your Head

As you read this book, you'll hear a voice in your head—it's me, your author (Joel Whalen). I'll be sharing ideas with you about effective communication. You'll be receiving pictures, sounds, feelings, and other sensations as we communicate with each other. In exchange, you will join me in this communications experience as you react to the ideas presented and sometimes engage me in active conversation in your mind. I expect you to join me in an interactive dialogue. This may be a unique experience for you: reading the words of an author who expects an active dialogue with you, without you actually answering back—because, of course, I can't hear your voice. Some may be disconcerted at this fantastical notion of two-way communication via a book. I am not. You see, I've spent decades in radio and television, sitting alone in a soundproof booth talking into a microphone, speaking to an audience that could not speak back. This type of communication seems natural and second nature.

TWENTY YEARS TALKING TO
PEOPLE WHO DON'T TALK BACK

I got my first disc jockey job in 1963 on weekends at WWIL-AM & FM Ft. Lauderdale (I was 15 years old). How could a child get a job as a disc jockey? Good fortune and stubborn determination: Each Saturday morning WWIL gave two hours of airtime to local kids to run their own radio show. Some guys from my high school were the announcers and for two glorious hours their voices were spat about the South Florida radio airwaves. To me there was no greater glory, no higher calling, than being a radio announcer; sitting in a nest of complex controls, knobs, dials, lights, switches, patch cords, and sound machines. The announcer was the captain of a vast electronic ship. Heady stuff to a gadget-freak like me. But the real fascination was in the power of communication; as he keyed open the mike, speaking in rounded, perfectly articulated tones, the announcer became one with thousands of other people, communicating with the three counties of South Florida (Dade, Broward, and West Palm Beach).

The energy was overwhelming; the power was mystical. I knew from the first time I stood at the back of that studio that I had to sit in the announcer's chair and fly that ship.

At noon, after the other kids left, I hung back, finding little services I could provide for the regular staff announcers: clearing the endless yellow river of paper from the AP and UPI teletypes, making coffee, filing records, answering the telephone. I'd find anything to do to be useful. Then, after weeks of waiting, the doors of opportunity swung wide . . . the FM announcer did not show up and Jay Carlson, the AM announcer (who was also the program director in charge of the announcing staff), was frantically running between the two studios keeping the records spinning—like the guy on the *Ed Sullivan Show* spinning pie plates. I said to Jay, "I can run the records in FM for you." Jay looked at me for a long second: he was a tall, weathered, reed-thin man, a poor station's Edward R. Murrow, with the mandatory cigarette stuck to his lower lip. The prospect was preposterous—you can't let a kid become a radio god—but Jay had no choice. In 10 minutes he had to start the *Old Trader Show* starring Jay as the "Old Trader"—hundreds of homemakers were already sitting by their phones hoping to talk with the Old Trader—their alleged purpose was to buy some garage-sale items over the air, but the real reason was that they all wanted to bask for a moment in Jay's honeyed-velvet voice. Jay loved it more than the homemakers. Jay's choice was simple: either cancel the *Old Trader Show* or allow this kid to roll records. "OK kid—but no talking, just do the ID." Hot dog, man-o-man, I was in.

BUSINESS COMMUNICATIONS
LESSONS FROM BROADCASTING

From those first moments on the air, the audience has been alive in my mind—I could actually see my family and friends in my mind, sitting, listening to me on their radios. Every time I plan a lecture, write a paper, create a commercial ad for a client, or anticipate an important telephone conference, my audience is vividly in my mind. You'll learn the importance of this fundamental skill shared by all skilled communicators—actors, announcers, CEOs, and politicians—the ability to see your audience.

Recommendation. Use this book as an opportunity to develop your mind's imagination. As you read, allow the *Theater in Your Mind* to make our communications more vivid. Picture me sitting across from you at your desk or sitting in my home office at my computer writing these words to you. I am thinking of you, so you think of me. It will open far more realistic communication. This is just as simple and powerful as the technique used by telemarketers—when you speak, smile. Though the other person can't see you, the smile on your face can be heard. Your tone of voice and your attitude change when you smile. Remember, your imagination and attitude are fundamental skills that yield substantial power in communication.

1

The Central Leverage Points
of Effective Communication

Y ou're about to explore a distinct set of ideas that will help make you a better communicator—we call them the Central Leverage Points. These are the underlying principles that drive this book. These are the critical factors that make one person more effective in persuasive business communication than another.

- *Mastery of message (ideas; analysis)*
  To be an effective communicator, you must know what you're talking about. In business, there is no substitute for excellence in analysis and planning. We can show you how to communicate effectively and persuasively, but you must first have something to say. Your message first evolves from your analysis and planning. Then you must find the fire and courage to show your vision to others.

- *Passion for message*
  Facts alone will not sell. Ideas that sit, flat and dull, on paper cannot move people to act. You must find methods to overcome the inherent inertia that holds people to the status quo, that binds them to their chairs, cursed by inaction. The surefire method that will move them is your faith, belief, courage, and excitement; in short, your Passion.
  Picture business as a long, beautiful train that is moved by the engine of emotion down the rails of analysis and planning. (Quite good for a 19th-century metaphor, huh?)

• *Credibility*
The most important factor of a communicator's effectiveness is credibility. Your credibility can be managed through the messages you send during your business relationships: messages about who you are, what you believe in, and your attitude toward your audience.

Factors that form the audience's perception of either high or low credibility for a businessperson include

Business credentials—For example, the firm you work with; your educational degrees and training; membership in professional, business, and social groups.

Relationship with audience—Simply put, you must communicate that you are motivated by the audience's best interest.

Love, not fear—Audiences want to know that you're dealing from a solid, moral, confident position of knowledge and good intentions, not from one of panic, ignorance, and fear.

Sharing and building, not ego—Speakers who believe that audiences are their partners working toward a common good have higher credibility than those who use their "airtime" to express their egos and dominate the group. Credible speakers are approachable, not distancing.

• *Knowing the audience*
The audience's motivation to follow your point of view are critical factors in persuasion. Motivation is the magical force that propels people to support you, but there are barriers and obstacles that will keep your audience from joining you. Some barriers are inherent in your plan and in human nature. Other barriers occur during a presentation or meeting. When you learn to deal with these barriers, you'll become a more effective communicator.

• *Knowing the rules—"Use the Rules and You'll Win"*
This book uses a rules-based approach. This effective method is based on the belief that people behave in society by a known and agreed-upon set of rules. Some rules are as simple as, "If I smile at you and say, 'Good evening,' " the chance is very good that you'll feel compelled to "Smile at me and say, 'Good evening.' " There is a set of business customs that forms the manner and conduct of

business in the United States; that regulates business meetings and business discussion.

The human thinking processes may also be modeled and understood as a set of rules. If you know the rules, you can know how people will react to information, how they will process that information as they think. Human behavior also has a set of rules that will be studied and utilized in this book.

The Whalen Approach
to Communication Training

I believe that superior communication and personal relationships are developed between the speaker and his or her audience through a set of attitudes and beliefs about how people should treat each other in communication. If you learn to follow these principles, they will help you become more persuasive.

PRINCIPLES

A communicator's generous, nurturing spirit
enhances the communication process.

The purpose of communication must be win/win—working for a common good. If not, the audience will raise barriers: It will stop listening to you; it will form aggressive counterarguments to what you're saying; it will not seek to clarify and work toward common understanding. Instead, listeners will project a benign, passive look as you present your ideas, then ignore what you've suggested.

A playful, entertaining attitude makes the speaker
and message more approachable and interesting for the audience.

Boredom and fatigue are your active enemies during a presentation. Your listeners are receiving messages that compete with yours—messages from their bodies and minds that may be more compelling than the one you're offering. You must capture and hold your audience's attention.

Business presentations too often fail not because they did not contain enough technical data, but because they were not interesting.

My concern for you is that in your rush to capture your listener's mind, you will fail to engage his or her soul and fail to gain her or his support.

Remember—to paraphrase the advertising master, David Ogilvy— "you can't bore your audience into being persuaded; you can only interest them."

To persuade, you have to entertain an audience—rational, logical statements are not sufficient.

To persuade, you have to arouse your audience's emotions— facts are not sufficient.

True, business decision making is very rational. Over the past four decades increasing use has been made of the objective, rational approach adopted from the physical sciences: namely, control, identification of variables, observation, hypothesis, measurement, and analysis. The great graduate schools of business spend a huge volume of time treating business as a rational science. Much of this book is based on the scientific paradigm.

Look to your own experience, too: In actual practice, how many decisions have you seen made based on force, on fear, on greed, on envy, by pressure of politics, or on other human factors? In fact, emotions and emotional information must accompany the facts that you present.

Emotions and facts together in your message allow your listeners to fully understand your plans and vision.

KEY People support fully only the things they understand.

Presentations should flow logically, while enjoying intuitive side trips.

Oral communication is not linear, it curves and takes trips down interesting side paths. Make sure that you digress; offer additional examples from other areas. Hope that your audience asks questions that will allow you to explore interesting intellectual cul-de-sacs with it. Don't rush hell-bent to your conclusion when the audience wants to play with ideas or needs clarification.

Persuasion can happen in an instant; but more often,
it happens over time.

You have probably spent considerable time and thought developing your vision. Your conclusions were reached at the end of a long analytic process—you drew upon experience, gut judgment, and instinct, along with hard data. Why expect your team, co-workers, or people outside your firm to grasp quickly the ideas that took you days, weeks, or perhaps years to understand?

Effective persuasive strategies consider timing. You may well find that other people must travel the same analytic path that you went down before they can fully understand, buy into, and thus support your vision.

Persuasion—changing a person's knowledge, attitude,
and/or behavior—is very similar to the educational process.

Picture yourself as a teacher rather than as a persuader. If you reflect upon the great teachers you've known, you'll realize that they were great persuasive communicators. Many principles recommended in this book are drawn from education.

People are persuaded voluntarily. You can't force people to be persuaded—you can only activate their desire and show them the logic behind your ideas. You can't move a string by pushing it, you have to pull it. People are the same. Their devotion and total commitment to an idea come only when they fully understand and buy in with their total being.

Forced attitude change lasts only for the moment. When the pressure you've exerted is removed, people will return to their prior position.

If the audience tunes the speaker out, even for a moment,
it isn't learning (being persuaded); and it will "tune out."

You must expect the normal human switching of attention (tuning out) and work to refresh your listeners' attention. Think of delivering your message in waves, with important content preceded and followed by light and interesting material. Ask your audience to attune in short bursts.

Professional broadcasters know that their audience is poised to punch out, channel surf to another program when the program's content fails to interest it. Radio and television announcers are taught to package their ideas into 10- to 15-second bursts of information. The faster pace keeps the message in concert with the audience's interest level and attention span. With more highly educated managers, you may well expand your information bursts to 25 to 30 seconds.

If you plan your communication, you'll communicate better . . . if you know how to plan.

Sure, you can successfully shoot your messages from the hip and you'll probably hit your target . . . at times. Good communication, however, takes advance planning. For example, factors you must consider include your audience's prior knowledge and attitude toward the topic, the optimal timing for delivering the message, and influential people who may help your persuasive effort.

The more you have at stake, the more important the outcome, the more you must develop your message and delivery strategy. *If you have a strategy, your communication has a better chance of getting you what you want.*

If you apply persuasion psychology, you can control people's minds and behavior . . . if you understand persuasion psychology.

Some college-educated people are suspicious of psychology. Yet most people who are exposed to formal education in psychology understand its utility and power.

Business managers use both mediated (thinking) and unmediated (un-thinking) responses to influences. This book will explore the mediated theories that predict how people will process and use information to make their decisions. In this book, we use the rational, thinking perspective. Nevertheless, there is much to learn from the unmediated theories.

You'll find that the unmediated theories are very interesting and useful. They have been brilliantly presented in a very readable book by Robert Cialdini, *Influence: The New Psychology of Modern Persuasion.* If you're interested in becoming a more effective and influential communicator, this is a must-read book.

Sensory communication is the best way to engage an audience: Visual symbols are the most powerful of the sensory communication tools.

You'll learn about the significant barriers to communication in this book. Most of these barriers are nested within your listener—selective attention and selective perception. And, there are inherent limitations to oral communication—which is a limited transmission vehicle; more about that later. In oral communication, the best messages are those that are directed toward your listener's sensory memory. You want to send words that trigger pictures in her mind.

Elaborate models are not useful for training people to become effective persuasive communicators. Models must be simple to understand as well as powerful.

Communication training is rife with models that are interesting and fun to study—but that are too elaborate and clumsy to use in actual business interactions. Under the pressure of business meetings, for instance, few of us can imagine, recall, and apply a 2 × 2 table of communication types.

This is a practical book. The ideas and models that are recommended are simple and powerful. They have been tested and found to be useful in actual business settings.

We avoid coaching you on "appropriate gestures" or "eye contact" or "picturing your audience naked."

Effective business communication is a two-way conversation between people. All too many "speech class" or "communication seminar" techniques sound good but in application turn the speaker into a stiff, artificial stooge. Such approaches to oral communication set up barriers to good relationships and to effective communication between speaker and listener. For example, we abhor speech anxiety reduction techniques that suggest you *"picture your audience in their underwear."* This book recommends more naturalistic methods of communication and relationships. We tap the great communicator in you by bringing out your personality, be you quiet and shy or quick-talking and effervescent. The last thing we seek to do is turn you into a robot.

Do what I say, don't do what I do.

I always tell my students and the participants in Joel Whalen, Ph.D. Effective Communication workshops not to mimic my presentation style. It's only natural that these communicators-in-training should imitate their teacher. You'll see that when I make presentations, I break all the "rules." I talk too fast; I don't complete my sentences; I've got a funny walk—like some invisible hand's pulling me up by the scruff of my neck. By genetic predetermination, I am one of the more hyper persons on the planet. Despite all my peculiar traits, I have enjoyed great success at reaching and influencing people through oral communication—because of the rules I do follow, the rules you'll discover in this book. I am persuasive and considered a good *Presenter*© in spite of my looks, personality, and "hyperness."

I believe that my success is solely due to the techniques contained in this book: message packaging and delivery techniques, attitudes of love and respect toward my audience, and sense of fun and adventure. I talk only about what I believe in, passionately. These are things you can learn, too.

Outcomes

By reading this book (and participating in a Joel Whalen, Ph.D. Effective Communication Workshop) you will learn to do the following.

Manage speech anxiety/stage fright (SA/SF©*)*

You will learn to understand the symptoms and stages of this powerful and debilitating phenomenon.

We'll show you how to predict when you're likely to develop it. When you develop it, you'll know how to reduce the uncomfortable, even painful symptoms that accompany speech anxiety/stage fright (*SA/SF*©).

I can't guarantee that you'll never suffer from *SA/SF*©. Rather, I predict that if you're pushing the envelope of business opportunity and taking risks, you're sure to experience *SA/SF*©. It's a natural though uncomfortable body state. You'll learn effective strategies and techniques for presenting while in that state.

Perhaps the most prevalent and debilitating effect of *SA/SF*©, is that at times we avoid making risky communications. I'll show you how to overcome these communication inhibitions.

Create and deliver more effective messages

You will learn how to package ideas for maximum reception by your listeners. You'll see how visual symbols (other senses) are your greatest communication tools and you'll begin to master their use.

You'll learn to design persuasion strategies based on the message, your relationship with your listener, and your listener's attitude and prior experience with the message topic. You'll learn how to plan your communication.

Manage and enhance your credibility

You'll become more actively aware of your credibility and how the things you say and do, and the things other people say about you, impact on your persuasive power. You'll learn to nurture and cultivate your credibility.

Redefine the manager's communication task

I hope you believe that important communication must be planned and that you'll embrace the attitude that developing plans are not enough, but that you must work to translate your ideas into forms useful and understandable to other people. You will learn the benefits of taking time to plan your communication.

Learn about "communications misconceptions"

If you've had formal training in communication, sales, and/or persuasion you've probably been exposed to models of communication that are misleading and, even worse, could cause you to build barriers to effective communication.

You'll see that many models are too complex to be useful in the business setting. Worse, many traditionally accepted models are too "one-way"— that is, sender to receiver—to be useful in business. You will learn the new, cooperative, mutual consensus-seeking models of persuasion and communication.

Never again will you see persuasion as a simple knee-jerk reaction by a listener to some magical words you spout. You will see communication as an organized process composed of many factors and influences.

Grow a maximally effective attitude

The key to top success as an oral communicator is an attitude of sharing ideas. You'll learn to talk **with** your audience, not deliver a speech **to** them. You'll look for ways to offer some light and intriguing messages that will entertain your audience. You'll conceptualize yourself as sharing your ideas or beliefs. Effective communication is not an exercise in ego for the speaker at the expense of the audience.

You'll experience firsthand the power of a positive enthusiasm for your message—and how the audience warms up to you as you express your enthusiasm.

Learn how to design and use visual information

Some simple but very important rules and guidelines will be offered on how to use visual materials like overheads and slides in your presentations. I'll show you how to make written materials more readable—what to put on the slides, for example, and how to integrate them into your presentation.

I'll show you how to handle *props* during a presentation. For example, how to hold a client's product.

Build delivery skills

Of course you'll learn about *stage presence.* Effective communicators give off a powerful but unvoiced message that says "I belong here," "I feel at home speaking with you." You may be surprised at how little time we'll spend talking directly about stage movement and how to hold yourself, or how to make gestures. There are some basic rules for getting around a stage, but for the most part what really matters is attitude.

Planning. This is essential to good stage presence: You must feel confident and prepared. The most important part of being a persuasive communicator is *mastery of your message.* Planning is an essential part of attaining mastery.

Team Presentations. You'll learn how to work with others in a smoothly integrated presentation team. You'll learn specific roles—*Host*©, *Presenter*©, and *Lucy*©—and how to use these roles to build mutual credibility and presentation power.

Voice. In oral presentation, your voice carries more meaning and content than do the words you speak. Many people find this hard to believe. Please take my word for it for the moment. I'll demonstrate this surprising fact to you later.

This book contains some exercises that will help you turn your voice into a more powerful and creative communication instrument.

Audience Relations. Your attitude toward your message coupled with your attitude toward your listener results in persuasion. You will learn to anticipate what type of relationship you currently have as well as the relationship you want with your listener in the future—and plan how to get what you want.

You'll also learn to read the audience's reaction to what you're saying and to adapt your presentation "on the fly."

| SUMMARY

To be an effective communicator, you must have

- Mastery of your message (ideas; analysis)
- Passion for your message
- Credibility

- Knowledge of your audience
- Knowledge of the rules of business communication and persuasion psychology

OUTCOMES—LEARNING CHECKLIST

- ☐ Manage speech anxiety/stage fright (*SA/SF*©)
- ☐ Create and deliver more effective messages
- ☐ Manage and enhance your credibility
- ☐ Continue to build presentation power and skill through Enlightened Self-Awareness

- ☐ Cultivate a maximally effective attitude
- ☐ Design and use visual information
- ☐ Build delivery skills
- ☐ Improve your communication planning, team presentations, voice, and audience relations

2

Effective Communication

Symbolically Sharing Your Personal Experience

"What we have here . . . is failure to communicate."

Communication was Cool Hand Luke's problem, and today it's a problem for all of us in business.

But it's not just businesspeople who have communication problems. To some extent, communication has been cited as the root problem in a galaxy of human relationships. Every day you see stories on the TV news and in the newspaper about conflict in marriage, race relations, employee/ employer relations, international relations, intergenerational communication . . . husband and wife, African American and Jew, sales manager and customer service, the United States and Japan. It may even affect you and your parents.

When communication is working, it's like love . . . nothing's easier. But like love, when it goes wrong there is nothing worse. It can ruin your day, your week, your job, and your marriage.

"Failure to communicate" is bad news and a big problem for business. The good news is that business communication, as practiced in the United States, is far easier to master than the other communication forms you use. One reason that the United States continues to be the world leader in business is our facile and efficient business communication system. I am not talking about faxes, telephones, and fiber optics. I am referring to the system of codes, symbols, behaviors, and rules that dictate how/when/why and with whom business communication takes place. Compared to learning how to communicate with your spouse, your relatives, and your government—learning to be an effective business communicator is a piece of cake (no-fat cake for the 1990s, of course).

Read this book, then practice what you learn and I promise you that you will become a better communicator.

DID YOU EVER THINK ABOUT
HOW COMMON COMMUNICATION IS?

I am about to make a bold assertion: *Communication is the fabric from which our society is cut and with which it is bound together.* Communication is at the core of your being. It is through communication that you decide how to spend your valuable and limited time and money; how you tell what is virtuous. Communication is the mechanism through which you select things that are beautiful and desirable and how you decide what to fear. Communication is the central and most important part of human activity.

IF YOU COULD READ MY MIND

Here is a thought that will make you believe I have read too much science fiction. Imagine this: What communication problems would we have if we were all perfectly telepathic . . . if we could share the same emotions and thoughts? Of course, we did not evolve that way. Long ago, our species learned to communicate by making abstract symbols: sounds originating in the chest, passing over sound-shaping muscles in the neck (vocal cords), and articulated with the tongue and teeth. By intelligently using these modulated airwaves we do most of our communicating. People use speech to order lunch, make love, get out of a traffic ticket, or place a buy order. But consider how our world would be if we did not have to communicate by modulating sound to create abstract symbols. Misunderstandings, desperate cries in the night that "You just don't understand me" would not be heard. Because we must depend upon the imperfect transmission of messages between each other for communication, to be understood . . . we will never be perfectly understood. We will remain isolated islands, signaling each other through the darkness with encoded flashes of light. It ain't easy.

BIBLICAL REASON COMMUNICATION'S SO HARD

Remember the Bible story of the Tower of Babel? After casting Adam and Eve out of the Garden of Eden, that was God's second challenge to humanity. I think that the Tower of Babel is more than the story of the scattering of humanity across the globe: People were estranged from each other by the different languages they spoke. I believe that this old Bible story is a metaphor for the silence and distance that separate us. We perform the act of communication through surrogate representatives of our inner thoughts and feelings—we send each other not the feelings and thoughts, but abstract symbols of those feelings.

I believe that oral communication is the most powerful form of communication for the average person. In close communication between two people, emotions can be transmitted directly, through tone of voice, facial expression, body posturing, and that magical energy we get from each other. The words we choose to use are poor, pale outlines of what we mean.

BREAKING THROUGH THE
SHELL OF HUMAN LONELINESS

We spend our lives succeeding or failing based on our ability to communicate. Not just to be understood, but to understand others. If we are understood, the loneliness that is an important part of our existence is relieved. But if we understand someone else, we can grow beyond loneliness.

True, you've learned many lessons in communication through the years. You have a bigger vocabulary than you did as a child, particularly in professional jargon. You've become more masterful in the display of the subtle, nonverbal messages that accompany speech—the raised eyebrow, the slight smile; you've got that nailed down tight. And I bet that you can talk to people today who used to intimidate you as a child. People in uniform or costumes can scare kids: police, medical doctors—I used to be frightened to death by clowns and department store Santa Clauses. You're a far better communicator now. I suggest, however, that you may have left some of your important persuasive communication skills behind in your childhood.

POUND FOR POUND, THE GREATEST
SALESPERSON IN THE WORLD: A KID

Think back with me now, to your childhood. I'll bet that when you were a kid, you were very persuasive. When there was something you wanted, you'd put considerable time and effort into getting it.

Remember the time you wanted to go to camp, or wanted a special toy—like an electric train, an oven that bakes, a Daisy Red Ryder Rifle—or to be given some new permission expanding your rights and privileges, to watch a PG movie, to stay over at a friend's house, or stay home without a baby-sitter? You had to convince your parent(s) to get what you wanted.

I'll bet you were quite slick and sophisticated. Think now of how you used Persuasive Communications. Use the following section, Communication Factors, to remind yourself of your communication power.

COMMUNICATION FACTORS

Who to ask? (Decider/Influencer)

_____

When to ask?

_____

What message?

_____

Multimedia

_____

PERSUASION GOT YOU WHERE YOU WANTED TO GO:
McDONALD'S FOR LUNCH OR SUMMER CAMP

You probably found that "when to ask" was a very critical factor when you were looking for something small, like permission to go to McDonald's after the ball game. You may remember that you increased the chance of success if you waited till your parent(s) was in a good mood (or at least a better mood) before you asked. You probably knew that you should wait till after dinner, or that it would be best not to grab Mom or Dad just as they were coming through the door after a hard day's work.

But for more important things, timing was less important than "who you asked" and "what you said"—already, you were very aware of the importance of the *Pitch,* your *Message Strategy.* For example, the conditional pitch: "If you get me the log cabin play set, I'll go to bed right at 8:30 and no fussing." Or the educational pitch: "Think of how much I'll learn by going to Europe by myself."

You may have used a multimedia approach, using newspaper ads and television commercials ("Look, Dad, see what that kid on TV has? I want one just like that."). Perhaps you enlisted the strategy of using Influencers, others who would help you with your pitch, such as grandparents or your friend's parents ("Jimmy's mother said he could.").

If you're blessed with children, you probably are very aware of how skilled they are at getting you to comply with their wishes. During the early years, children use melt-your-heart looks and god-awful, high-decibel screams to get what they want. Later they become skilled pitch artists, gifted with words, psychology, and razor-sharp timing.

HAVE YOU LOST A FEW STEPS AS A PERSUADER, NOW THAT YOU'RE AN ADULT?

Let's think now about you as an adult businessperson and how you use persuasion with your bosses, co-workers, suppliers, and customers. Most people tell me that they have lost a few steps in their "persuasive fitness" compared to when they were kids. They spend less time preparing to be persuasive, less time planning, anticipating, and running scenarios of how the pitch will go down and be received by the decider. How about you? Could you use more time planning and timing your pitch, bringing allies to help you persuade, making a longer search for evidence to support your case?

Think about the roles of timing, message strategy, persuasion psychology, the assistance of others, and multimedia techniques in your professional life today. Perhaps you could become more persuasive if you recalled your childhood and brought forward some of the excitement, importance, and urgency you felt then.

COMMUNICATION BREAKDOWN

Sometimes communication gets tangled, and the reason is hard to fathom. Other times the cause of the miscommunication is easier to find. Read the following paragraph and see if you can diagnose what went wrong. When you figure it out, you've learned the first important lesson in becoming a better communicator.

> Your food stamps will be stopped effective March 1992, because we received notice that you passed away. May God bless you. You may reapply if there is a change in your circumstance. (From a letter to a dead person from the Greenville County, South Carolina Department of Social Services)

Miscommunication is a great source of laughs. Next time you're watching the comedy channel notice how many jokes are about misunderstanding, misuse of words. Comedy is the flip side of tragedy. Miscommunication can be tragic . . . and funny.

I've shown this tangled letter to hundreds of people and asked them to tell me what the communication problem is. The first answer a person gives is: "They're writing to a dead person." That is a correct answer; the writer is addressing the deceased **and he is also writing to the survivor.** The letter writer is addressing two people and not communicating well with either one.

This is the first lesson in becoming a more powerful and effective communicator. When you begin to plan your communication and as you proceed to communicate, you must have your listener/audience clearly in mind. The bureaucrat writing from the office of the Greenville County, South Carolina Department of Social Services seems like a nice person— trying to be helpful and even keeping the door open for further assistance, "if there is a change in [the] circumstances." But he made the mistake of trying to hold two different audiences in mind at once: the survivor and the dead person. What made the letter so confusing was that the survivor and the dead person have two different sets of needs and should be addressed with two different message strategies. The strategy for reaching the dead person is either (1) hold a seance or (2) don't try, the person is dead. You can visualize the poor writer, sitting at a gray metal, government-issue desk, surrounded by an ever-building mountain of paperwork, taking the time to craft an individual, customized letter to his client. But as he began to write, the two disparate audiences began to shift in his head. One moment the message was being addressed to the survivor and the next minute to the dead person.

The principle of effective communication that you can learn from this letter is always to have a clear picture of your audience in mind as you plan your communication. I recommend that you actually picture your audience in your mind as you are writing. Work to talk with your listener as you write down your ideas and words. Communication is a conversation between two people. You'll never address a crowd. Even if you're given the opportunity to address ten thousand people in a stadium, you'll only be talking with one person at a time. When I go on television or radio and speak to hundreds of thousands or millions of people, I imagine that I am speaking to just one person.

VISUALIZE YOUR UNSEEN AUDIENCE
AS A SINGLE PERSON

A technique professional radio and television announcers use can help you vividly picture your audience. Did you ever think how difficult it is to sit alone in a soundproof room, speaking into a microphone to thousands of people you don't know and can't see? To make their listeners more real, announcers create a vivid image of one person in their mind. They picture this person as they are speaking. Writers use this trick, too. As I am writing this book, I am picturing you answering my questions and reacting to the things I write. Of course, I don't know what you look like, so I'm not really picturing you. The face I see, the voice I hear, is that of a little old lady. She's been with me since I was a 15-year-old disc jockey on WWIL-AM/FM. She joined me at my first broadcast and has served as my audience surrogate ever since. I have never given her a name, but she definitely has a personality. She's a cold-hearted, cynical, small-minded old grouch. And that makes me a better communicator. If I can communicate with her, nice people like you are easy.

Right now, you do the same thing. Picture somebody in your mind. It doesn't have to be anybody real. In fact, it's probably better if the person isn't real. If you select somebody familiar you could have a problem, because that one's interests, knowledge, personality, and attitudes will be confused with those of your true, intended audience. Your audience stand-in must change attitude, profession, and job title to fit your audience.

My little old grouchy lady takes on the characteristics of the audience I am addressing at the moment. Today, as I write, she is standing in for you. So far this year, she has helped me prepare my communications with my graduate students at the Kellstadt School, a senior advertising executive, a marketing professor, undergraduate marketing students, high school sophomore student leaders, a Swift Butterball Turkey Home Economist, Japanese health and beauty aid business executives, a team of T-shirt salespeople, and, unfortunately for me, an IRS auditor (who turned out to be very nice). Why should you imagine your stand-in having a bad attitude? If you write and/or plan your oral presentation to deal with the biggest cynic or the most ignorant person you can imagine in your audience, everyone else will be overwhelmed. You may not choose to deal directly with the issues your imaginary cynic raises, but you'll have plenty of ammunition ready should you need it later, in a meeting or when making your presentation.

Communication Defined

Communication is the central human activity. Before we realized how bees and dolphins and other living beings communicate, we used to say that the ability to communicate separates human beings from the animals. If we still believed that, I bet you could point out lots of people who aren't human, because they surely can't communicate.

Take a few minutes and scan this list of definitions of communication. You may be impressed by two things:

1. Many disciplines have their own, distinct definition of communication, and
2. Communication, as defined, is critical to that discipline.

VARIETY OF COMMUNICATION DEFINITIONS

- *Mechanism by which power is exerted* (Political Science)
- *Process of transition from one structural situation-as-a-whole to another, in preferred design* (Time)
- *Discriminatory response of an organism to a stimulus* (Behavior)
- *Introduction of additional bits of unique information into a system* (Systems Engineering approach to information theory)
- *Transportation of air and matter into and from an organism* (Biology)

- *Change in potential from one circuit element to another* (Electronics)
- *Means of sending military messages, orders, and so on, as by telephone, telegraph, radio, couriers* (Military)
- *Process that links discontinuous parts of the living world, one to another* (Geography)
- *Verbal interchange of a thought or an idea* (Speech)
- *Process by which we understand others and in turn endeavor to be understood by them. It is dynamic, constantly changing and shifting in response to the total situation* (Understanding)
- *Act or process of transmission of information, idea, emotion, skill, and so forth, by using symbols—words, pictures, figures, graphics, and more.* (Dance, 1970, pp. 204, 208)

Perhaps as you read the inventory of communication definitions, you noticed that each discipline defines communication in terms of what is central and important to accomplishing goals and conducting the process involved in that discipline.

DO WE NEED A DEFINITION OF COMMUNICATION TO COMMUNICATE?

Yes, it would be great if we had one. To master something, you have to understand what it is. Perhaps we need a functional definition rather than a conceptual definition. A *conceptual definition* abstractly defines some phenomenon or thing by using other abstract concepts. For example, you can define *marketing* as "facilitating exchange"; interesting, but not really that useful—it's too abstract. Conceptual definitions are commonly bandied about by academics. We professors love to create and use conceptual definitions—it's a great mental exercise.

Greater understanding and utility can be found in *functional definitions,* defining something by what it does. If you know how something works you are better able to use it. Let's look for a functional definition of communication. An early model that is widely used and taught is the Shannon-Weaver model.

SHANNON-WEAVER MODEL

Shannon and Weaver were engineers working for AT&T. They were given an important problem to solve. Senior planners at AT&T wanted to know the

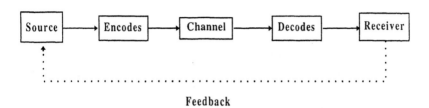

Feedback

Figure 2.1 Shannon-Weaver Model of Communication
The popular Shannon-Weaver Model of Communication, developed to analyze telephone utility line capacity, is too one-way and static to represent modern business communication.

maximum volume of telephone calls that could be handled by its system of wires, switches, and sending and receiving equipment. In the 1940s AT&T didn't know, and this was a big problem. It's like a manufacturer not knowing the production level of his or her plant. The problem was bigger for AT&T, because existing models of manufacturing plant process efficiency did not seem to apply to its communication system. Nothing seemed to fit. The bright minds at AT&T realized that they needed a new conceptualization of the problem. Shannon set about the difficult task of creating a model of a telephone call. Today it seems simple, but before Shannon's breakthrough work it was a mess. In fact, Shannon's contribution was so significant that he and Weaver won the Nobel Prize for their model of telephone conversation (see **Figure 2.1, Shannon-Weaver Model of Communication**).

Let's walk through the model together. Imagine that you're the *Source* of the message. The setting is your office on a bright, beautiful Monday morning. You feel great. You've had a fun weekend; you got plenty of deep, restful sleep. Also, you have some really interesting things to do today. You are one with the universe and you feel powerful and ready to get started. (Work with me now, I realize that this is total fantasy. It's not like any Monday morning you've ever had. It's just a learning example—trust me.) Now, you see your friend Kathy (she's going to be the *Receiver*). You're glad to see her and you want to share this great Monday with her.

So you *Encode* a message (you select a big booming, full-of-life, "Good morning, Kathy, how's everything with you?"). You select Speech, and the *Channel of Communication* will be air. Your voice modulates the air molecules between you and Kathy. They vibrate her eardrum and that signal is converted to nerve impulses that travel down her auditory nerve to her aural thalamus, where the message is *Decoded* in the thalamus, to the amygdala and the cerebral cortex.

Now, what you didn't know is that Kathy is hung over, she had a big fight with the love in her life, and she's really down. She reacts to your message with a look of pain, saying, "Sheesh, hold it down." This is *Feedback*—it lets you modify your message.

Incidently, the feedback loop was Weaver's contribution to the model. Shannon had developed the whole thing when Weaver looked at it and said, "You need something here showing the *Receiver* can communicate back to the *Source*." For that small but important observation, Weaver shared the Nobel Prize with Shannon. Just another example of the importance of timing in life and success.

PROBLEM WITH THE SHANNON-WEAVER MODEL:
IT'S TOO ONE-WAY

The Shannon-Weaver model worked beautifully. AT&T managers began to understand their telephone system. Over the past five decades the Shannon-Weaver model has been taught widely and has been expanded to serve as a model of all types of communication. The model has shaped the way most people think communication operates. This is a problem. The Shannon-Weaver model, though offering some interesting and useful insight into many types of communication, does not really capture what goes on at a business meeting.

For example, imagine that you're the *source* at a meeting; the *receivers* are your co-workers. They give you *feedback* through their nods and verbal statements of affirmation like "I see," or objection statements like "No way." So far the model is working just like Shannon and Weaver predicted. But when your co-workers start to share their point of view, the *sender/ receiver* roles shift, your co-workers become the *source* and you become the *receiver*. As the tempo of the dialogue increases, as conversation changes topics and takes on new information, the *source* and *receiver* roles shift back and forth during the meeting. The dynamic, interactive nature of business communication is not captured by this static model. Round and round the message goes without any change taking place except the roles of the *sender* and *receiver*. And change is what a business meeting (and all communication) is about.

The Shannon-Weaver model does not allow us to study and to understand two important aspects of business communication:

1. The goal-driven, change-oriented nature of business meetings, and
2. The sense of teamwork, of striving for a consensus of opinion, of working for agreement that typifies the business climate in the 1990s.

Today's boss is not a decision-tyrant *source* barking out orders to a passive *receiver* employee. The boss's goal is to delegate, to drive power down the organizational chart empowering the entire workforce. Ideas and change that make companies competitive come from the bottom up. The Shannon-Weaver model conceptualizes the communication process as too one-way. The message is pitched like a baseball thrown from pitcher to catcher. The inherent vision of the model is an active speaker and more passive audience. The *source* in effect says to the *receiver,* "You keep quiet and sit there. I'll do all the talking."

Simply put, the problem with the Shannon-Weaver model is that it is one of communication dominance rather than communication sharing. It's also static, there is no change in the model's elements as a result of the communication: The message just goes round and round. The only dynamic thing about it is the fact that it may be conceptualized as having the role of source and receiver traded during the conversation—and, frankly, that may be a stretch that the model's creators did not envision or intend.

BUILDING A NEW MODEL
OF BUSINESS COMMUNICATION

Let's think about another way of modeling the business conversation. We need to understand communication as it takes place among co-workers at a business meeting. Let's start fresh and work from the ground up. Let's examine the most basic elements of communication. We know that communication is very complex, very important, and a central element in all human activity. Also, we know that each specialist, the electrician, the botanist, and the English teacher, redefines communication to suit her or his professional purpose. We see communication in terms of our own field and its particular point of view.

Let's erase our minds, throw old assumptions out the window, and grab a fresh, clean sheet of paper. What is communication at its most basic?

BUILDING BLOCKS OF COMMUNICATION

Everything can be broken down into its most basic elements. A building is made of bricks. Bricks can be broken down into sand and binding material. Sand can be broken down into silicon and organic and inorganic elements. Silicon and organic and inorganic elements are composed of molecules and atoms. Atoms can be broken down into protons, neutrons, and electrons. Now understand that 175 years ago, when I studied science, we stopped breaking things down at those three subatomic particles: protons, neutrons, and electrons. I am now told that scientists have further reduced subatomic particles into quarks—the most basic element of matter. Don't ask me what a quark is. I've asked hundreds of my students, including chemists, engineers, and technicians of all types, and nobody seems to know. Maybe someday the folks at Fermi Labs will invite me to present a communications seminar and then I'll find out. There, I am confident, in the great Midwestern citadel of physics, the hallways are filled with people who are savvy about the quark.

THE BASIC ELEMENT OF COMMUNICATION:
THE SIGN

The most basic element of communication is the *sign*. A *sign* is a symbol. A *symbol* is something that stands for something else.

For example, a map is a symbol that represents an actual physical, geographic territory. Look at the maps of my home state, Florida, in Figures 2.2 through 2.5.

SYMBOLS ARE NOT THE
OBJECTS THEY REPRESENT

Look at my beautifully handcrafted maps of Florida. They are not really Florida, are they? You knew that, but you agreed, for a moment in time and just for the sake of communication, that we'd use my inarticulate squiggles

Figure 2.2 Basic Map of Florida

to represent Florida. What did you receive from my communication? Did you see a real Rand McNally map of Florida, or did your mind see an overhead satellite photo of the state? When you looked at the Mouse Hat did

Figure 2.3 Map of Florida With Lake Okeechobee
Here is Lake Okeechobee.

Figure 2.4 Map of Florida With Mouse Hat
Here is where you go to play with the mice at Disney World. This is a Mouseketeer hat, in case you didn't recognize it.

you see Mickey or Disney World? Have you ever been to Disney World? If you have been, then your interpretation of these symbols would be different from only having seen Disney World commercials. What sunset did you see in Key West? If you have not seen a Key West sunset, whatever your mind conjured was a pale, inadequate substitute. (You've really got to see a Key West sunset—it's amazing, soul shaking, and can't be captured on film or video. You have to be there in person. Promise me that you'll go.)

THEATER OF THE MIND

The magic of communication is that you agreed to suspend reality for a moment and enter the theater of your mind and your experience to share my vision with me. I could not force you to do this . . . to invest the mental effort necessary for a communication event to be shared. If you're pressed for time or you're finding this text to be unimportant or boring, you may have skimmed quickly and not expended the mental effort necessary to

Figure 2.5 Map of Florida With the Keys Added and Pointer to Key West
Here are the Florida Keys and here is Key West. When you visit Florida, be sure to make the trip to Key West. Get there in time for sunset—its one of the most magnificent shows on earth. And be sure to rent a convertible: You'll look marvelous with the top down.

receive the message I was sending you in those maps. See, I did not really send it in the Shannon-Weaver sense. I merely offered it to you, held it out for your consideration. If you wanted it, you had to bring something with you from your experience, your memory.

I hope that you agree that symbols are important elements of communication. Let's examine symbols in some detail.

TYPES OF SYMBOLS

We human beings are symbol-seeing critters. Everything in our world that we can visualize or sense has symbolic meaning and can be used in communication. The more able and facile you are at summoning, selecting, and sending symbols, the better a communicator you'll become. (See if you can say that last sentence without slobbering.) Now, come with me on a little road trip as we explore some symbols and see what they mean to us.

• *Color*
Colors are rich in symbolic meaning. What does the color red mean?
Red = blood, violence, death
Red = stop sign
Red = anger
Red = hot
Red = Communist (a less-prevalent meaning every year)

As a color, red has a variety of meanings, but notice how they tend to be active and powerful. Can you think of a calm, passive meaning for the color red?

Consider the color green.
Green = money
Green = ecology; environment
Green = oxygen tank
Green = life
Green = mint-flavored candy
Green = lemon-lime flavored soft drink
Green = envy

• *Costume*
Do you ever think of business dress as costume? Would the costume you wear to a first job interview be different from the way you might dress after you get the job? Maybe not?

Would you wear the same outfit to a meeting with your banker to present a business plan seeking a loan as you would to a meeting with the creative group at your advertising agency?

PREDICT DR. WHALEN'S BUSINESS COSTUME

Recently, I had 45 minutes to present my plans for a seminar to the top two executives of a $450 million dollar company. It was our only meeting. Realizing the importance of costume as a symbol set, and knowing that with little time I must use every communication channel to my advantage, what set of costume symbols did I choose? The answers are in **Table 2.1, Dr. Whalen's Presentation Costume.**

What color was my suit? _____

What color were my shoes? _____

What color was my briefcase? _____

What brand name was my watch? _____

Here is a more personal example. Let's use you. Imagine that you're walking down a public street at 9:30 p.m. You see Harry coming the other way. Now, you don't know Harry, but he starts walking toward you and says, "Hold it right there." What do you do?

Scene One. Harry is 5' 10" tall and weighs approximately 175 lbs. He is about 35 years old. Harry is wearing an old, soiled, army-issue olive drab field jacket. His shoes are ancient, nondescript, and shabby. He is wearing a black knit watch cap.
  What do you do?

Scene Two. Harry is 5' 10" tall and weighs about 175 lbs. He is about 35 years old. His shirt is a light blue. He is wearing black pants and on his feet are bright, spit-shined black shoes with rubber soles. The hat he wears is a peaked military type with an interesting badge on the crown. What really gets your attention are his accessories. Harry is wearing lots of chrome and leather accents including handcuffs, truncheon, badge, Mace, and, most impressive, about five pounds of gunmetal-blue revolver in a worn leather holster.
  What do you do?

The only difference between the Harrys is what they are wearing. Business costumes are as important as any public safety officer's uniform. They help identify us and help us take command. Just as a police uniform increases the power and authority of a cop, the correct business clothing will send out the right signals about you.

TABLE 2.1. Answers to Dr. Whalen's presentation costume

What color was my suit?	Grey
What color were my shoes?	Black
What color was my briefcase?	Black
What brand name was my watch?	Rolex

TIP   Upon an initial meeting, upper-echelon executives often assess each other's relative status and "club membership" by noticing accessories, particularly shoes and briefcase. Don't economize here. Spend what it takes to get the right symbolic accessories for you. *Warning:* Don't try to take too giant a leap ahead. A $1,000 handmade imported leather briefcase on a $45,000 a year salary sends out the signal that you don't know how to spend money. Who wants to trust business decisions in the 1990s to a spendthrift?

• *Lines*

Here are two people:

Person A

Person B

- Which person would you like to sit next to on a four-hour plane trip?
- Which one would you like to dine with?
- Which one would you like to have as a project team member?
- Which one do you want to handle your lawsuit against a bungling, substance abusing surgeon who has mutilated someone you love?

• *Shapes*
What is the meaning of the following shapes?

Look here. Go in this direction.

Stop.

• *Gestures*
These meaning-rich symbols are some of the most powerful communication tools we have. When you're speaking, some gestures have standard
meanings—for example, touching and tapping your forefinger to the top
of your head means I am thinking. A slight variation with a single rapid tap
means I have an idea.

Other gestures are more simple. An extended arm can have a variety of
meanings, merely depending on what position the hand is in and how it is
moving. The symbols for "come here" and "go away" are very similar, the
difference is just in the way your hand faces.

Most of the gestures you use in oral communication have no standard meaning. Their meanings come as they modulate in a beautifully articulated dance with your words, facial expressions, tone of voice, and body movement. Your hand and arm gestures, shoulder shrugs, body stance, and rolls of your head all dance in rhythm and tempo with your words and the passion of your ideas. Much of the all-important emotional information comes from this elegant, articulate movement.

• Mathematical/statistical symbols
Perhaps the most concise and accurate set of symbols comes from the highly codified and agreed mathematical symbols:

$$\leq \quad \Sigma \quad \div \quad \infty \quad \Pi \quad \text{Å} \quad \Delta \quad [\,] \quad \theta$$

Which of the above symbols have meaning for you?

• Space
Countless messages are communicated by how people use the space about them, how they claim that space for themselves, or how they share it.

Researchers led by Nancy Henley, Director of the University of California at Berkeley's Women's Studies Center, traveled the world taking hundreds of candid photographs of people in public places: sitting on park benches, walking in malls, dining in restaurants. The people were not aware that they were being photographed, so they were captured in their "natural state." Of the many interesting things that Dr. Henley noticed in the photos was how differently men and women use space. Men sprawl and take up lots of space; women tend to be more compact and hold themselves in. Men will splay their legs out, sit back and form a tent over their heads with their arms, hands folded behind their neck. Women sit with their hands in their laps and legs tucked inward, held near their body. Dr. Henley says that men communicate superior power or dominance in a group by taking up more space and making themselves appear bigger. Woman show less assertiveness, even submission, by making themselves smaller. Next time you are seated at a conference table, watch how men and women tend to use space, including how they place their papers and other materials about them on the conference table and on adjoining chairs. You may find that men and women are still occupying different amounts of space not indicated by relative rank in the group or in the organization.

The codes and manners in business were established by men. Men still dominate business, particularly in the upper echelons. Women can learn to adapt these ways of using space to their advantage. Men can learn to be more gentle and less aggressive in the way they use space.

It is important that you effectively communicate your status and power to others. And you can push the envelope of your power by subtly using power symbols that are not strictly appropriate to someone of your current status. You can use power symbols that are less obvious than a raised voice or accompanying physical gesture—for instance, when you sit at a conference table the way you arrange your papers in front of you communicates silent but powerful messages to the people seated around the table.

Space = Relationship

Next time you're in a public place with a few minutes to observe people, notice how couples (male and male, female and female, female and male) walk and stand with each other. You may be amazed by your ability to guess the nature of their relationship just by noticing how much space they maintain between themselves. You will be able to discern if they are business associates or lovers. Their use of space will tell you if they are just beginning a relationship, like a first date, or if they are in a long-established union. You'll also spot those who are having a fight or are feeling the flames of love. As you study these couples, describe what you're seeing in words. You'll find that the way they use space has great symbolic meaning to their relationship. If you were to ask them how they decided to set the space between themselves, they would look at you blankly. Most of the time we don't make this decision consciously—but if the space is not correct, we know it and adjust.

I have more to share with you on space and communication when we talk about making standing presentations before groups (see **Chapter 7, "Oral Communication: The Words You Say Are Less Than 10% of the Message"**).

• *Touch*

Like space, touch says volumes about a relationship. Touch communicates symbols of power and dominance. For example, should you and I meet in a class or Effective Communication seminar, and you stand near me, see what it feels like to reach out and touch me on the shoulder. You will probably feel an invisible power shield about me. That's because of our relative ranks and roles within our professor/student relationship. Now, I don't feel that same barrier with you. I would feel perfectly natural touching you, in a neutral area of course: top of arm, hand, or top of back on the shoulder.

With coequals, in a group of the same or similar relative status, touching has a different meaning than between persons of different rank. When a person touches another person of the same status, it communicates comradeship. The appropriate amount of time must have passed since the initial meeting, however, or the friendly touch may be interpreted as an attempt at dominance and may communicate the wrong message.

When the relationship is forming, and you want to assert dominance or communicate friendliness, measure the time you've spent, determine the dynamics of your relative status, then go ahead and give a friendly touch (on a neutral body part like the forearm) or a pat on the back; you'll communicate lots of good things. If the person jumps as if touched with a live electric wire, you've touched too early in the relationship.

• *Smells*

One of the most powerful memories we have is olfactory. Our minds recall with maximum clarity the things we have smelled. Scent is able to kindle volumes of other memories. When you recall the smell of pine, you might remember being in a forest with the hushed rush of air through the trees or the soft, loamy feel of the pine needle carpet beneath your feet.

Smells can have symbolic meaning, too. Real estate agents suggest that if you want to sell your home, you should put cinnamon sticks in a pan of boiling water. The homey scent will communicate just the right message to potential buyers. I coached a home builder client to have his salespeople bake cookies in the model homes. Certainly the scent of fresh-baked cookies would send the same signals as the boiling cinnamon; and cookies gave the salespeople the chance to engage in the relationship-building act of sharing food as they offered the cookies to prospective buyers.

A theme that keeps running through all I've told you about symbols is *meaning*. Perhaps you've noticed that symbols and meaning have an important relationship. Is the color red really more active than green? Is cinnamon really a homey smell? What is inherently homey about cinnamon? That spice's meaning comes from our prior experience with cinnamon: growing up with that smell and the activities that we were engaged in at the time forms its meaning today.

SUMMARY

Communication is the central human activity—*it is the fabric from which our society is cut and with which it is bound together.* In business, oral communication is the most powerful form. Through oral communication we transmit the meaning behind our words through tone of voice, facial expressions, body posturing, and that magical energy we get from each other. Symbols are the building blocks of communication. We give symbolic meaning to everything in our world. People assign meaning to colors, space, lines, clothing, shapes, gestures, and even silence.

3

The Search for Meaning

Symbols Get Meaning From Social Experience

Wearing a flannel shirt is a special act to me. It has loads of wonderful feelings and memories; it is a very satisfying symbolic act. Slipping on a flannel shirt is a signal of a day off, a private day. A day where time is under my own command. A plaid flannel shirt is a masculine, fatherly shirt to wear. It is warm and soft and comforting. When I see a flannel shirt and think about it, or when I actually decide that a flannel shirt is the right shirt to wear, these are the feelings I get, if you'll allow me: These are the messages I get through self-talk with a flannel shirt.

Nowadays, the meaning of my excellent collection of well-worn flannel shirts has changed. Young people are wearing old flannel shirts, thanks to the "Seattle Grunge Movement." A flannel shirt's symbolic meaning has dramatically changed to a very non-fatherly, non-masculine domain. Now when I wear my beloved flannel shirts out in public, I run the risk of being trendy, God forbid. I received some bad psychic scars during the Disco Scare of the late 1970s. I was trapped, locked in a radio control room for three or four hours every day, forced to play and listen to disco records by a deranged program director and a listening public gone mad. But, enough about me.

The idea you'll want to remember is that symbols take their meaning from social experience and agreement among people. For example, imagine a grand dinner where you are the honored guest. What meal would you be served? Perhaps, champagne and steak. Why do we honor people by serving those two foods? True, they're expensive, but they have no other inherent characteristics that would give them celebrity status.

Now pretend that you're being honored by a celebratory meal in the mountains between China and Tibet. As guest of honor you would be offered that region's highest celebratory dish: live, eviscerated monkey. To that culture, scooping out live monkey guts is the height of social status. Perhaps this is akin to eating the worm at the bottom of the tequila bottle or having your choice of turkey part at Thanksgiving. I know that those last few ideas are quite raunchy, but I want you to realize fully the power of symbols . . . even if they are little scratches of ink patterns on white paper. They can still shake your bones and rattle your cage.

TYPES OF MEANING

As you may suspect, we in the communication sciences have decided that symbols are so important to the world that different signs should be given different names and assigned to precise, functional categories. Two of those symbolic categories have important information that will help you deliver more effective messages.

• Denotative symbols

Businesspeople love to use Denotative Symbols. As Dragnet's Jack Webb was fond of saying . . . "Just the facts, ma'am." When you're presenting hard data, you're using Denotative Symbols. A Denotative Symbol is a concrete object and the sign attached to it: for example, the **Grand Canyon.**

When you read the words Grand Canyon, as I shoot that symbol into your mind, there is little error. The chance is very good that you've pictured the huge natural wonder in the American West. The only chance for miscommunication would be if you had never seen or heard of the Grand Canyon, or if your brain had slipped a synapse and you thought of the Grand Caymen Islands, another natural wonder like the Grand Canyon, only much more moist. The communication is accurate and the probability of error in transmission and reception of that message is very low. When you want your message to be accurate you select Denotative Symbols from your lexicon. Businesspeople need to send many accurate, factual messages loaded with Denotative Symbols.

DENOTATIVE SYMBOLS ARE POPULAR WITH BUSINESSPEOPLE, BUT ARE POOR PERSUADERS

The problem with *Denotative Symbols* is that they are not persuasive. If you build your message with mostly factual, accurate symbols you'll inform your listener, but you may not move her. If you want to be persuasive and a leader of people, you must mix in the right dose of *Connotative Symbols.*

• *Connotative symbols*

As you may suspect, because *Denotative Symbols* are very accurate, the other major category of symbols, *Connotative Symbols,* is inaccurate. You're right. The inaccuracy comes from the rich constellation of meaning that surrounds *Connotative Symbols.* The meaning of a *Connotative Symbol* varies from person to person. For example, the meaning of the symbol "excellent meal" will change from person to person and from event to event. An "excellent meal" to some people is measured in the quantity of food served, for example, "Country Buffet" or Shoney's "All You Can Eat Breakfast Bar" would constitute an excellent meal to a group of fraternity boys after a beer party. Compare the meaning of an "excellent meal" in the context of entertaining a senior executive—selecting a restaurant that furnishes a large bib, a bucket, and big spoon to each diner may not be appropriate. You and the executive might seek an "excellent meal" at one of Chicago's elegant dining establishments. The meaning of a word can change from person to person based on their experience. For example, the word *mother* conjures the meaning of a warm, feminine, nurturing person. Among the lessons our society has learned in the past five years, however, is that the word *mother* can also signify an alcoholic and/or drug addicted, abusive, pain-inflicting source of despair. In another dimension, think about other *Connotative Symbols,* like "love" or "fairness" or "success." Compare the meaning of "love" to a newlywed couple with that of "love" to a recently divorced mother of five children. Or "success" to a business major with "success" to a student of philosophy or the fine arts. Which would tend to equate dollars and cents with success?

I am sure that you are aware that *Connotative Symbols* are very imprecise. The sender must be aware of the impact of these symbols on his or her listener. The meaning will vary from listener to listener and from time to time for the same listener. The power that *Connotative Symbols* deliver is in their ability to arouse emotion in both the speaker and the listener. These are the words that inspire us. When Franklin Roosevelt wanted to stir the souls of the American people during the Great Depression (1929-1940), he selected the simple but rich *Connotative Symbol* "fear." Roosevelt told the American people, "We have nothing to fear, but fear itself." Certain *Denotative Symbols* can arouse emotion, but they must be linked to a strong *Sensory Modality.*[o] For example, when Winston Churchill appealed to the people of England to rally behind him during the Blitz Bombing of World War II, he selected the set of *Denotative Symbols,* "Blood, sweat, and tears." As they affect our emotions, *Denotative Symbols* can produce a reaction. "I've torn my guts out over this presentation." "There was blood all over Wall Street today."

PERSUASIVE MESSAGES USE BOTH
DENOTATIVE AND CONNOTATIVE SYMBOLS

Accurate (denotative) symbols appeal to the listener's head. They allow you to reason with him. But reason will not move most people. You can't depend upon people to act on facts alone. Often, the facts don't have any meaning without a context for analysis: their impact upon the firm, its employees, and its customers. This impact is best presented and given meaning and salience through symbols (connotative) that arouse the listener (see **Figure 3.1, Persuasion = Facts & Emotion**). It's not enough to present the facts for decision making. You must also provide the motivation for action. Providing facts for consideration is reporting, it is a staff-level function. Motivating people to action is leadership, an executive quality.

• *Contextual meaning*
We give symbols meaning based on two types of context: (1) the physical and social environment in which the symbol is used, and (2) the symbol's semantic context with other symbols, that is, words modifying the meanings of other words.

For example, the physical/social environment will change the meaning of the *costume symbol* of a bathing suit. Visualize yourself wearing a bathing suit on Oak Street Beach. You're standing with volleyball players,

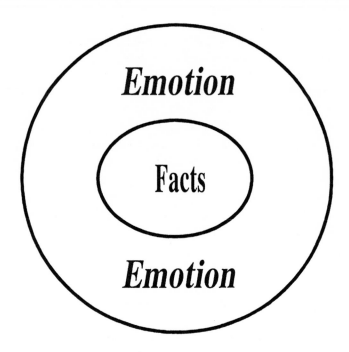

Figure 3.1 Facts/Emotion Figure

sun-soakers, and people whizzing aerobically by on skates or bikes, and jogging. What symbolic meaning does your suit have? Perhaps positive messages, like "dressed appropriately," "summer time," "athletic," "sexy," "with-it fashionable," "fun," "healthy," "time off." Or perhaps negative, shameful messages like "human stick" or "beached whale" come to mind. Now, visualize yourself wearing your bathing suit on the floor of Chicago's Options Exchange. There you stand, in that huge open room with hundreds of frantically active people wearing their multicolored barber jackets that symbolize their firm affiliation. What messages come to mind: "nut," "embarrassment," "exhibitionist," "law breaker"?

The physical/social environment changes the meaning and the impact of your language on other people. Think of the meaning and impact of using profanity in church versus using those same words in a softball game. A more subtle change takes place in the impact of your words when you use the full extent of your considerable vocabulary and skill with technical words in a business meeting, or when talking to the person who is fixing your car. In the business meeting, you'll be accepted and probably be very effective. The same use of education with a mechanic or other blue-collar worker can be distancing, emphasizing the difference in your social groups and relative status. You may alienate the mechanic and cause your bill to rise.

Words also take on meaning as they are nested together in sentences. Remember how you learned to read and, working like a detective, figured out the meanings of new words by studying the other words in the sentence? You did not have to go to an adult to get the meaning of every new word you encountered. This was an important step in becoming an independent learner.

THE BIG LIE: LITE BEER

Professional persuaders know how to use words to change the meaning of key words. For example, the geniuses at Miller Beer's advertising agency created a new product category with "lite beer." The truth is, no beer is "lite." Every beer made will pack on the pounds, as millions of gullible American males like me have found out. How much beer would they have sold if they called it "Miller's Diet Beer"? In fact, previous attempts by other major brewers to sell a low-calorie beer failed, in part because they selected the wrong contextual symbols to position their beers. They used the lower calorie/diet context.

BIGGER LIE

In revitalizing the nation's stagnant economy by multi-billion dollar military spending and creating unprecedented levels of national debt, President Ronald Reagan brilliantly used contextual meaning to sell his plan. He combined two very different words into a new, powerfully persuasive image: "Peace-keeper missile." Taken alone, the word *missile* has very negative meaning, particularly to those Baby Boomers who remember under-the-seats-duck-and-cover drills during the cold war. We can still see vivid pictures of incoming missiles and flaming death in the theater of our minds. The other symbol, however, "peace-keeper," is beautifully selected. *Peace* by itself has very positive meaning to the voting public. The word *peace-keeper* sends our minds back to the days of the old West, when one clean-cut sheriff faced down the bad guys at high noon. It draws from the heart of our greatest tradition: independence, justice, and controlled skill and power with firearms. As John Steinbeck observed in *Travels With Charlie,* "every American male thinks that he is a born hunter, a dead-shot with rifle or gun. Without any special training he is ready to gun-down armies of advancing Redcoats." A "Peace-keeper missile" becomes the perfect sidearm for the new marshal on the world stage: the United States, the only law west of the Milky Way.

SYMBOLIC COMPLEXITY

The more important a thing or idea is to a culture, the more names it will have—the more symbols we will attach to it. When we can label something or assign a symbol to it, it becomes easier to see; to perceive. The more names you give an object, the better you can study it.

For example, consider snow in Chicago. It's fairly important to us: It affects our lives over several key months when business activities, particularly travel to meetings and to work, can be impeded. Snow is important. Now, pick up your pencil and list all the different names you can think of for snow. If you like winter sports, like skiing, you probably can think of a few more symbols.

• Names for snow in Chicago
  1. _____
  2. _____
  3. _____
  4. _____
  5. _____

After you've finished your list, look below to see a few of the 30 different words Eskimos use for snow.

How important is snow to you compared to an Eskimo? Even with the rapidly "modernizing" social/technical world that today's Eskimo lives in—the impact of improved communication, transportation, and accelerated economy from the Northslope oil fields and the Alaska Pipeline—snow is still an important part of the Eskimos' culture. Because the Eskimos have more words for *snow*, they can perceive more types of snow than you or I. If you give something a name, you can see it better.

- Eskimo words for snow
  - *Masak* (wet, falling snow)
  - *Qanik* (snow in the air)
  - *Aqilutag* (new snow)
  - *Aput* (snow on the ground)
  - *Natiruvaag* (drifting snow)
  - *Suagutisik* (very fine snow)

Eskimos have more than 30 different words for *snow*.

Consider now a practical example of symbolic complexity taken from your everyday work: *Technical Jargon.*

TECHNICAL JARGON = MANY SYMBOLS

Consider the complexity of the symbols you use in your profession. To a lay person, the myriad things you deal with professionally may have but a single name. On the other hand, to you, the professional, those objects are complex and therefore require more precise names. For example, look at what a big deal I've made of the terms *word* and *symbol*. As a communications professional I've added complexity to help you see those terms in greater detail, and hopefully, have added clarity to your understanding. You master communication by giving lots of names to the building blocks of communication: signs/symbols.

In my field of advertising, for example, the "ad" or "commercial" has many names:

spot	10-sec spot	60	30
facing	double truck	gatefold	10 panel
quarter page	reversal	teaser	spectacular
insert	pitch	reader	fact sheet
classified	display	institutional	local
sales-promo	national	make-good	bumper
telegraph	promo	first-in/first-out	
free standing insert (FSI)			

Don't get me started . . . I can go on and on. If you're in advertising, I'll bet that you have thought of many variations and could add a dozen more names for "ad."

Each profession has an expansive list of precise symbols to describe, perceive, and thereby analyze and control key phenomena. For example, look at the following list of common names a lay person would give an object. Think for a second how many different names the working professional can and will use for that simple, lay term.

- Financier: *Investment*
- Advertiser: *Ad*
- Chef: *Knife*
- Accountant: *Analysis*
- Dentist: *Tooth*

Now, think about your professional domain. Select a term that a lay person, some new client or person off the street, would use. Then list the different names and/or terms somebody in your profession might use for that phenomenon:

- Lay person's word for your professional object/concept

Word _____

- More precise technical jargon used in your profession

1. _____
2. _____
3. _____
4. _____
5. _____
6. _____
7. _____
8. _____
9. _____
10. _____

I've probably not given you enough space to list all the terms that come to mind. If you had a week to build your list and you consulted with others in your profession, I bet the list would really grow.

ADVANTAGES OF JARGON (TECHNICAL SYMBOLS)

Consider some good things that flow to the person who is facile and in command of the vocabulary of his or her profession.

Added Credibility. As you will learn in **Chapter 6, "First People Must Believe You: Managing Your Credibility,"** among the important things you can do to build your perceived credibility with your listener is to display a command of your profession's technical symbols, its jargon.

Group Membership. One of the educational passing-rites for entrance in your profession is to learn the technical symbols and when and how to apply them. It's not enough to "know" what they are—you have to deliver them smoothly, like second nature. This verbal fluidity is the mark of a professional and it should be. It takes time and practice to command the professional language—it's an artifact of experience. They say that the first few years in medical school are primarily spent learning the vocabulary.

Group Status. The progression from novice to member of the profession is marked by the mastery of language. The more advanced, exalted members of the profession have access to a larger lexicon to describe their professional activities. The symbols you acquire are concomitant with your mastery of your profession. Part of the passing-rite of acceptance by others in your profession is your mastery of the vocabulary. You can make yourself more persuasive by easily and accurately applying the proper symbol.

Added Precision. When something has myriad symbols attached to it and those symbols apply to different aspects of the phenomenon, the great precision lets you see and understand more of it. For example, imagine that you're playing volleyball and the ball is set up to you—you jump up, make a brilliant spike and return to earth at the wrong angle. Your foot twists in the sand, gives way, and you feel a "snap." The pain is instantaneous. Your teammates help you to the sidelines. Your friend looks at your foot and says, "Your ankle is really swelling up fast, we'd better get you to a doctor." At the hospital, the doctor examines your foot. Her ability to name and therefore perceive the hundreds of bones, muscles, ligaments, and tendons in your foot gives her the ability to diagnosis your injury more rapidly. What to you is "my twisted, swollen, and painful ankle," is to your physician a far more complex and therefore treatable condition.

There are many advantages to mastering and using a technical language. Be careful when dealing with others, though; it can be dangerous.

DISADVANTAGES OF THE
TECHNICAL VERBAL ADVANTAGE

Can Intimidate and Distance the Lay Audience. It's nice to have the authority that vocabulary gives you. But that authority can build big walls between you and your listeners. People with less education and experience need to understand you. Remember, your success will come from not just your authority and expertise but by getting others to embrace your ideas and vision. People only buy into what they understand.

Can Be Too Precise and Leave Out Important Meaning. You can wander through your thick, professional forest where each tree is another term, model, or interpretation and forget that you're in the woods. Too much precision can lead to micro-analysis. The danger is that you end up heading down one path, with rigor, forgetting other possibilities—or worse, forgetting the factor of importance and the impact of your ideas. Thinking simply is beautiful. Without clarity of thought, you can risk *losing track of the big picture*—the leader is responsible for knowing the direction the group is heading and why.

COMMUNICATION IS HOW YOU FIND REALITY

Earlier, I made a rather bold assertion: Communication is the fabric from which our society is cut and with which it is bound together—and that communication is at the core of your being and my being. Let me take that conceptual territory a giant leap forward—I'm going to plant the flag of communication on the heart of your world. I declare to you that communication is how you know reality . . . how you perceive your inner self, how you see the outside world, and how you manage the relationship between the two.

IT'S ALL IN YOUR MIND

Where do you live in your body? Ask a child where he lives and he's likely to point to his chest, around his heart. As that child gets older, he'll probably move up in his body. He'll change where he resides in his body to his head. Highly educated people like you live in their heads. Through observation of the world, analysis, and self-talk, we live in our brains.

You are in your brain. If you are a trained athlete, you probably are adept at focusing your consciousness on various parts of your body and can examine or regulate the activity taking place there. But you're only there for a visit. You spend most of your time, particularly your time interacting with co-workers, clients, and superiors in the pursuit of your business day, living in your head.

YOUR "SELF" WAS FORMED OVER TIME

The brain is essentially blank at birth. Recently, we've discovered that significant learning occurs while you were in utero; you were very active during the time spent in your mother's womb, in the last trimester. It was a time of great growth and, perhaps, a time of learning. For all practical purposes, however, vast regions of your brain were blank at birth. In fact, the first two to three years of your time on earth was characterized by an explosive growth in the number and type of your brain cells. Did you know that you had more brain cells at age two than you do now? And it's not just because of all those undergraduate kegger parties. The brain expands vastly, then determines what general sets of brain cells will be needed and draws back on that expansion, reducing the number of cells that are maintained throughout adulthood.

SOME BRAIN PATTERNS ARE ON-BOARD AT BIRTH

We've learned that other parts of the brain are "hardwired," that there are genetically determined traits that have an important role in your life. But by far the larger aspects of you, your skills, your worldview, your knowledge, your disposition and temperament, are the result of the patterns of cellular interconnection in your brain; of the information and analytic processes, the reactions stored in your thinking and unthinking brain.

BRAIN PROGRAMMED
THROUGH SENSORY INFORMATION

All that you are came through your interaction with the world. All the information that you have taken in, all the experiences, interactions, and observations, have been delivered to you through your sensory organs. If you had no sensory contact with the world, your brain would lie fallow and undeveloped. It is through the things that your eyes see; the sounds that your ears hear; the sensations of pain and pleasure, heat and cold that your skin senses that the outside world communicates to your brain.

The only pathways to a person's brain are through the sensory organs. Communication, the messages you send to and receive from other people, is sent through the sensory organs (eyes, ears, skin, tongue, nose; see **Table 3.1, Sensory Modality**). This is the only gateway to communication with other people: sensory communication (with all due respect to those individuals skilled in psychic communication—I don't know how to teach that skill).

SENSORY MEMORY AND ORAL COMMUNICATION

Later, in **Chapter 7, "Oral Communication: The Words You Say Are Less Than 10% of the Message,"** you'll discover how limited oral communication is. Think of communication as the sending of bits of information to another person. The volume of bits that you can transmit using strictly oral communication compared with the number of bits you can send via a photograph or a written report is quite small. You'll find that very little denotative, factual information can be communicated verbally. Oral communication is a very inefficient method for sending facts to another person. Later, we will talk about how important and powerful oral communication can be if you focus your communication strategy on developing stronger, more reliable relationships with other people, and you'll see how powerful oral communication is in persuasion.

As you apply the principles taught in this book, you'll be amazed at how little your listener(s) remembers what you've said. You'll spend hours creating the most perfect presentation you can imagine. You'll load up with interesting and important facts. You'll use every bit of your considerable

TABLE 3.1. Sensory Modality

Sense	Sensory Organ
Aural	Ear
Visual	Eye
Visceral-Motion-Emotions	Body
Smell	Nose
Taste	Tongue
Touch	Skin

The human senses and the sensory organs that detect messages directed to them.

intelligence to construct an airtight set of logical conclusions. Speaking smoothly and confidently, you'll lead your listeners through your message. Perhaps you'll even use overheads with key words, graphs, and charts. With this considerable barrage of information directed at a collection of some of the brighter, more highly motivated people in the Chicagoland area, few facts get through and into their memory. What do they remember? They instantly remember the strong sensory messages you send them. Ask your audience to write down what they remember and you'll see a consistent pattern of sense memory. Things that you described, visual pictures that you shot into their minds. Sounds you suggested, textures and shapes that you portrayed. The smells and feelings that sparked the powerful sensory stimulation that burned your message into their minds. When you went into the theater of your memory and described to your audience what you saw, felt, smelled, and heard there, your listeners were with you. They went to their past experience and retrieved from long-term memory their recollection of similar experiences.

A LITTLE BIT OF SENSORY MEMORY
STIMULATION WORKS WONDERS

When you work with sensory memory, you don't have to become a master storyteller. It's not necessary to weave a tapestry of words, sights, sounds, and celebration to use sensory memory. In business, if you overdo the description and become too verbose you'll turn the audience off. You'll lose credibility as your listener(s) decides you're a b.s. artist.

SECRET BEHIND USING SENSE MEMORY

St. Augustine said, "God is in the details" (popularized by Mies van der Rohe). The key to activating your audience lies in picking just a couple of sensory-rich details and planting them in your message. If you want to bring home the impact of company layoffs, all you have to do is paint a single, vivid picture. Make it a small picture that illuminates a detail.

> It's in their eyes . . . the shocked look in a man's face as he picks up his last paycheck. You know he's thinking, "What am I going to do now?" . . . and you know he thinks that we've betrayed him.

You've seen this technique used often by skilled leaders like Ronald Reagan and Bill Clinton. They boil down complex social/political programs to their essence. They use highly visual examples, usually a story about some single citizen and how the program impacts that person.

It's easy to do: We live in a sensory-rich world. You'll find examples all around you:

> Waking up Saturday morning to the aroma of fresh-brewed coffee that someone else has already made.

> It's the sinking feeling you get in the pit of your stomach as the elevator starts down too fast.

> You'll see it in the early morning mist on a mirror-flat lake.

> It's a child's laugh, the ring of the cash register; it's the excitement in their eyes.

Make sure that your important points are communicated by addressing sensory memory.

SENSORY PREFERENCE—
DIFFERENT SENSES FOR DIFFERENT PEOPLE

Some people, in fact most people, are visually oriented—they have a preference for seeing messages. They prefer that you send your messages

TABLE 3.2 Verbal Clues to a Listener's Preferred *Sensory Mode*©

Preferred Sense	Things the Listener May Say
Visual (seeing)	"I see what you mean" "I get the picture" "That's very clear"
Aural (hearing)	"I hear you" "Sounds good to me" "Doesn't ring true"
Visceral (body)	"I can't get my hands on it" "I can grasp what you mean" "Things are well in hand"

Determining a listener's preferred sense by the things he or she says.

in pictures. If fact, they'll tend to receive and decode what you're saying using primarily visual sense memory.

I tend to be more acoustically oriented. You'll find that each individual you deal with may have an orientation different from yours.

Sometimes people give you clues to their preferred mode of sensory communication. They'll tell you if you listen (see **Table 3.2, Verbal Clues to a Listener's Preferred *Sensory Mode*©**).

HOW THE INFORMATION
YOU SEND ATTAINS MEANING

Earlier, we talked about how symbols get their meaning through experience as the result of common agreement among people (consensus) and from the environmental/social context in which the symbols were first experienced and the objects/concepts they stand for.

What is your prior experience? Are you afraid of dogs? Do you love math? Think that hot dogs are fun food? Think that French is a romantic language? Feel more comfortable with shorter men? All of your complex (and not so complex) attitudes, beliefs, and orientations about the things in this world came through your experience. People's reactions to the symbols you communicate come from their prior experi-

Me   You

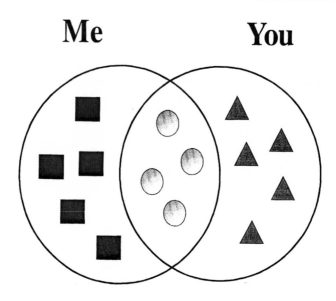

Figure 3.2 Frame of Reference

If I wish to communicate with you, I mean really engage you, your brain, your feelings, give you strong understanding and felt sense, I am wise to pick symbols from your frame of reference (triangles) or from our commonly shared frame of reference (circles). If I select symbols from my frame of reference (squares), I am making you work too hard to receive my message. I am also creating a real barrier between us. Try as we might, and as motivated as we both may be in trying to communicate—you just have not been there and so can't understand. At best, I can try to build bridges for communication by selecting symbols/experiences derived from your frame of reference.

ence with that symbol and the thing(s) it represents. Please look at **Figure 3.2, Frame of Reference.** This Venn diagram represents everything you and I have experienced and gives us some insight into how well we will communicate—our probable strengths and weaknesses as communication partners.

In the diagram you'll see some things that you have experienced, and I haven't, represented by the triangles. Each triangle is a symbol/meaning that has a unique meaning to you because you have experienced it (and I have not). At the intersection, the little circles are the symbols/meanings that we share in common. The squares in my area are the symbols that have meaning only for me, because you have not experienced them.

NOTHING IN COMMON

I was reared in Florida. Did you play ice hockey? Go cross-country skiing? Ice-skate outdoors? I never have. If you want to share your experience with me you have to find similar symbols that I have experienced, if you want to give me understanding.

I've been in hundreds of television and radio commercials, love to sail, skin-dive, and scuba dive. Have you ever pulled a lobster from under a reef? I've never ice fished. I've never met your spouse, your parents, or visited your high school.

The challenge and struggle of education is to share experience with those who wish to gain it. You have command of your profession. How would you begin to teach me how to do your job? Let's make it harder for you by imposing some restrictions. I can't go to your place of work. We must meet once a week in a classroom. You can only talk to me and give me things to do and to read. This is the challenge of communication, to relate experience and vision. Experience is from your past; you draw from your memory and as you communicate you relate what you see, hear, and feel as you look back into your mind. Your vision for the future is what will help you become a business leader, a successful person who can create value, build organizations, and gather people about you. Your vision comes from the bedrock of your past experience, your knowledge of market data, and your firm. Understanding is the product of your interpretation of the predictive marketing, economic, and financial models. This is your vision: What will happen. To lead, you must share your vision in powerful, meaningful, truthful communication. Later in this book we'll talk more about how your listener decides if what you're saying is the truth. By *truth* I don't mean "not a lie." The truth that we seek in persuasive business communication is far more powerful. It is the truth of a shared experience from the past and a shared vision for the future.

SEEK TO SHARE UNDERSTANDING

If you wish to lead, to persuade, to share your vision with others, there is one surefire goal that will make you successful as a communicator: work to share understanding with your listener. Seek to create a feeling in your listener that she really understands. It's not enough to have your listener agree with what you're saying, to know the facts. Earlier, I suggested that a persuasive message be composed of *factual symbols wrapped in emotional symbols.* Can you visualize that? Let me add a layer to that image. Persuasion—understanding—is a reaction between mind and body. Your mind and body work together to help you decide if what you're thinking is accurate, if it is the truth. You may think of your body confirming your cognitive judgment as "gut feeling" or "instinct"; psychologists call it "Felt Sense."

FELT SENSE: YOUR BODY KNOWS

Imagine that you're leaving your home for work. You grab your briefcase and bag and head for the door. Just as you reach for the doorknob you get this feeling that you're forgetting something. It's a rather unpleasant sensation in your body, perhaps a grab in your stomach, a tension running through your shoulders, a tightness in your back.

From experience, you know that those sensations come from your body telling your mind to double check, you're forgetting something. You begin to run a mental inventory of all the things you may have forgotten. You think about file folders, your wallet, your keys. That's it, your keys; you left them on the bureau. How do you know that this was the right item on your checklist? Your body goes to work and tells you with a strong feeling, a rush of energy, that you're right—it is your keys that you're forgetting. As you visualize the bureau and perhaps see your keys on top you get the feeling. This feeling is "Felt Sense," discovered by some brilliant psychologists including Eugene T. Gendlin at the University of Chicago (Mathieu-Coughlan and Klein, 1984). Working with people from all walks of life, psychologists have developed felt sense as a very useful tool for showing people how to rely on their body to confirm what their mind is thinking.

MORE FELT SENSE AT WORK

Let's say that as you ran through your mental checklist, you got a *Felt Sense* when you thought about your keys, but you could not remember where you left them. Tension builds within you. You're starting to run late. Now you think of all the places you could have left them. You scan your memory, thinking of all the places they might be. Suddenly as you think to yourself, "Are they on my bureau?" you get a strong, welcome rush of feeling that tells you your keys are on your bureau. Your body has confirmed what your mind has considered. Your body/mind truth detector works for you again with *Felt Sense.*

YOU'RE REALLY COMMUNICATING WHEN
YOU'RE GIVING AND GETTING FELT SENSE

When you're making a superior presentation or you're involved in a wonderful one-on-one conversation with somebody you really like, you and your listener are getting lots of felt sense. When you work to share vivid symbols that are both denotatively logical and connotatively emotional, and you're speaking the truth from your memory of past personal experiences or you're relating a vision that you see for the future, you're creating a felt sense in your audience.

Your listener knows that what you're saying is important and true, not just because her mind tells her that what you are saying makes "sense." Her body is working with her cerebral cortex to form the felt sense experience that tells her that what you're saying is the truth as she has come to know it. That, my friend, is shared understanding and what we call persuasion.

Communication Conceptually Defined

Here is what we believe good, effective business communication is. As you read the following ideas, you may well say, "Not at my firm we don't." Perhaps together we can prepare you to improve your communication skills and make you ready for the day when you can change the way your firm communicates.

1. *Communication is sending and receiving pictures.*

Visualize communication between two people as sending and receiving pictures. When you speak to someone, you're activating pictures in the theater of his mind.

2. *Communication is shared meaning.*

To be understood, for our meaning to be received by our listeners, we must choose symbols either from their exclusive experience or through our shared experience. We don't have to have lived the same life as another person to communicate. By developing our abilities in empathy, learning about our work partners' backgrounds and experiences, we can draw on the rich experience that they bring to the communications event to communicate to a superior degree.

3. **Communication is agreed definition; it is the process of seeking a consensus on the meaning of things.**

We come to understand the meanings of things through communication. Rather than the transmission of facts and ideas from one person to another, business communication is the process of seeking consensus. In a conversation, we don't just pass a verbal beanbag back and forth till our time is up. Communication is a goal-directed behavior; we seek to find agreement and greater clarity in understanding by modifying our vision. We triangulate reality through the interchange of ideas.

4. **Communication is a cooperative, mutual event undertaken by active participants.**

Listeners are alive, reacting, thinking. An audience is not a dormant set of faces . . . an audience feels and reacts. Communication is a goal-directed dialogue. Your audience may not answer back verbally, but feed its reactions back with facial expressions, body movements, and sounds of assent or disagreement. If you believe that you're talking with an audience instead of at it, you'll be far more effective and engaging.

When two people begin to communicate, they are agreeing to join actively in a goal-directed behavior. Their purpose is to explore ideas and to share perspective. Perhaps you've noticed that you really begin to understand your ideas after you struggle to explain them to another person.

LET'S DEFINE COMMUNICATION

Having said all of that, now I feel we're ready to define *persuasion,* a special type of communication—it's a communication with a goal, it's a process.

A professional persuader, whether a car salesperson, missionary, professor, or IRS agent, begins by deciding where the listener is—his knowledge, his experience, and his attitudes—and where she wants the listener to be—what the listener will know, experience, and believe because of the persuasive communication. We think of where the person is at Time One (see **Figure 3.3, Definition of Persuasive Communication**) and decide what the person should know, believe, and do at Time Two, after receiving the persuasive communication—or more likely, undergoing the persuasive communication process. It can take time to persuade someone. When persuasive communication is ethical, two people (the persuader and the person being persuaded) enter a process of discovery and change. The persuader must undergo a process of enhanced knowledge about the listener and, because of the consensus-seeking nature of business communication, become a bit more enlightened herself.

Knowledge. Persuasive messages can be designed to change people's knowledge set on a topic. To suggest that persuasion is the transmission, reception, and adoption of information may strike some as unique. In classical and traditional speech training, a speech to inform is not considered persuasive. I believe that in today's competitive information environment, where managers are bombarded by an avalanche of information—e-mail, phone calls, faxes, meetings, seminars, books, magazines, newsletters, and confabs over coffee—we first have to convince our colleagues to expend their effort to receive the information. In postgraduate training, both at the great universities and in private seminars offered to working professionals, the "Edu-tainer" is the more successful communicator.

Feelings. People's attitudes and feelings can be either roadblocks and obstacles that inhibit their ability and desire to change, or catalysts that make that change happen faster.

Professional persuaders realize that change is difficult for all of us. As my friend and colleague, Dr. Dave Drehmer says, "The only person on earth that likes change is a wet baby." We all resist change, particularly change that comes to us from outside forces (government, spouse, boss, even the weather). To persuade somebody, you must convert the emotional obstacle into motivational attitudes.

Behavior (Doing). Frequently the object of your persuasive communication is to get others to change their way of doing things, to get them to join in a process, attend an event, or perform a task in the best possible way.

Which do you think you should do first: Change a person's way of doing a task or get him to change his attitude toward doing it?

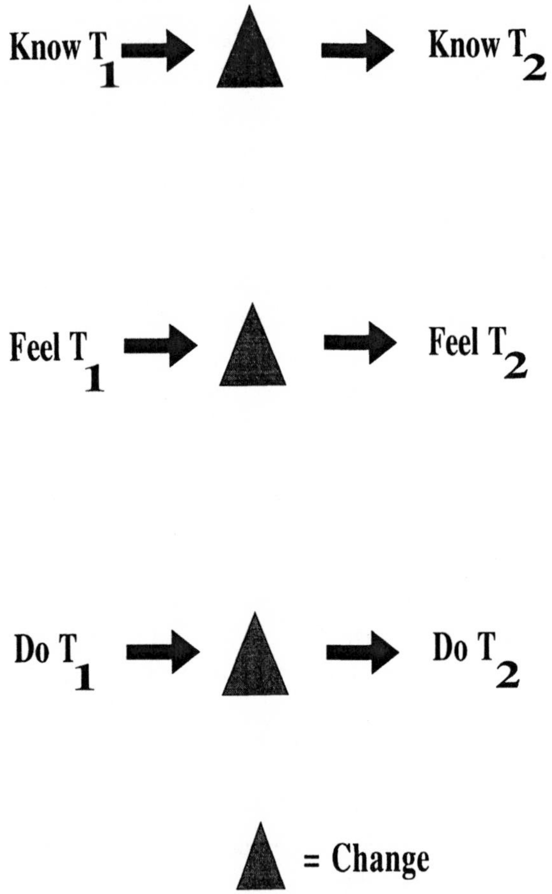

$$\text{Know T}_1 \implies \blacktriangle \implies \text{Know T}_2$$

$$\text{Feel T}_1 \implies \blacktriangle \implies \text{Feel T}_2$$

$$\text{Do T}_1 \implies \blacktriangle \implies \text{Do T}_2$$

$$\blacktriangle = \text{Change}$$

Figure 3.3 Definition of Persuasive Communication
Persuasive Communication is the Change (Δ) in a person's knowledge (know), feelings (feel), and behavior (do) as the result of your message.

Most people would say "change her attitude first." A couple of decades ago, even persuasion psychologists believed that behavior followed attitude, that is, people first change their feelings about an idea, then they begin to act like their feelings indicate they should. We now know that behavior comes *before* attitude.

Unless the person has big feeling-based obstacles that prevent her from doing what you want, your best first strategy is to change her behavior, her attitude follows.

Dr. Daryl Bem said that people see themselves behaving and adjust their attitude to conform with what they just did. Procter & Gamble's brilliant advertising campaign that used "Mr. Whipple" to sell Charmin bathroom tissue, used Dr. Bem's principle of "get them to behave first." Mr. Whipple would not let you squeeze the Charmin, remember? When that advertising campaign came out, I remember seeing my first package of Charmin in the store and could not resist reaching out and squeezing it to see what it was all about. Did I put it back on the shelf or in my cart? The cart was easier. We don't spend tons of time or considerable mental effort sorting out our toilet paper buying decision. It's what we marketers call a routinized decision, for a low-involvement convenience good. But by getting us to *do,* by engaging us in the physical action of picking up the product, Procter & Gamble also made a sale. Can you sell all products and ideas with such a simple behavioral strategy—get the buyer to pick up the product? Not really; the more complex the product the more steps you must use to persuade a person.

As these thoughts are recorded in my notebook computer, I am sitting in one of the most beautiful parts of the world: Napa Valley. There are lush vineyards 20 yards away and beyond them the green mountains. The wise vintners know that if they give you a glass of their fermented grape juice, you're likely to buy a bottle or case. The simple act of sampling a product does more than allow you to investigate the product's characteristics—it begins the path of what psychologists call *Commitment and Consistency.* Once we've started down a behavioral or attitudinal path, we adults are compelled by the need to be consistent, to follow through. Think of a time when you put your foot on a new path of personal growth. When you searched for more information, you began that path. When you told significant others in your life (boss, co-workers, spouse, friends), you took another step in product purchase. Major decisions begin with small steps.

Ultra-savvy automobile sales organizations realize the importance of getting the customer to do, to engage in the desired behavior. For example, when they get you to sit in the car or to take a test drive, to get your car appraised or "run the numbers" to see what your payments would be, you're taking an important behavioral step in the process of persuasion. Your pride in personal growth and the pride you feel for your new car is attitudinal, but it began with behavior—things you did.

Yes, attitudes can well precede behavior, but for the professional persuader the surefire method is to get the buyer to take a small behavioral step . . . like you did when you picked up this book and started to read.

| SUMMARY

Symbols take their meaning from social experience and from context, that is, from other symbols around them. Your past experience with symbols gives them meaning for you.

Persuasive messages must have both facts and emotion. Technical jargon is how we give important things many names. It can add precision but can also create distance and confusion for lay people.

The listener's senses are key to effective communication: hearing, sight, touch, taste, smell, and visceral (motion and emotion). You can only count on people to remember things that reach their sensory memory. Visual sense is most people's favorite. *Felt Sense* is your body confirming what your mind is thinking. People believe that they understand your message when it gives them *Felt Sense*. When you send messages designed to reach people's senses, you give them *Felt Sense*.

Effective communication can be accomplished if you send and receive pictures. Communication is the process whereby people work to find a shared meaning. Persuasive communication is designed to change a person's knowledge, feelings, and/or behavior. If you wish to change a person's attitude, first plan to change his or her behavior.

4

When You're Afraid to Communicate

Understanding Anxiety and Fear

I hope to convince you that fear of public speaking is a normal feeling that everyone gets at one time or another. Let me repeat that: Everybody gets Speech Anxiety/Stage Fright (*SA/SF®*). I hope that you'll also come to realize that you can manage and can tap into the power lying dormant within you—a positive power that actually comes from the same source that causes *SA/SF®*.

WHY MUST YOU MANAGE YOUR SPEECH ANXIETY?

Have you ever avoided speaking in front of a group? Have you ever "stepped aside" so another person could take your place as speaker? If not, I say good for you. Many of us have stepped aside or avoided opportunities to speak because we have a real or imagined fear of making fools of ourselves.

If you are among the courageous people who accept speaking opportunities, let me ask you a question. Although you take the responsibility to speak, have you ever actively and aggressively sought out speaking opportunities? If you're serious about success, I strongly recommend that you do everything you can to become a skilled, popular, and frequent speaker.

GO FOR MASS MEDIA

How would you react if you received an invitation to appear on television as an expert in your field? Would you leap to accept the invitation or leap away from it? If you're among the bold few and see yourself accepting the invitation, have you made an effort to appear on television or radio, or to talk with newspaper and magazine reporters? These omnipotent media have made presidents out of idiots and fortunes for simple people who were blessed with the ability and the courage to present themselves well on television. Imagine if someone with your ability, intelligence, and education were to appear in the media, and do well—how far could you go? How far do you want to go?

Here is why you must remove the barriers that prevent you from doing your best in public speaking and public communication. People rate good speakers as superior to less able communicators on a number of important dimensions:

- More intelligent (not explained by IQ)
- Better looking/more attractive (not supported by photo judging)
- Better candidates for leadership

A series of experiments was conducted to test the power that superior speaking ability gives to a person. Two speakers were matched on all characteristics and given the same message to deliver to several different audiences. One speaker was highly trained and used every positive speaking technique to enhance his performance. The other speaker was coached to deliver a below average presentation. In audience after audience, listeners rated the better speaker as more intelligent, better looking, and a superior leader.

• Speaking gives you power: The bigger the audience, the greater the power

Though big audiences and big speaking occasions, like appearing on radio and television, are more scary and intimidating than other venues, you can train yourself to enjoy the rush of energy you get from the experience and surf across that wave of energy to success.

• May not get rid of the butterflies, but you'll get them flying in formation

Although I cannot nor will I guarantee that you can train yourself never to get *SA/SF®*, I am confident that you can learn to manage the symptoms and turn them to your advantage. You must find opportunities to speak. They will accelerate your success.

In this chapter I'll show you how to do the following.

• *Predict when you'll get speech anxiety*
I'll show you how to know when and where you're likely to experience this unpleasant body feeling. Forewarned, you'll be ready to take action and get things under your control.

• *Recognize the 10 major symptoms* (see **Table 4.3, Speech Anxiety/ Stage Fright Symptoms,** later in this chapter)
Repeatedly, people experience the same body feelings during episodes of *SA/SF.*© Many of these feelings are part of your fight-or-flight protective mechanism. This physiological response is wonderful if you're in combat or trying to survive in the Amazon Rain Forest, but if you're wearing a business suit and trying to win friends and influence people, it really gets in the way. You'll learn about the source of the feelings, where they originate in the body, and why they feel the way they do.

• *Manage yourself when you're in the grip of SA/SF*©
Great sailors learn how to navigate during storms. I'll show you how to maintain the strain, to look good and perform well even though it feels like giant waves are breaking on the rocks in your stomach.

• *Manage your runaway SA/SF*© *metabolism*
Using relaxation and visualization techniques perfected by clinical psychologists, I'll show you how to grab the reins and control your runaway metabolism.

IF YOU NEVER GET *SA/SF*©,
YOU'RE A RARE BIRD

In fact, over the past 12 years, working with thousands of executives and students to make them better communicators, not one person has claimed never to get *SA/SF*©, I've yet to meet the person who has never experienced *SA/SF*©, I've heard some wild symptoms described and some very unusual occasions where people get *SA/SF.*© For example, some students and clients have told me that they don't feel any symptoms before or during the speech, but after their presentation the symptoms hit them like Robocop beating up a bad guy.

SA/SF ©: THE SILENT ENEMY OF SUCCESS

Few of us experience a career-capping opportunity of addressing thousands of people. And rarely, if ever, will your career be built upon this type of venue. More likely, your success will come from communications in more informal venues: small meetings, telephone conversations, one-on-one sidebars with supervisors and colleagues. If you're like most businesspeople, I'll bet that anxiety before a communications event may be inhibiting your success. You may artfully avoid making the communication by not attending a meeting or not speaking up once there. Or you may hold yourself back, either corral your ideas or hood your passion and intelligence, due to fears we call *SA/SF.*©

This *non-speech, speech anxiety* is a prevalent problem in business (as well as in social and family life). If you're like most people, this type of "speech anxiety" may be limiting your career because it's making you avoid certain business conversations. For example, have you ever avoided or postponed making a telephone call? You knew that you had to make it, but as you thought of what you'd say or imagined the other person's reaction, you began to have second thoughts; perhaps you just decided "to do it later." This is a very subtle, more insidious form of speech anxiety.

AMERICANS' GREATEST PHOBIAS

Phobias are *irrational fears* like fear of tall people, open spaces, examinations. I bet that each of us has experienced a fear that another person would consider irrational. Look at **Table 4.1,** *Chicago Tribune* **Survey,** for the result of a survey conducted by the *Chicago Tribune* that asked people, "What are you afraid of?" Then look at **Table 4.2, Ranking People's Greatest Fears,** to see how the people surveyed by the *Chicago Tribune* ranked their fears.

TABLE 4.1 *Chicago Tribune* Survey: Peoples' Greatest Fears

Rank your fears on this list of people's greatest fears:
Rank   Rank

_____ Death   _____ Heights

_____ Flying   _____ Insects

_____ Financial difficulties   _____ Deep water

_____ Public speaking   _____ Illness

_____ Other   _____

People's greatest fears—from a *Chicago Tribune* survey.

TABLE 4.2 Ranking of People's Greatest Fears

Rank	Fear
1	Public speaking
2	Heights
3	Insects
4	Financial difficulties
5	Deep water
6	Illness
7	Death
8	Flying (or crashing; not-flying)

How people ranked their fears in a 1991 *Chicago Tribune* survey

WHEN IT'S YOUR TURN TO SPEAK,
DO YOU GET THESE SYMPTOMS?

Fear of speaking produces a distinct set of physical feelings in everyone. For example, you may be speaking before a group of 15 co-workers, or perhaps you're just sitting around the conference table at the opening of a meeting; the chair says, "Why don't we begin by introducing ourselves," and you get a rush of feelings. Look at **Table 4.3, Speech Anxiety/Stage Fright Symptoms,** and identify the feelings that you've had.

TABLE 4.3 Speech Anxiety/Stage Fright Symptoms

Check the ones you experience:

☐ Increased heart rate	☐ Dry mouth
☐ Pounding heart	☐ Muscle tension in shoulders and neck
☐ Sweaty palms	☐ Cold, clammy hands
☐ Butterflies in stomach	☐ Mind "blanks out"
☐ Tunnel vision	☐ Other _____

Physical symptoms people report during Speech Anxiety/Stage Fright

Let's explore the source of these physical symptoms. It all starts in your brain.

YOUR BRAIN IS THE BOSS

I promised you that we'd find the source of these feelings, and here it is: the Locus Coeruleus. Located in your brain stem, this organ is the unthinking brain that controls many of your body's most important functions, like body temperature and breathing. It does not think, it just does. Some people call it the alligator brain, because the brain stem is a remnant of earlier evolution. It was the first brain found in reptiles and lower life forms.

Besides running your body's metabolism, the brain stem is in charge of sensing danger. When your locus coeruleus senses that you're in danger or threatened, it overrides the thinking brain (cerebral cortex), taking over the operation of your body and mind. One of the first things it does is send out a master chemical (catecholamine) to direct the sympathetic nervous system. **Table 4.4, Sorting Out What You're Feeling,** has a list of the physical changes in your body and what they feel like. The locus coeruleus is the biological source of your *SA/SF*© feelings.

Your heart is racing, your blood pressure's up. You've got lots of sugar in your muscles and adrenaline is speeding up your body. The fighting muscles in your upper body are tense with anticipation. You're primed and ready to kill. You could fight off a room full of savage invaders or rip a telephone book in half, but you have to be cool. Wow! It's tough.

TABLE 4.4 Sorting Out What You're Feeling

Alligator Brain's Action	Your Symptoms/Feelings
increases blood flow to major muscle groups	increased heart rate
sends sugar to muscles	shakes
increases adrenaline	butterflies in stomach; shaky feeling
ignites fighting muscles	upper body tension
lubricates grasping appendage	sweaty palms
diverts control from thinking brain to alligator brain	mind "blanks out"

The brain-stem-caused body response to Speech Anxiety/Stage Fright and the accompanying physical feelings.

WHAT'S THE DIFFERENCE BETWEEN SPEECH ANXIETY AND STAGE FRIGHT?

Let's clear up what you're feeling. If the speaking occasion has not happened yet, then you're feeling the effects of Speech Anxiety. If you're just thinking about it and you get the *SA/SF*© feelings, you're anxious. Anxiety is the fear of a pending event, something off in the future. Stage Fright happens when you're in front of an audience and looking the people right in the face. You're introduced, your metabolism takes off, and you've got *SA/SF*©, Stage Fright is fear during the presentation.

Imagine, for example, that you're driving across railroad tracks and your car stalls. The first thing you think is, "Oh, no—what if a train comes?" What you're feeling now is anxiety. If you see a light coming down the track and hear the train's whistle, that's fright.

WHEN YOU'LL GET IT

To prepare to deal with *SA/SF*©, you'll want to know how to predict when you'll get it. For most people, the type of audience and the purpose of the talk is critical to getting *SA/SF.*©

There are four factors of a communication event that occur when you have a high probability of getting *SA/SF*©:

Factor One: Purpose of the communication

The outcome is important. You want to do well for personal or professional reasons.

Factor Two: Audience composition

The audience is composed of your professional peers.

The audience is in a position to decide or approve your plan or to affect your career to a real degree, for example, presenting to an audience of supervisors.

Factor Three: You're risking important things

• your plan's on the line
• your reputation
• your self-esteem

Factor Four: You're not a master of the message

This is the worst catalyst for getting SA/SF.[©] If you don't know what you're talking about and you have any risk of failure, like speaking before people you care about, you're almost sure to get SA/SF.[©]

STRATEGIES FOR WHEN YOU'RE
NOT A MASTER OF THE MESSAGE

I recommend that if you're asked to speak on a topic you haven't mastered and the audience is familiar with the area, you should refuse the opportunity to speak. Your risk is too great.

If You Can't Refuse. If the boss says you have to give the talk, a good strategy is to talk only about what you know well. You can find some area of the topic that you can expand on or can relate to things that you do know. The standards of logic are far more loose for oral communication than written. You may get away with it. But remember my first advice: Refuse to talk; weasel your way out of it. Get somebody to take your place.

If you can't refuse—can't find a way out of having to make a presentation on a topic that you know nothing about—I have only one piece of advice left to give you: Fake It. You'll find more advice on putting on a stiff upper lip and a brave front in **Chapter 7, "Oral Communication: The Words You Say Are Less Than 10% of the Message."**

Did you notice a common pattern in the factors that lead to *SA/SF*©? For most of us they are negative outcomes, visions of failure, and embarrassment. Often, we don't really have a clear idea of what we're afraid of or anxious about. That lack of specificity makes fear a foggy monster, without a form that can be wrestled. Let's give that monster a face so you can deal with it. Take a few minutes now, or when you can find time to concentrate privately, and build a list of things that you fear about making speeches or talking with other people. Imagine the fearful outcomes you envision happening when you think of communicating with others. Use a speech situation, or making a telephone call, or talking during a one-on-one interview. You can pick a single communication venue or a variety. It's important that you pick the things you really fear. The fear does not have to be rational, in fact the things we fear are usually not rational. I'll show you how to use this list of fears to reduce your *SA/SF* © in the next chapter.

List of Negative Audience Reactions

1. _____
2. _____
3. _____
4. _____
5. _____
6. _____
7. _____
8. _____
9. _____
10. _____

Some General Thoughts on
Getting SA/SF© or Not Getting SA/SF©

If you never get speech anxiety or stage fright you may have an uncommon physiological response, your metabolism may be set at a very low level.

Or—and this is a problem if you never experience *SA/SF*®—you may be playing it too safe. You might not be risking enough—you've got to take risks to grow. Remember, in business and in life, the bigger the risk, the bigger the gain—and the bigger the risk, the bigger fool you'll appear if you screw up.

I believe that the **Key** is: **Fear of losing face.**

Anxiety is normal—we all get it. Today's world is full of stress producers: job, family, school, children, taxes, and the dangers, both physical and psychological, that surround us.

Anxiety is OK in speaking circumstances, it's only a problem if it causes you to avoid opportunities to speak with people, keeps you from expressing your vision to others, or if the physical and psychological experience is so intense or so unpleasant that you're very uncomfortable. The next chapter offers some tried and true suggestions for managing *SA/SF*® that have been used successfully by thousands of executives.

SUMMARY

Fear of speaking is a normal feeling that everyone gets. *SA/SF*® becomes a problem if it keeps you from speaking when you want. You can't eliminate speech anxiety nor would you want to. You must learn to manage speech anxiety and turn its power into useful energy.

You can recognize the distinct set of physical symptoms that indicate speech anxiety. *SA/SF*® is caused by your brain stem trying to protect you from physical danger. You'll get *SA/SF*® when it's important that you do well, when the listener(s) can judge you, when you're at risk, and when you're not a master of the message.

5

Managing Speech Anxiety

Action Steps You Can Take

I n this section, we're going to talk about six action steps you can take
that will help you manage yourself in stress-inducing communication
venues.

ACTION STEPS YOU CAN TAKE

Action Step One	Ride it out, it will pass.
Action Step Two	Be here now.
Action Step Three	Think about the positive outcomes.
Action Step Four	Fill your conscious mind with positive thoughts.
Action Step Five	Manage your metabolism.
Action Step Six	Know your topic.

Action Step One:
Ride It Out, It Will Pass

Researchers measure pulse rates to test for speech anxiety/stage fright.
Pulse rate is a good surrogate measure for the increased metabolism that
accompanies stage fright. Across all types of speakers and in a variety of
speaking venues, a single pattern of pulse rate emerges. Researchers at Florida

State University and cooperating universities, led by the internationally recognized communication researcher, Dr. Theodore Clevenger, measured executives, students, and television performers. The speaking venues were business meetings, in-class speeches, and nationally broadcast television shows. The pattern of physical change during speech anxiety and stage fright is shown in **Figure 5.1, Speaker's Pulse Rate While Presenting.**

In the graph in Figure 5.1, the speaker's pulse rate is on the vertical axis and time runs along the horizontal arm. The first thing you may notice is that the speaker begins talking to his or her audience with an already elevated pulse rate. The typical resting pulse rate is 50 to 60 beats per minute (bpm) for trained athletes, and up to 70 bpm for average people. You can see that most speakers, even before getting up to speak, begin their talk with an elevated heart rate of 90 to 110 bpm. As they progress into their talk, their pulse accelerates rapidly. When it's your turn to speak, as you are introduced and walk before your audience or as you are ushered into the boss's office, your pulse may climb as high as 170 to 180 bpm.

During these initial minutes you're temporarily insane. Catecholamine is released into your body and brain. You hear your pulse pounding in your head because there is a major artery that passes near your ears. You have trouble inhaling because the intercostal muscles between your ribs are tense and tight, along with the "fighting muscles" used in hand-to-hand combat: the upper back, neck, and arms. Your body is demanding lots of oxygen to service the runaway metabolism. Your field of vision may narrow. You feel slightly nauseous from the adrenaline flowing in your blood. Adrenaline causes that feeling of butterflies in your stomach. Yet you've got to appear poised and cool and deliver a smooth presentation. Good luck. There is good news. Notice that after three to five minutes your body begins to settle down and your pulse drops dramatically. It doesn't return to a normal resting rate, but by comparison to the runaway freight train you've been riding, it seems much more normal. So your task is to make it through the first few minutes of your presentation; this is where most people experience the most intense Stage Fright.

MORE ON BUTTERFLIES

Remember the feeling you experienced when having dental work that required novocaine? Dentists give adrenaline along with the injection of

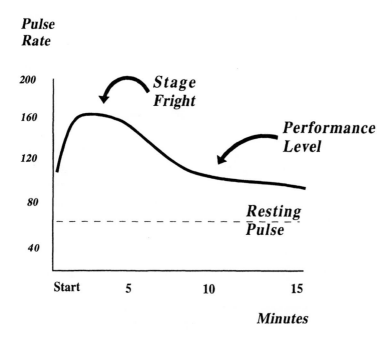

Figure 5.1 Speaker's Pulse Rate While Presenting
The speaker's pulse first soars to intense levels usually associated with physical exercise, then after three to five minutes lowers to 90 to 100 beats per minute (bpm).

novocaine because it acts as a vasoconstrictor. Adrenaline causes the capillaries to squeeze down, reducing any bleeding that might occur. It's great for the dentist because it makes the operating field easy to manage. The dentist leaves, saying, "I'll be back in a few minutes to see if you're good and numb." You're sitting there trying to relax, and fighting a losing battle. You're trying to think positively and minimize your fears, but all along you've got a tremendous flock of butterflies in your stomach and that slight nausea that signals fear. You don't realize that the butterflies are caused by the adrenaline injection, you think you're scared. Psychologists call what you're thinking an *internal attribution*. We'll discuss attribution theory next.

Mental self-management is vital to professional communicators. You are what you think. You create and control your own state of mind and sense of well-being. The following section on attribution theory will give you a thorough understanding of how your mind and body work together and how you can learn to exercise superior control over your state of mind.

ATTRIBUTION THEORY

Attribution theory—a popular psychological theory—is a very rational approach to understanding how we think. Unlike other theories that describe human behavior as driven by internal states or by personality, attribution theory starts with the premise that people are thinking, rational beings. People think like scientists even though they don't have formal scientific training. We watch other people notice the world's events, and we try to make sense out of them. Though much of what we see appears to be chaotic, we still try to sort it out and create order.

For example, we use formalized and well-established systems of thought to organize what could be random behavior. Imagine what chaos business would be if accountants didn't have rules and rational ways of dealing with money as it flows in and out of a firm. Or if marketing people didn't have methods of getting money for accountants and finance people to play with.

ATTRIBUTION THEORY—THE SCIENTIST OBSERVES

We watch the world about us, explaining the events we see, why they happen, assigning cause for effects we observe. For example, imagine that you're sitting on the shore of a lake watching a sailor in a rowboat that is moving across the lake. You want to explain why the boat is moving.

As an intelligent person, trained to use attribution theory, you rely on two fundamental rules to explain causes of effects: *Can* and *Try.*

1. *Can:* Does the person have the ability to cause the effect? If the answer is "Yes," the person may be responsible for causing the effect. But even though it's necessary, *can* information is not sufficient. The person has to try, too.
2. *Try:* Did the person exert effort?

Together, *Can* and *Try* evidence are excellent explanations for responsibility.

As you look at the sailor and the boat, what *can* and *try* information do you have?

Test One. Does the sailor have oars or sails? (*Can*)

Test Two. Is the sailor working the sails or pulling on the oars? (*Try*)

If you answer "Yes" to Test One and Test Two, you will attribute cause to the sailor. The sailor is responsible for the boat's progress across the lake.

But if the answer to either the *Can* or *Try* Test is "No," you'll make attribution to forces outside the sailor: For example, the passive sailor in the powerless boat may be moving due to the wind or current.

The next idea I'm going to share is a bit slim in form but powerful in utility, so may I ask you to sharpen your attention a bit more?

ATTRIBUTION PRINCIPLE:
"INTERNAL OR EXTERNAL LOCUS OF CONTROL"

The *Locus of Control* is the *Source of Power* or force that causes things to happen. It's the mojo that moves people, places, and things, it empowers actions and causes results. There are two Loci of Control: Internal and External. The power resides or originates either within or outside the person. If you believe that the motivation comes from within the person, you'll make the attribution that the person is the cause, that the person is responsible. Or, if you believe that forces outside the person were the cause, you would not hold that person responsible.

IT'S A FOUL ASSIGNMENT AND
YOUR NAME IS WRITTEN ALL OVER IT

For example, consider the internal (inside) forces that would cause your supervisor to give you an undesirable assignment. You receive a voice mail message from your superior assigning a nasty, bothersome little project that no one in their right mind would want. What caused her to give it to you? Here are two lists of possible causes. The first list contains only internal motivations. The second is a set of external attributions you could make to figure out your supervisor's actions.

- *intelligence:* she knows that you handle messy projects well

- *prejudice:* she believes people of your gender, racial or national characteristics, or sexual preference like this type of work
- *greed:* she will look good in the eyes of her superior
- *knowledge:* she knows that you won't turn her down or fuss too much
- *love:* she wants to see you succeed; though undesirable, this project will show how tough you are and spotlight you to others in your organization

If you believe that any of the above reasons were deterministic in her giving you the assignment, you'd blame her.

Now, consider this list of external attributions for cause:

- *other people:* her supervisor expressly suggested that you be given the assignment
- *systems:* as part of your company's operating policy, miscellaneous assignments are given in strict rotation according to seniority and the last project assigned—your name came up
- *forces of nature:* everybody else is sick, you are the only one available

If you make the attributions for the cause behind your supervisor's assignment to be external forces, you'll be far less likely to blame her.

PERRY MASON USES ATTRIBUTION THEORY

Juries make decisions of guilt or innocence using attribution theory. If they believe that a defendant's motivation was due to internal forces, they will bring back a verdict of guilty. If the defense can successfully demonstrate to the jury that external forces were at work, the defendant is pronounced not guilty.

For example, in a criminal case, the jury must decide why a wealthy young man killed his butler.

External. The butler went berserk and attacked him with a lead pipe in the library. Verdict: not guilty, self-defense.

Internal. The butler was blackmailing him with candid photos that showed him committing adultery. Verdict: guilty, murder.

In a personal injury case the jury decides why the patient died. They determine if the doctor was at fault.

External. The patient had a rare fungus that quickly enveloped his body; there was no known cure. Verdict: not guilty.

Internal. The doctor was drinking and ingesting prescription medications and misdiagnosed the case. Verdict: responsible for the patient's death.

WHY FAILURE IS AN ORPHAN

Something extremely useful to managers or group leaders is people's reactions to success or failure. When asked, people will make an internal attribution for successful outcomes and external attributions for failures.

For example, you get an A on a test and I ask you why. Within the normal bounds of modesty, you say, "I studied really hard"; "I have a talent for this subject"; "I'm a good student." All are internal attributions of cause.

But, imagine that you get an F on a test. NOT THAT IT WOULD EVER HAPPEN. But just pretend you failed a test and you're asked why. Likely answers would include, "The test was too hard"; "I had to work and could not study"; "Not a single thing the professor told us to prepare for was on the test." Failure generates external attributions for cause, it's human nature.

The same factors apply if your plan is approved by upper management or when you hit a home run in softball. Even when your children do well in school, it's probably due to your great genes and how well you've reared them.

TEST OF CHARACTER

Watch out when you have to assign cause (blame). You can predict that the person you have to blame will have some automatic thinking patterns. You can bet that he or she will shift blame to external factors. Perhaps you should follow Dale Carnegie's advice and avoid ever assigning blame to another person.

If you have to assign blame, do not refer directly to the person responsible as a source of cause. Say, "That project is slipping behind schedule" rather than "Your project is slipping behind schedule"—or worse, "You're behind schedule." It makes it easier for people to step forward and take responsibility, or at the very least, keep their defensive shields lowered.

Also, may I suggest that you watch yourself when you are the recipient of negative evaluations or outcomes. It is a sign of higher character to resist an automatic thinking pattern and to seek "truth" and accept the responsibility.

HOW TO USE THE POWER OF ATTRIBUTION
THEORY TO MANAGE SPEECH ANXIETY

Just as we assign cause for other people's actions and the outcomes of events, we all use attribution to explain why we feel the way we do at any given moment. We humans experience a wide range of emotions: anger, fear, love, passion, envy, desire, greed, anxiety, elation, and many more. As an adult, you have become very sophisticated in detecting the various types of emotions you experience at any given moment. Although you may feel an extensive set of emotions, the physical feelings you're having are quite limited. In fact, the same chemicals flow through your body during almost all emotions. Emotion is rather simple chemically, but it is very complex attributionally. This limited set of physiological responses/feelings is explained by external cues. You use information from your environment to explain your feelings.

For example, imagine that late one night, after shopping, you're walking out of the mall just as it is closing. Suddenly, out of the corner of your eye, you see a stranger jumping out at you from a dark corner. You take that set of information—human form, sudden, aggressive movement toward you, the fact that you're in a vulnerable situation—and you attribute the cause of the sudden rush of feeling to fear.

Now, change the setting in your mind to a romantic, softly lit watering hole. You're sharing a lively, loving conversation with a person of the gender you prefer; this person is attractive and you experience a slowly building set of physical feelings that, when they reach their peak, are almost identical to the body chemical that you generated when you were surprised by the stranger as you were walking out of the mall. It's the very same set of chemicals producing the very same body feeling. One is unpleasant and frightening, making you hope in your heart of hearts that it never happens again. The other is a moment that you wish could go on forever, one that you'll choose to return to again and again in your memory.

SITUATIONAL INFORMATION
DETERMINES YOUR FEELING

If you're opening a letter from the IRS, you may label your feelings "anxiety" or "fearful expectation." Should you find yourself speaking before an audience, you could attribute your enhanced physical state to the fact that you're about to seize a thrilling opportunity—one that will confirm your exalted status and knowledge. Or, you could decide to believe that you are a victim trapped in a frightening experience—one that will mean huge risk and probably failure and humiliation. How do you decide? Do you realize that the attribution you make is entirely up to you? You pick the one you most believe in. That will determine how you feel and will regulate how you speak.

WHAT IS THE CAUSE OF THESE FEELINGS?

During significant business communications your body is alive. Adrenaline is flowing, your blood pressure is up, your heart is pumping. How do you explain these symptoms? Possible attributions could include that you're weak, vulnerable, that you've got a sick feeling. Or you could choose to attribute the feelings to excitement and power: that you're sensing that the audience loves you—that you're feeling totally alive. That second set of attributions—the feelings of power—is what successful business leaders make; that is what they tell themselves. And they really believe it.

IS IT FUN OR SCARY?

Think about the first time you went downhill skiing or skin-diving or rode a roller coaster (or pick your own sensory-rich, body-rush-producing experience). Did you like it? Was it exhilarating or scary? Were you challenged, or did you feel like you were a prisoner on a freight train to hell? Did you feel powerful and alive or frightened and in physical danger?

During the first few moments of these experiences you make a decision, an attribution for the profound set of body feelings you're having. If you think that downhill skiing is exciting, when you get to the bottom of the run you can't wait to get on the lift and go again. On the other hand, if you were frightened by the feeling, felt that you were out of control and in danger, when you finally made it to the bottom of the hill you probably kicked your skis off, headed to the lodge, planted yourself at the bar, and vowed never to let yourself be trapped in a situation like that again.

Business communication is like that. You can convince yourself that you like the feeling, that the body-rush of adrenaline and accompanying sensations are the result of power and excitement rather than uncontrolled danger. You are what you think.

INSIGHT INTO ATTRIBUTION FOR FEELINGS

Let me share some objective scientific evidence that will clearly demonstrate to you how people label their body feelings based on information about the setting they are in. In these psychological studies, undergraduate male students at a leading university were given heavy, soundproof headsets to wear, like the headsets that airport ground crews wear as they wave your plane up to the gate. The experimenters convinced the young men that what they were hearing in the headsets was their own heartbeat. The young men were given an album filled with photos of nude females. As the subjects looked at certain preselected photos, the experimenters turned up the subjects' "heart rate." At the end of the experiment, the men were encouraged to select one of the photos (their choice) to take with them as a reward for having participated in the study. Each time, the young man selected the photo that accompanied his faster "heartbeat." What makes it more interesting is that the photos were prerated by a panel of judges for attractiveness. The experimenters increased the heart rate for the photos that were consistently rated as less attractive. The subjects made the attribution: "I liked her best."

If you found the first experiment interesting but of questionable ethics or taste, wait till I tell you about the second experiment that was conducted. Everything was the same as before: Young males listening through headset to "heartbeat"; looking at nude females. But this time, a picture of a nude male was inserted in the midst of the album. Guess which picture the experimenters increased the heartbeat on this time? Right you are. And guess what reaction these young men had, at an age where much of their sexual identity was being established? Subject after subject began to believe that he was gay, even though his sexual orientation was heterosexual. The experiments went into greater ethical jeopardy as they did not adequately debrief the subjects and explain what they had been through. This series of studies profoundly demonstrates the power of attribution. If young men can be convinced that they have an attraction to another person based on heart rate information, you can convince yourself that your heightened metabolism is the result of excitement and power, not fright. This is exactly what I recommend you do—convince yourself that you're excited, tell your listeners that you're excited to be speaking with them. More on this idea later.

KEY | You are what you think.

HOW TO TAKE CONTROL OF YOUR BODY AND MIND

As you're waiting to speak, feeling anxiety surge through you, there are positive steps you can take to manage your metabolism and reduce your anxiety. Remember the graph of how your pulse rate changes during a presentation? You remember that the most challenging part happens at the beginning because your initial pulse rate, just before and immediately after you're introduced, is the highest. A good plan is for you to work to lower your pretalk metabolism as you're beginning to feel anxiety. Controlling your metabolism at this stage will make the opening of your talk much more enjoyable for you and your audience—and reduce your feelings of anxiety.

Action Step Two: *Be Here Now*

This tip may sound a bit "groovy": *Be Here Now.* As you're getting ready to speak, think about the present. Don't let your mind wander to the near future, when you're going to be speaking. Remember, anxiety is fear of impending danger. If you are literally living in the present moment you will be invulnerable to anxiety. So, keep your mind in the present; think about the things you'll say; review your speech. Don't visualize yourself delivering it, just think about your ideas.

While you're waiting to speak, find a position in the room that lets you see your audience's faces. Study the audience, pick out people whose faces you like. For some wonderful reason, some people are more appealing to us during that fast flashing moment of a first impression. Maybe they look like somebody we know and like. Perhaps they just seem friendly. As you study the audience, you're living in the present moment, and you're gaining the additional bonus of taking a set of intimidating strangers and turning them into more familiar friends. When you begin to speak, when your metabolism is at its highest level, you'll want to talk exclusively to the faces you like.

Here is another trick for *Being Here Now* that I learned from a gentleman who teaches people who suffer from chronic and debilitating fear of flying how to overcome their disability. Harith Razah works as an executive, but part-time he conducts seminars for American Airlines. Mr. Razah suffered from crippling fear of flying and learned to manage his fear. The trick he uses (among other techniques) is to give a thick rubber band to each of his students. When they feel anxious, they snap it on the tender flesh of the wrist. This sharp blast of pain brings them back to the present moment. They concentrate on the sensation in their wrist and in those moments of minor pain they get an important relief from their escalating anxiety. They are thinking about the pinch of pain instead of all the things that could go wrong with the plane.

Try the wrist snap, or if your metabolism level is not that high, study the back of your hand, your pen, or the paper your notes are written on. These will all bring you to the present moment where anxiety cannot get you.

Another idea is to listen to the other speakers. Really concentrate on what they are saying. Do not allow yourself to think about your talk or what will happen when you get up. Don't worry about being ready when you're introduced, you'll have all the time you need to bring yourself to the peak of performance for your talk.

Action Step Three:
Think About the Positive Outcomes

If you feel anxious and you insist on thinking about the impending communications event, think positively. Allow yourself to think only about the wonderful, beneficial things that will happen. You'll begin to feel powerful and energized. For example, picture the audience being delighted with your speech. Rehearse parts of your speech and visualize the positive response that you'll get from the people in your audience. Think about what will happen after you've spoken and your vision is adopted by the group. Visualize the benefits you'll accrue from speaking.

TAKING CONTROL OF PERSISTENT FEARS

Fears of all types are a very common human problem. Clinical psychologists have developed techniques that will help you prepare to manage yourself and to deal with all types of stress-inducing fears. Dr. Ralph Iennarella, of Northwestern University, taught me how to reduce fear using this simple, three-step process.

Fear, particularly anxiety over an impending event, is a nasty, annoying emotion to live with. Our brains prefer to think about negative, fearful incidents. Unless you take control of your thoughts, left to its own resources your brain will choose to pay more attention to fear information than to positive information. Your brain would rather think about the bad stuff that could happen than the good things that probably will happen. Think about all the things you've been worrying about over the past few months. Now, how many of those disasters actually happened? Few, if any, I bet. Next, think about the lousy things that did happen to you. How many of them did you anticipate, think about, and develop a nice set of anxiety over? The answer for most of us is that 90% of the things we worry about, even lose sleep over, never happen. And of the things that actually go wrong in our lives, few of them were expected.

FALSE ALARMS GOING OFF IN YOUR HEAD

Our brain stem is not very good at understanding the dangers we face today. When our brain stem comes to our rescue because we feel threatened or are feeling anxious—it can make speaking harder. I think that our brain stem is a lot like the character played by Joe Pesci in the *Lethal Weapon* movies starring Danny Glover and Mel Gibson. Like Pesci's character, the brain stem is well meaning but totally out of touch and unequipped to deal with the problem at hand. Just like Pesci's character, your brain stem can shoot you in the foot while it's trying to help you fight the bad guys ("OK? OK? OK? OK? OK?").

Here is why: Our reptilian brain was developed millions of years ago when all the dangers we faced were physical. For example, a cave dweller was threatened by a saber-toothed tiger or by running off a cliff, not by having her co-workers laugh and ridicule her when she presented her financial analysis. To protect our ancient ancestors, the brain stem responded to danger by pumping out a rush of chemicals that made them stronger, faster, and their bodies better able to stand and fight or to run from danger (fight or flight). Unfortunately for us, our society has evolved faster than has our brain stem. The dangers we face today are social, not physical. When you get ready to present your ideas, your brain stem senses your fear and thinks that you are in physical danger. It rushes in to rescue you: It shuts down the cerebral cortex and all brain activity is diverted to combat condition red; it reduces blood flow to your extremities so if you suffer a cut you won't bleed to death; it increases your heart rate to pump blood to your upper body's fighting muscles. Sugar is shot into your muscles. You're powerful; your arms shake with energy. If your mission was to tear phone books in half or leap into your audience and kill 20 people, you could. Your body is ready. But your job is not to become a killing machine, your job is to be cool. You are supposed to project calm, confident control and make your audience believe that you are in charge.

If the brain stem were properly designed to rescue us from the dangers we face today, it would not turn us into fighting machines. Rather, it would produce chemicals to heighten our intelligence and charm. For example, if our brain stem were the type of ally that we need during an important business meeting it would send chemical messengers to relax our muscles, allowing us to move gracefully and to gesture smoothly. Rather than making our mouth dry, it would order the production of extra saliva to lubricate tongue and lips so we would speak with great fluidity. The brain stem would release endorphins to give us a feeling of well-being. Other chemical messengers would be released to heighten our intelligence, decrease our cerebral cortex's processing time, and make retrieval time from memory more rapid allowing us to assess ideas and questions with greater brilliance. Peripheral vision would be enhanced allowing you to see more of your audience—you could read every person's reaction to your ideas (the opposite usually happens: a narrowing of the visual field, like tunnel vision). And perhaps the brain stem would help us become more socially attractive by releasing a chemical musk scent that would make us more sexually attractive to our listeners. Now, that is the brain stem we need when we're under social danger—something to turn us into Cary Grant, not Rambo.

YOUR BRAIN STEM IS OBSESSED WITH FEAR

Time and time again your brain stem makes you miserable. It gives you rotten feelings when you should be feeling excited and powerful. It makes you stupid when you need to be intelligent. You become a klutz when you need grace and charm. But just because it has this consistent track record of failure doesn't prevent the brain stem from obsessing about things that will go wrong. Fear and anxiety are very hard to let go of. Your brain stem thinks that it's protecting you. In reality it may be harming you with pent-up stress and preventing you from optimal performance.

You must make an extra effort to deal with these pesky, anxiety-creating fears.

The key is to take your recurring negative thoughts through a systematic analysis. At the end of this process, you'll find that your fears will be greatly reduced and, best yet, they won't recur as much, if at all. This technique has been known to rid people of their nagging fears forever. If you like, practice this technique by returning to your **List of Negative Audience Reactions** (in Chapter 4) to put yourself in a state of speech anxiety. The more vividly you recollect the fear, the more you'll experience this technique.

Step One: Sense fear and its cause. Visualize the fear, the negative, very clearly. You want to really feel the anxiety.

Step Two: Write down or say aloud exactly what you think will happen.

Describe the disaster in clear terms. HINT: You must not just think about the fear. The fear must be brought out into the clear light where you can examine it by writing it down or saying it aloud.

Step Three: Rank the magnitude of the fear on a scale of 1 to 10.

Assume that your worst fears come true. How bad would that be? Or, how severe a fear is it? Let 1 be hardly any fear at all, a very, very minor fear and 10 be the end of your world as you know it. The worst outcome you could imagine.

Step Four: Reassess fear and likely, realistic outcome.

Next, revisit the potential situation that is causing the anxiety. Describe it either by saying it aloud to yourself or by writing down what, rationally, will probably happen.

Step Five: Re-rank magnitude of fear on scale of 1 to 10.

Finally, sense your fear level and re-rank the magnitude of your anxiety. You'll find that fears that started out to be 8s or 9s have dropped way down to 2s or 3s. You'll find that they aren't even worth thinking about.

This technique allows you to put fears under the microscope. Fear is sneaky. It lurks in the background, in the shadows, whispering at you. So, your fears may be hard to grasp and deal with. To take back control you must bring your fears out, one by one, onto center stage. Put fear in the spotlight and give it a microphone. In that cold rational light, it can be dealt with.

Give this technique a try. Return to that list of negative outcomes you put together earlier in this chapter. Pick a really ugly, scary fear and use these five steps to whittle that redwood of fear down to a toothpick.

Action Step Four:
Fill Your Conscious Mind With Positive Thoughts

Filling your mind with positive thoughts will give you two great benefits: (1) You'll be able to reduce your anxiety and fill your body with positive energy, and (2) you'll become more powerful. Your audience will sense your positive energy. It heightens your leadership quality and credibility.

Remember, you are what you think. The great author Kurt Vonnegut told us, "We are what we pretend to be." Your state of emotional well-being, confidence, and dynamism is the direct product of your last sequence of thoughts and experiences. You can test this fact yourself. Next time you're lifting a heavy object, perhaps working out in a gym, test the power of a positive mental state. As you lift say the word *strong* or *power* to yourself. Concentrate on that word. You'll sense an immediate upward change in your physical power as you exert yourself against the weight. Next, try thinking the words *weak* or *heavy* and you'll notice that your power rapidly drops off. If a simple word can change your physical strength, what do you think profound and detailed thoughts can do? By programming in a sequence of positive thoughts, derived from the real experiences you have had, you can generate a positive push wave of energy. People will follow you and believe the words you say (see "The Fourth Component of Credibility" in **Chapter 6, "First, People Must Believe You: Managing Your Credibility"**).

HOW TO BUILD YOUR POSITIVE
LIST OF PERSONAL POWER THOUGHTS

Think about things in your life that make you confident and happy, things you've done to help people. Think about the people who love you and trust you. Visualize their smiling, loving faces. Remember the times you've been the big winner: in business, in sports, in love? Recall the times you were hired, promoted, landed a contract, had your ideas accepted? Were you ever a hero?

Next, you must record these private moments of victory and accomplishment in a list. You will want to have a set of 10 things that will instantly make you feel good about yourself the second you think of them.

KEY The list must produce strong, positive emotions and tie into visual memory. You must see the event vividly in your mind, so you can really feel it.

Ten Things That Make Me Feel Good

1. _____
2. _____
3. _____
4. _____
5. _____
6. _____
7. _____
8. _____
9. _____
10. _____

Action Step Five:
Manage Your Metabolism

This section prescribes physical exercises that you can do to reduce the heightened metabolism you experience during *SA/SF®*. Again, the idea is to begin with less stress so you'll enter into the communication setting with a lower level of stress.

Do stress-reducing exercises to help you relax as much as you can.

> **Exercise One.** Take 10 long, slow, deep breaths. Hold each breath and let it out slowly, between your teeth. If nobody is around, make a hissing sound as you exhale.

I'll bet that you may need only five or six breaths before you feel much better.

Caution: Watch out for hyperventilating by taking in too much air. You may need just a few breaths to get the benefit . . . too many will leave you lightheaded and giddy.

Next is a variation on taking 10 long, slow, deep breaths. Here we add a private message for your mind. The deep breaths address your body. The silent messages of *calm* and *down* soothe your troubled mind.

> **Exercise Two.** Before you go on stage, take a very deep breath. As you are inhaling, say to yourself: "Calm." Hold your breath for a few moments, then exhale. As you release your breath, slowly say the word "Down."

> **Exercise Three.** Do stretching exercises to remove tension from your upper back, shoulders, and neck. This tension makes your throat feel thick and your voice sound funny. Tension makes you look nervous.

> **Exercise Four.** This is a chance to apply your increased knowledge in visual memory to help you gain control of your mind and metabolism. Think of a place where you feel very relaxed. Practice thinking about that place. For example, if your favorite relaxation place is lying on the hot sand at the beach, picture yourself there.
>
> Use each of your senses—touch, taste, hearing, smell, and sight—to remember that favorite spot. For example, you can smell the salt air and

the breeze, feel the warmth of the sand, see the bright, light blue sky, hear the waves and far-off conversations.

The longer you practice remembering this, the more powerful and automatic it will become. The calming effect is wonderful and always at your command.

Exercise Five. Hum forcefully. This will relax your throat muscles and let you speak with greater ease. It will remove any trace of tension from your voice. You will not sound nervous. As you feel your throat begin to relax, hum more gently.

Action Step Six:
Know Your Topic

Earlier, I made what I hope is a convincing case for being a master of your subject matter before you speak. Let me also suggest that you demonstrate that mastery in the way you deliver your talk. Speak from an outline, have the general points you want to cover well in mind, or, even better, on overheads or handouts. Carry on a conversation with your audience—a good presentation is a lively exchange between your listeners and yourself.

Never, never, never, never memorize your speech. Note that I did not say sometimes, or usually. I insist that you never attempt to memorize a speech. **Exception to that rule:** If you are so talented that you can take prewritten ideas and deliver them with such elegance and fluidity that your audience is not aware that you're speaking canned words, do not go into business. A fortune and tons of fun are awaiting you in showbiz. If you want to stay in business, you can: Be your own manager.

The rest of us cannot take things we've memorized and deliver them in an *audience-engaging manner.* Sure you'll get the words out, and to some extent you'll be an effective communicator—because part of your vision will be communicated. Your audience may well receive some logical content. But the major message you send them is, "Shut up, don't participate, I'll do the talking, you just sit there." Your stilted, memorized tone creates a barrier between you and your audience. In this course, we will work with you to break down that barrier—making you a more powerful speaker.

THE DEER-IN-THE-HEADLIGHTS LOOK

Person after person has told me that one of their biggest fears about speaking before important people is that they will go blank during their presentation. They imagine themselves standing, mute, before a group of people who think that they are an idiot.

A great reason not to memorize a speech is that during a presentation everybody goes "blank"; we all forget a train of thought or lose a word for a moment—it's normal. But if you blank in a memorized presentation, as you probably will, it's like death. You stand there frozen, your mind races, you fight panic. You either stand there repeating the last line you said, hoping to recover the link to the idea that you've forgotten, or like a third grader delivering the Pledge of Allegiance, you have to start over at the beginning. Either way, it's not a pretty sight.

DEALING WITH BLANKING OUT

First, you can expect to go blank at least once during a talk. It's natural and it happens. In fact, the better you speak—the more spontaneous, the more involved you are, the more your audience is hanging onto your every thought—the greater the chance that as you're creating this lively communication experience you'll fail to find the right word or idea right away. This natural blanking can be exacerbated by panic. If you tense up and panic, you're dead. The audience realizes that something is wrong and transmits fear back to you.

STAY COOL, MON

Relax, forgetting is natural and only lasts for a few seconds at the most. See for yourself. Next time you're engaged in a conversation, notice how often you fail to find the right word or how often you lose your train of thought. My recommendation is to handle it the very same way you do in a casual conversation. Just wait, think, and it will come to you. But a persuasive business communication, particularly at a meeting before an important executive, or in a formal setting before a large group, is different from a casual conversation.

TWO DIFFERENT SPEED ZONES—
YOURS AND THE AUDIENCE'S

Besides the level of tension within you, there is another factor that makes blanking in a presentation especially difficult: *Einstein's Time Shift.* The audience and the *Presenter* are moving through two different time continua. For you, the speaker, time moves very quickly. It seems that you just got up to talk and time is up. For your audience, time moves in the other direction—it's moving very slowly. When you go blank, you feel like you've been standing mutely before the audience, sweating bullets, with everyone staring at you, for minutes; but to your audience, it's only the blink of an eye. If you make too big a deal out of blanking, the audience is likely to be puzzled over what you're talking about. To the audience, you just seem to pause. So relax, take a few seconds to think about what you want to say. Usually, your forgotten thought will come to you. Your audience believes that you're thinking. Makes you look smart and in control.

MOVE TO THE GROOVE:
USE BODY MOVEMENT
TO UNSTICK YOUR MEMORY

If you've waited and the thought doesn't come to you, use the same trick that athletes use to get in the groove and improve their performance: move. Standing frozen in the spotlight makes it worse, but moving, taking a step, will unlock your mind. The same trick works when you're sitting at a table and you go blank. When you shift your body position, rapidly and with confidence, that body movement will trigger recall.

JUST READ THE WRITING ON THE WALL:
USE VISUAL CUES

You can always glance at your visual supporting aids, like notes, or much better, the overhead projection of your outline. It's best to have your talk's key words on overheads (see **Chapter 11, "Visual Tools for Presentation"**).

CONFESSION IS GOOD FOR THE SOUL

If all the above methods fail you, be honest. Tell the audience you forgot what you were going to say. Your candor will build a bridge between you, enhance your credibility, and bring the audience closer to your side. And, just as in everyday conversation, as soon as you tell your listeners that you can't remember what you wanted to say, **you will remember it.**

Seven Keys to Managing Speech Anxiety and Stage Fright

Here is a list of seven practical keys that will help you manage yourself when you're experiencing *SA/SF®*.

KEY 1 The natural chemicals that are flowing through your body and mind as a result of your excitement give you a case of "temporary insanity."

- During the opening part of your talk you're under exceptional stress and elevated pulse rate. You may not remember the things you wanted to say during the first few moments; you may feel like you're riding on a runaway freight train.
- Have extensive notes or write out the first 30 seconds of your talk. After you get through that first section, you'll be fine.

KEY 2 Let your heightened metabolism work for you.

- It's energy, so use it. Move, be dynamic, be excited. Tell your listeners that you're very excited to be speaking to them. Elaborate and tell them why: Because your ideas are superior, you have found solutions, or best yet, because they are impressive, important people and you realize the magnitude of honor bestowed upon you by being allowed to speak to this esteemed group. Remember that you must be sincere. If the audience believes that you're just stroking it, we'll have to hose you off the sidewalk. You will have killed or badly wounded your credibility.
- Don't try to be cool, whatever you do. Your body is alive with power and energy. Your muscles are filled with adrenaline and sugar; they shake with strength and drive. Your breathing rate is faster and deeper as your body demands more oxygen to maintain this heightened metabolism. You'll only increase your stress if you try to stand still and look cool. If you're taking small

cautious breaths, you're not feeding the animal you've become. Breath deeply, drink in the oxygen. Move, too.

KEY 3 If you think your excitement is showing . . . tell your audience that you're excited to be speaking to them.

- The audience will attribute your obvious agitation to your excitement and will be flattered.
- Result: The audience will like you better, and you'll be building credibility.

KEY 4 Remember that the audience is on your side.

- Especially during the opening moments of your presentation, your audience wants you to speak well. Have you ever been listening to someone and said to yourself, "I surely hope that this speaker is boring"? Your listeners want an entertaining, informative presentation.
- Think of your listeners as partners in your presentation; that is, you're trapped together in the same lifeboat.

KEY 5 Try to meet the members of the audience before you speak, shake their hands and look them in the eye.

- Tell them you're one of the speakers. Thank them for coming. This human contact will greatly reduce your anxiety over being a stranger in the room. Even if you know the audience and work with them every day, a couple of moments of human contact will greatly enhance your sense of ease and their sense of participation in the talk. Together you'll have a better communication experience.
- A tip for meeting strangers is to look them in the eye. See if you can guess what type of person he is—friendly, serious, analytical, humorous. See if you like him or feel an affinity toward him. Most of us make a rapid, if not accurate, determination during the first few moments when we meet somebody: either we like her right away, don't like her, or find it hard to get a reading. Perhaps she reminds you of someone in your family, or someone you work with or have met before. If you begin your talk with a handful of people that you like, you're way ahead. You're going to focus your attention on them initially. More on this technique in **Chapter 7, "Oral Communication: The Words You Say Are Less Than 10% of the Message."**

KEY 6 Just before you're introduced, study the faces of your audience. Look for friendly faces.

- This is an application of the "Meet the Audience" technique just discussed. You'll find that some people are naturally better listeners. They give feedback; they look at you with expressions of interest and liking on their faces. You'll find that trying to talk to people who have blank or hostile faces or who are looking down is very disconcerting. But by focusing upon the good listeners, people you like, you'll begin to get and feel the good feedback and participation that you need to hit your tempo.

- As you begin to hold these individual conversations with the good listeners, the others will begin to tune in and become part of the communication experience. Focusing on the bad listeners or those who are tuning out will throw you off by giving you false feedback.

Talk to the "good listeners" in the audience.

KEY 7   Focus on the audience and your message.

- Concentrate on your ideas, not on yourself. If you're aware of how you are gesturing or of your physical symptoms, you'll heighten the $SA/SF^{©}$ reaction. You'll get nervous if you think of yourself too much. Think hard about how best to express your ideas.

- Look at audience members one at a time, hold brief conversations with each person, moving from one good listener to another.

- Forget about yourself. You don't have to spend your limited mental awareness and thinking ability on worrying about how you're conducting yourself. You have been beautifully reared and have fine business manners. Your natural gestures, the ones that you'll make during a presentation, are fine.

- What counts most in business presentation is a communication with the audience of facts and emotion, spontaneously delivered by a well-prepared authority on the topic: You.

- Great speakers are hungry to share their ideas with the audience; they really don't think about what their body is doing. Their motions and gestures become automatic. Train yourself to avoid "Self-Monitoring Behavior."

SPEECH ANXIETY: BARRIER TO SUCCESS

What keeps people from finding success and recognition in their business lives? Lack of planning? Bad luck? Too little effort? Lack of capital? Sure, these reasons have been the cause of business failure and lack of advancement. Think about yourself and your career. Like many people, you may find that anxiety in speaking has held you back. Not just because you got cold feet at the prospect of addressing the 5,000 national sales representatives and distributors at last year's national meeting. That would scare anybody. I am talking about the times you did not speak up at a meeting, the times you held back or were held back by anxiety or an unfocused, confused mind. How often have you not made or not returned a phone call because you did not want to speak to another person? Perhaps you were afraid of some unknown factor. How often, after the meeting was over and you were perhaps sitting at your desk or riding in your car, have you kicked yourself for not having spoken up? The regrets that we have are more often for the things that we did not do . . . not the things we did.

|SUMMARY

Some of the steps you can take to manage *SA/SF* [©] include

- riding out the increase in your metabolic rate, knowing that it's only temporary and will pass
- convincing yourself that you're excited (not nervous)
- thinking about the present moment so you'll become more calm—if you think about the near future (speaking), you'll become anxious
- filling your mind with only positive thoughts of the results of your communication
- lowering your metabolic rate with relaxation exercises
- never, never, never, never memorizing your presentation
- relaxing, if you go blank: You'll remember your thought in just a moment

KEYS TO MANAGING *SA/SF* [©]

☐ Have the first 30 seconds of your presentation memorized to get you over the high adrenaline hump that accompanies *SA/SF*[©],

☐ Let your higher metabolism work for you—it's energy, so use it as power, enthusiasm, and drive.

☐ Don't try to act cool when your engine is over-revving. Tell your listeners that you're excited about meeting them and excited about your topic.

☐ Meet the members of your audience before you speak—that familiarity will give you friendly faces to speak with.

☐ Before you speak, look into people's faces, look for people you like or are comfortable with.

☐ Talk only to the good listeners—the others will then tune in to your energy.

6

First, People Must Believe You

Managing Your Credibility

The single biggest factor in delivering a great presentation is a passionate desire to share your ideas and knowledge with your listener.

Two key factors must be present for a great presentation:

1. passion to communicate
2. mastery of message

If you really know what you're talking about, have prepared your ideas and how you want to share them, then you're ready to rock 'n' roll.

Now that you're prepared, there is one additional thing you'll need to do to make your presentation outstanding and persuasive. After all, this is the real reason for reading this book. You want to be persuasive.

SINGLE BIGGEST FACTOR IN PERSUASION:
YOUR CREDIBILITY

Of all the variables under your control during a presentation, the one that contributes most to your persuasive power is credibility. It's the single biggest variable under the speaker's control during the presentation.

I suggest that you must include messages designed to enhance your credibility in the presentation. Credibility messages are things you say and things you do. These communications are designed to answer the audience's key question:

"Why is the speaker telling me this . . . what is her motivation?"

KEY | Answer the underlying question in the audience's mind.

Listeners believe that a high credibility speaker's motivation is to the listener's benefit—that if they follow the speaker's plan they will benefit.

CREDIBILITY AND THE TEAM PLAYER

Of course, your foremost goal is to build credibility for yourself. But some magical things happen when you wisely take time to craft credibility for your teammates and for your firm.

You see, building credibility for others builds credibility for you. As their status and estimation builds in the eyes of the listener, your credibility grows through association. The attribution is "birds of a feather." In communication, we call it the *halo effect*. Around election time you'll see those masters of persuasion, politicians, flocking together to share the wonderful warm glow of the halo effect. When the president comes to town notice how they all cluster together, having their photos taken. When the president is in trouble, they run from the White House spotlight for fear that their credibility will be denigrated by association.

Source Credibility

High credibility is generally desirable, it's something that you want to acquire. Here is why: When your audience believes that you have high credibility, some wonderful things happen.

- People will listen more intently to what you say and for longer periods of time.
- A high credibility communicator is more persuasive than someone with lower credibility. In study after study, speakers with equivalent speaking skills and styles of delivery gave the same message to an audience. The only difference between the two was their credibility. For example, one speaker might be presented as an expert in the field and the other as a well-informed amateur.

The expert was far more persuasive than the well-informed amateur. (More on the characteristics of a credible communicator later in this chapter.)

◻ You'll enjoy more control over the communication situation. People will respond to your questions; the audience will conform and follow you during your presentation. You'll benefit from this heightened degree of audience cooperation.

TWO WAYS OF LOOKING AT SOURCE CREDIBILITY

We in communication research have learned to look at credibility in two different ways: the Source's personal characteristics—for example, job title, gender, age, education, level of expertise, occupation, income—or the things that the communicator does. Here is the key: While preparing your persuasive communication you can't do much about your characteristics. Growing older quickly or attaining another graduate credential is not a good short-term strategy. Controlling what you do and say, however, can be managed in the short term.

LESSONS FROM THE PERSUASIVE MASTERS

I trust that you've advanced in your education or in your personal development to the point where you can utilize the lessons of older cultures. (I've noticed that when people with lower educational skills are presented with ideas from a generation or two ago, they are skeptical. Should some well-meaning person suggest that they embrace ideas that come from far older civilizations, they tune out completely.) That is why I feel comfortable sharing insight into persuasion that comes from the greatest group of persuasive individuals in the history of this planet: the ancient Greeks. I believe that this group of constant debaters, who made all decisions in open public forums, akin to the New England Town Meetings, developed and honed their persuasive communication skills to a razor-sharp edge.

ANCIENT SECRETS OF CREDIBILITY

We modern scientists have used all our advanced skills and technology to uncover the most powerful secrets of persuasion. First at Yale during and after World War II—then at Stanford, Michigan State, Florida State (Go 'Noles), and Columbia Universities, and other leading communication research institutions—endless experiments, surveys, and Adelphi Think Groups have been conducted. After hundreds of hours of mainframe computer time and hundreds of scholarly articles, we've managed to confirm what the ancient Greeks knew all along. The following is the list of ancient secrets:

1. Listeners believe that a high credibility communicator is far more persuasive than a low credibility speaker.
2. Credible people have three characteristics:
   ◻ expertise
   ◻ trustworthiness
   ◻ goodwill

Not to sell modern communication scholars too short, we have discovered some useful facts about credibility and persuasion. I'll share those with you in a second. First, let's talk more about the three personal characteristics of a highly credible communicator and how you can enhance your credibility in the eyes of others.

Three Pillars of Credibility: Expertise, Trustworthiness, and Goodwill

Credibility Pillar One: Expertise. You are what you know

What have you accomplished in your life: what degrees do you hold, what honors have you received? What can you do: operate software, fix things, find things, create ideas? What do you know: technical facts, financial analysis, foreign languages? Think about the *specialized training* you have taken, the *facts you have at your command.* You demonstrate your expertise as you present your ideas. People infer expertise to you through the speed, accuracy, and facility with which you use jargon and terminology and how well you can translate technical terms for them (lay people). Expertise is demonstrated through your job title. Some job titles are more credible than others. For example, "Sales Representative" carries lower credibility than "Marketing Executive."

Perhaps that is why IBM began to call their sales representatives, Marketing Executives. They found it easier to get in the door to see prospective customers, that is, get the first appointment. Soon most corporations began to assign the title Marketing Representative or Marketing Executive to their sales staff. I think that IBM has raised the ante. One of my outstanding graduate assistants, Mike Gomol, landed a job at IBM just after he completed his MBA at DePaul. He phoned me with the exciting news that he was now a Market Manager for IBM. I was beyond impressed, I was amazed. "Wow," I thought. I knew Mike was ultra sharp, but to be given product design, advertising, promotion, pricing, and production-level responsibility right out of grad school was unheard of at IBM. Of course what had happened was IBM now called their Marketing Representatives, "Market Managers," thereby staying semantically one step ahead of the industry. Mike left IBM within two years to join a more entrepreneurial firm.

Other Professionals' Esteem. A surefire way to build powerful credibility for yourself is to have other people in your profession speak highly of you. Have you ever noticed how physicians and lawyers are reluctant ever to say anything against another member of their profession? Should your surgeon accidentally sew your foot to the top of your head, another surgeon if pressed to comment on her colleague's work would probably say, "The stitches were beautifully executed, notice how closely placed and even they are." Physicians and lawyers clearly understand how important it is to maintain each other's esteem, at least as communicated to lay people and outsiders. They have strict formal and informal codes to maintain this very important source of credibility.

Educational Degrees. Fine evidence of your expertise is advanced educational degrees. They are external and objective evidence that quickly communicate who you are through what you've achieved. Educational degrees will also serve as evidence of your self-discipline and, thereby, your trustworthiness. The pedigree of your alma mater is important, because the reputation of the school awarding your diploma extends to you, through the halo effect. Simply stated: You are who you hang with.

Expertise Takes Time to Build. If you've got an important meeting coming up, you can't rush out and buy yourself a set of expertise. Expertise can be communicated but can't be instantly created. You can't get more expertise during a presentation.

Credibility Pillar Two: Trustworthiness

We all like people who do what they say they are going to do. It's an increasingly valuable trait. When we think about a trustworthy person, we think of rather lofty attributes: honor, truth, and even ethics. But trustworthiness can be as simple as showing up for a meeting that you had promised to attend or completing a project by the deadline. Trust is "can I take your word and believe that you'll give me your honest opinion." For example, there is an art to letting the boss or an important customer know when they are wrong.

Trustworthiness takes time to build. You can't expect people to trust you upon first meeting. We all put new acquaintances and business associates on a rather short leash until they have demonstrated to us, through performance, that they are trustworthy and will deliver what they promise.

Without trustworthiness your credibility is worthless. The business world is filled with untrustworthy people who are highly expert.

Today, people are very skeptical of experts. They wisely believe that there is danger from experts who don't use expertise "to help." For example:

Finance	*Insider trading; reverse blue-lining*
Marketing	*PowerMaster beer; adulterated baby food; discounts*
Government and Politics	You can *just name it*
Law	*Excessive and even exaggerated personal injury suits* that set precedence for a continued lowering of *the individual citizen's acceptance of personal responsibility.*

Time is the big limitation on trustworthiness. There is no such thing as **Instant Trustworthiness**—just add water and microwave. You have to build a track record before your trustworthiness will be well known. Perhaps that is why personal recommendations are so effective in gaining new accounts, jobs, and access in the business community. There is nothing like a hearty recommendation from a person who can vouch for you to some new associate to get your credibility off on the right step.

Credibility Pillar Three:
Goodwill toward your audience

Now for the good news. The most important part of your credibility—communicating an attitude of goodwill toward your listener—can be managed during the presentation. You can build and manipulate your listener's perception of your goodwill during the communication. Actually, it is during the communication that your listener will decide how well you rate on this dimension of credibility.

ARISTOTLE'S IDEAL COMMUNICATOR

The ancient master of persuasive communication, Aristotle of Athens, called the ideal communicator a "Man of Goodwill." He called credibility, "A mantle of reputation and personality worn about the speaker's shoulders."

THE SECRET BEHIND PROJECTING "GOODWILL"

You have to feel it. You can't fake goodwill unless you're a very talented actor. People are very sophisticated at detecting insincerity. We're like dogs sniffing for fear. Think about the time when you were a little kid and were going to visit relatives or a family friend. They had a dog and the adults told you how to act when you first meet a new dog. They probably told you not to make any sudden movements: to hold out your hand and not to show fear. The same principles apply to business communication. You must project your feeling of goodwill to your listeners. Sure, you can communicate your goodwill with words, but unless you've got the attitude to back it up, your listeners will not fully believe you. Words can ring hollow.

SET YOUR ATTITUDE BEFORE YOU MEET

Work to place the good of the other person in your heart. As you are packaging your message, consider how your vision will affect the listener. How would he like to learn about your plan? It's not enough to present your ideas with a spirit of goodwill—you've got to develop those plans with the other person's best interest as your highest interest.

YOU MUST RESPECT YOUR LISTENERS

Have genuine respect and admiration for the audience. This is the first step in setting your mind and attitude for optimal communication. You don't have to agree with everything another says, is, and does. But you must find something that you admire about your listener before you can project goodwill.

LOOK IN THE MIRROR

Look in the mirror and see the other person's reflection, not yours. See things from the other person's viewpoint first. You may feel uncomfortable in focusing your attention on the other person's perspective. Perhaps you'll fear losing "what I want to say"; or perhaps you're concerned that you'll end up changing your viewpoint or plans. Don't worry about forgetting what you want to say. You'll remember when it's your time to speak. More on this in **Chapter 7, "Oral Communication: The Words You Say Are Less Than 10% of the Message."** You'll find great success as a speaker, leader, and persuader when you learn how to communicate from the listener's frame of reference.

THE FOURTH COMPONENT OF CREDIBILITY

I know that I told you that there were three major components of credibility: Expertise, Trustworthiness, and Goodwill. That is true, these three have been with us since ancient Greece. But modern research has uncovered another component, and I think it's important: Dynamism. People are persuaded by dynamic speakers. Not just pulpit pounders like Reborn Christian Preachers; nor even Fiery Stage Pacers like Management Guru Tom Peters (an excellent thinker and speaker). You don't have to use bombast and dramatic explosions to be effective. Your dynamism can be communicated with enthusiasm. Remember that I said that Mastery of Message was the most important ingredient in persuasive, effective business communication? Well, when you free yourself to talk about ideas that you really understand and you take time to think about how to communicate them from your listeners' viewpoint, you're ready to be dynamic. All you have to do is care if they get it. That is all you have to do, care—and show that you care. More on this in **Chapter 7, "Oral Communication: The Words You Say Are Less Than 10% of the Message."**

FLUID PRESENTATION—ANOTHER TYPE OF DYNAMISM

To talk freely with your listener, letting the words flow from your mind unedited, is a very powerful dynamism in presentation. It's OK to search for the right word, to let your audience see you struggle for the right expression of your idea. It shows that you care. But coolly searching for the right way to spin the phrase is not dynamic and will lower your credibility. Remember that great *Saturday Night Live* character "The Liar Guy" by John Lovitz? You always knew when he was about to lie because he'd pause, loose his fluidity, and stall . . . "You know, my wife . . . ahhhhh . . . Morgan Fairchild . . . that's the ticket." If you're trying to be too cool in a presentation, without meaning to, you'll come off like The Liar Guy.

CREDIBILITY THROUGH THE AUDIENCE'S EYES

So far, we've looked at credibility as a set of characteristics possessed by the speaker (age, gender, education, job title) and as things this communicator does (goodwill, dynamic delivery). Next, we're going to shift perspectives and use an information-processing model: Attribution Theory. We'll look at how the listener uses information about the communicator and information from the communicator's message to determine the communicator's credibility.

Note to reader: If you haven't read **Chapter 5, "Managing Speech Anxiety: Action Steps You Can Take,"** and/or are not "top of mind" with attribution theory, please go now to Chapter 5 and learn about the Attributional Perspective. This next section will make little sense without that background knowledge.

ATTRIBUTION THEORY AND CREDIBILITY

After reading this section you will be able to look at your various communication events as they are seen through your listener's eyes.

You'll remember that attributional perspective shows us that people are rational scientist-types who are trying to explain why things happen—to explain the causes behind the events and effects they see.

When your listeners think about your message, they think about the logical and emotional ideas you're sharing, the vision you want to communicate. They ask big credibility questions: "Why is that person saying those things?"; "What is her motivation?"; "Is the speaker's motivation based on objective facts or his bias, is it for my good or only to line his pockets with my money?"

What do you think the following communicators had as motivation for delivering their messages?

- "No new taxes." *George Bush*
- "I'll love you forever." *Aggressive Male, to Female*
- "This is the perfect car for you." *Car Salesperson*
- "Attribution Theory can help you be more persuasive." *Dr. Whalen*

Are they sincere (trustworthy), do they really know (expertise), do they care about me (goodwill)? Do they have an information bias? For example, you may believe that Dr. Whalen is an expert and as an educator is trustworthy and motivated by a sincere desire to help you learn important ideas. But what if he is limited in his knowledge? What if he is so caught up in psychological theory, stuck living in an Ivory Tower, that his knowledge—though accurate and well meaning—is out of touch with reality? Whalen's opinions could be the result of his limited and biased information set.

Research has shown that people tend to consume information that supports their narrow expertise or social/religious/political bias. Liberals don't read *National Review* or listen very long to Rush Limbaugh without switching stations in disgust. Conservatives don't attend many National Organization for Women seminars.

CREDIBILITY FLOWS WITHIN
YOU AND WITHOUT YOU

Remember how the sailor and the boat were moved either by internal (rowing, effort, ability) or external (wind, current) forces? The cause of the boat's movement was either the sailor (internal) or nature (external).

Your listener will ask the same question: "What is the locus of control—internal or external?" We all know that persuaders with internal motivation for their messages have low credibility, but speakers with external motivation have high credibility.

For example, forces within the source that will lead the listener to draw the conclusion that the speaker has low credibility include

- ignorance
- greed/gain
- information bias

Forces outside the source that lead to attributions of high credibility are

- facts
- truth (observable)
- consensus of opinion (other smart people agree)

It is important that you are aware of this powerful effect as you make your presentation. You will receive a higher credibility rating from your listeners if they make an *external locus of control attribution* for your motivation for being persuasive than you'll get from a glowing set of *source characteristics*. I am saying that goodwill (external motivation = good outcome for the other person) is more powerful than a big job title and advanced degrees. We prefer a skilled doctor who shows tenderness and a good heart over a world-class bastard.

Look at **Table 6.1, Credibility and Attribution** and make some attributions for the persuasive attempts presented earlier in this chapter.

So, open up, let your listeners know that you like them. Be sincere, speak from your heart, be enthusiastic, and show your honest emotions. Don't strain to generate emotion, it will flow, but be sure to let emotion come, don't try to be cool. The audience will trust you more.

CREDIBILITY BUILDERS: SOME TRICKS OF THE TRADE

Professional advertisers and salespeople know that when you're selling there is a real danger of blowing your credibility with the buyer by promising too much. Salespeople can get themselves in trouble by weaving too elegant a tapestry of wonderful benefits for their prospective clients.

TABLE 6.1 Credibility and Attribution

	Low Credibility Internal Locus	High Credibility External Locus facts
Persuasive	ignorance	truth (observable)
Communicator	greed/gain	consensus opinion
and their message	information bias	(smart people agree)

"No new taxes."
George Bush

"I'll love you forever."
Aggressive Male to Female

"This is the perfect car for you."
Car Salesperson

"Attribution theory can
help you be persuasive."
Dr. Whalen

Locate the speaker's internal or external motivation in making these statements.

You can make a big mistake by claiming too many wonderful things for your product, your ideas, or yourself (whatever you're selling).

YOU CAN'T BE THE GREATEST IN EVERYTHING

While we're toning down our pitch to be more moderate in claiming our product's/service's superiority, what do we throw away? I suggest you follow the plan of disclaiming, or throwing away, the least important attribute. Of all the things your product can do for your client, only one or two will be the things she really wants. In sales we call the product features that the audience really wants the buyer's hot buttons. As I was taught by former master salesperson, and now attorney, Ken Platt, "You can see their eyes dancing up and down when you describe the benefits to them."

For example, imagine that you're buying a car. The model that has captured your fancy has a list of 10 features that you want. Only one or two of those product attributes will be very important to you, say price and styling. Several more will be of moderate or low importance, for instance mileage, *Car and Driver Magazine's* high-praise review, the options' package, and the dealer's reputation for fair dealing and good service. One or two elements of the attribute set will be of little or no importance to you, such as the 0 to 60 m.p.h. acceleration and the size of the ash tray. A savvy salesperson will have astutely guessed that you probably aren't a speed freak and don't smoke. She'll say, "Our acceleration is slow, so you're in no danger of whiplash when you take off from a light. But, we're top-rated on gas mileage and that's a benefit many of our customers prefer."

By disclaiming or throwing away one product attribute (acceleration), she is free to place extra emphasis upon the product's other attributes. When astutely applied, this message strategy has been demonstrated in experiments (Mitzerski, 1978) to also heighten the speaker's credibility. Lesson learned: A little "aw-shucks" modesty can pay off. If you choose to be modest about an attribute that the listener places lower value on, you'll be more persuasive, too.

HOW MADISON AVENUE MADE US LOVE THE VW BEETLE

An early use of the technique of disclaiming the least important product attribute in advertising catapulted Volkswagen from an obscure German car—fighting for a foothold in post-World War II sensitive United States—to a market-leading best seller.

It is necessary to understand the automobile market in the late 1950s and early 1960s. Detroit was making giant, chrome-coated gas-guzzlers. These vehicular dinosaurs were perfect for the vast roadways and the country's newly opened expressway system. Wrapped in 18 gauge steel, passengers rocketed straight down the highway, at very high speeds, in great comfort. Better yet, the cars' planned obsolescence, big tail fins, and *look-at-me* shiny chrome appealed to the male ego during a time of great national prosperity, when Dad was the exclusive decider of which "Chariot of Steel" the family would own.

Then on the radar screen of market research appeared a new consumer—younger, upwardly affluent, rejecting the empty values of ostentatious consumerism that made Detroit's gas-gulpers so attractive. They wanted basic transportation, in a car that offered high quality and economy. The new generation of car buyers rejected planned obsolescence and garish design. The Volkswagen Beetle was perfect. The humble Bug offered a design that was improved each year but looked the same, model after model. The engineers improved engine performance and economy, the size of the glove box and braking speed, not the size of the tail fins. To sell this modest little gem, ad genius Bill Bernbach decided to grab attention and heighten his ad's credibility in one fell swoop. He used the startling headline "Ugly is only skin deep" and showed a humble little Beetle car, looking . . . well, ugly. The body copy under the photo went on to tell the reader that yes, it's ugly, but it will get 30 miles per gallon and never need antifreeze, because the engine is air cooled . . . and so on. By disclaiming or throwing away the product attribute least important to the target buyer, "physical beauty/appearance," Bernbach was free to make grand claims for the rest of the car's many features.

HOW TO APPLY DISCLAIMING
TO BUILD YOUR CREDIBILITY

If you're selling professional services admit that you're not an expert on the unimportant issues, then claim expertise on the issues that are important to your potential client. You too will enjoy greater credibility and persuasive power. For example, today most professionals are specialists. If you're offering financial planning services you may say, "If it looks like capital gains tax issues are going to be an issue, we can call in Jane Franks—she's our tax law expert. My area is mutual funds, that's what I really know."

John-the-Baptist® TECHNIQUE

The *John-the-Baptist®* technique is a wonderful technique that you've probably already used without realizing it. Let other people build your credibility by relating your credentials to the listener for you. Among the first recorded uses of this was Christ and John the Baptist. If you think of it, John the Baptist was the world's first advance man.

If you've studied the New Testament of the Bible, you'll recall that before Jesus of Nazareth began his ministry he spent time in the wilderness. Fundamentalist thinkers believe that Christ was "wrestling with the devil" for 40 days and 40 nights. A less representational interpretation suggests that Christ was "wrestling with ideas and beliefs," preparing for the ministry. This is the time of the Christian Church's Lenten season. Just before Jesus of Nazareth left the wilderness to rejoin humanity, John the Baptist went about the countryside heralding the Messiah. He would say, "Christ is coming, wait till you see him, when you look in his eyes you'll know that you've met Christ the Lord. He'll turn water into wine, make the blind see, the lame walk." People became very excited. They were so filled with anticipation for this wonderful Christ they had heard about that, as Christ emerged from the wilderness, he found large welcoming crowds. These crowds already had vivid expectations of and well-formed attitudes toward Jesus. Christ enjoyed the benefits of high credibility. This positive credibility helped Jesus of Nazareth as he talked with various groups of people—he was far more persuasive then he would have been without John the Baptist.

Consider the alternative. If there had been no John the Baptist, Christ would have had to do his own advance work. He'd have had to tell people who he was. "Gather near me, here my words. I am God. I'm going to make the blind see and turn water into wine." Of course, Christ could pull it off and deliver, but to a real extent he'd have had to begin his ministry appearing to be a braggart.

John the Baptist was the world's first advance man. I suggest that you need an advance man, too.

YOU'RE A PRODUCT

In many ways you are a product, you take yourself on the open market to find a job. You sell yourself to suppliers, co-workers, supervisors, and customers. At home you're still a product. You sell your spouse that you love him or her and that you are worthy of love, trust, and commitment. If you're blessed with children, you probably balance yourself between salesperson and tyrant. If you interact with neighbors, shopkeepers, lawn care experts, exterminators, plumbers, and cops, you're in sales.

When you first meet people you want them to know how wonderful you are. You want the benefits of high credibility. How can you let them know about your expertise, trustworthiness, and goodwill?

You don't want to have to recite your own credentials. You'll either come off as a braggart or have to hold back the volume of your braggadocio. Either way you end up with lower credibility.

THE SOLUTION: GET A *John-the-Baptist*©

If you've ever been interested in meeting someone and one of your friends knew the person, I'll bet you said, "Say something nice about me." Then after your friend made the Cyrano/Christian pitch on your behalf, I'll bet the first thing you asked your friend was, "What did you say about me?"

When professional persuaders make sales calls in teams, you will hear them conference on two major points before they call on the customer: (1) Who takes the lead during the meeting (to prevent stepping on each other's toes), and (2) double check on what aspects of each other's set of credible credentials they want their partner to pitch to the customer.

John-the-Baptist© IN JOB INTERVIEWS

If you want to project an aura of power, leadership, and high credibility, talk about what you believe in, your vision for the future. Let other people, your résumé, letters of recommendation, and other "objective" material present your expertise and trustworthiness. When you talk about what you see for the future, your philosophy of business, how you see the markets and effective internal operations, the image of leadership flows to you. If you talk about your credentials, no matter how well or elegantly, your self-promotion is not as effective as it would be if someone else were to do that for you.

THE SINGLE MOST EFFECTIVE
POLITICAL COMMERCIAL

When selling a candidate, I always use a standard format that is effective when the candidate speaks to a group live or in a radio or television commercial. (I've run three successful political campaigns: School Board, Secretary of State, and State Senator.) In a commercial, the announcer comes on first and recites the candidate's credentials in glowing terms and then says, "Meet Senator Harriet Firecracker." Then Senator Firecracker talks about her vision for the new state, what she believes in. It works beautifully. For more on using the *John-the-Baptist*© technique in team presentations see **Chapter 9, "Strategies for Formatting Presentations: How You Say It."**

WARNING: HIGH CREDIBILITY CAN
BACKFIRE ON THE PROFESSIONAL—
CREDIBILITY AND TECHNICAL REPORTS

If you are like many businesspeople and professionals, your credibility is very important in communicating the complex, technical ideas that are part of your professional life, such as financial and business plans or medical diagnoses. You'll be making recommendations and trying to influence decisions on big deals like capital installations.

These persuasion events not only require a special type of skill in manipulating your message and how you deliver it; you must also take special care with your credibility.

Too much credibility can be just as harmful to selling your plans as too little credibility. That may not make sense now; it didn't to me until I saw the experimental evidence for myself (Whalen, 1986; Whalen and O'Keefe, 1987).

WHEN HIGH CREDIBILITY CAN KILL YOU

You can incur risk from your high credibility, because when the buyer can't adequately judge the product/service/ideas, he will make the decision to buy/not to buy by judging the *Presenter.*[6] In this type of persuasive situation, establishing credibility is paramount. For example, consider your thought processes when your physician suggests that you follow a change in diet or submit yourself to a surgical procedure. You largely take her word for it. Although she may offer a fine explanation of the diagnosis, the procedure that she's recommending, and the likely prognosis, she doesn't make a complete technical presentation. She doesn't send you home with a stack of medical journal articles that relate the complete story of the etiology of the disease and the conduct of the procedure. You just take her word for it. It's good that you do: Most physicians can be trusted; their judgment can be verified easily with a second opinion from another medico. You use the physician's credibility to make your decision: *expertise* (medical training), *trustworthiness* (other patients, references, your past relationship as a patient), and *goodwill* (she's a healer and is devoting her life to serving humanity). You probably think for only a second, if that, about the thousands of dollars that will flow into her bank account when you buy the surgical procedure.

CREDIBILITY AND THE BUSINESS PROFESSIONAL

Unlike the physician's, your persuasive job is far harder, you can't let your high credibility get in the way—and it will. There can be a real danger in letting the person take your word for it.

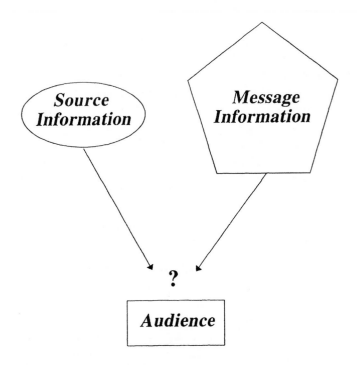

Figure 6.1 Credibility and the Technical Message
The listener selects between two types of information in making a decision, (1) source information, and (2) information contained in the message. When the message is technically complex and too challenging for the listener, the path of least resistance will be taken; use the source credibility information to make the decision and stop attempting to comprehend the message.

Using the Attributional Perspective, we see that your decider/audience is weighing two different types of information during your presentation (see **Figure 6.1, Credibility and the Technical Message**): (1) information about you as the source (credibility), and (2) message information (ideas), that is, the data in your presentation. Now, your listener can choose to make judgments based on the facts you bring forward in the presentation, in other words, the *message,* or on the information on the *Presenter's*[©] *credibility,* or on both.

When the message is complex, for example, highly technical, mathematical, or statistical in nature and outside the listener's area of expertise, he will prefer to take your word for it. He will use source information, credibility, to make the decision for him. The listener will transfer responsibility for decision making over to you. Just like you did when the physician recommended your surgery (in the example above).

The person you're persuading will listen attentively to you, thinking about what you say until two things happen: (1) you've established your expertise and goodwill toward him so he trusts you, and (2) he decides that the issue is more complex than he wants to, or can, deal with. He stops listening to you, stops the rigorous mental effort it takes to process the data that you are transmitting to him, and takes your word for it. This will happen more frequently when the listener is under work pressure or is short of time.

Your high credibility allows the buyer to shift attention from "message" to the *Presenter's*® "Ethos."

HERE IS THE PROBLEM

Problem: They'll remember less about what you've said. They can't remember why they were persuaded (the facts), but they will remember you. If they have to take your recommendations to another person, the boss, who is the "real decider," you're in trouble. The boss will say, "Tell me, Harpwell, what do you think we should do, buy the property in Ireland and build a factory from the ground up or convert our St. Louis factory?" Harpwell will say, "Boss, you've got to meet that financial analyst, he was really sharp. I believe that we must go to Ireland and set up shop." The boss says, "OK, tell me why." Harpwell searches his memory and can't remember much. Your messenger is dropping the ball and your deal is slipping away. Sure, it's all in the technical report, but Harpwell, the trusted assistant, is making hamburger out of the presentation because he was so overwhelmed by the data and so taken by you. The curse of charm—you've faced it all your life.

TURN DOWN THE CREDIBILITY

Many times when you're presenting highly technical or complex plans, the person you are presenting to is not the final decider. Often, you know that your plans will proceed through the organization, escorted by others, and you can't go with them. You've got to implement a strategy that ensures that your listener will remember what you say. Here are some suggestions for dealing in this High Credibility/Low Comprehension Technical Presentation Dilemma.

- Build in lots of decision points or choices for the listeners. This gets your listeners involved and forces them to use higher-order mental processes to think about your questions and make a choice. Because of this mental muscle movement, they'll remember more.
- Present two sides of the issue to create some doubt in their minds. Of course you present the weaker version of the other issue. Again, this gets them thinking and remembering.
- Say, "I work for North American Gumbo Corporation and while I really think that this is the best solution, I have not fully explored the other options. You've got to make a decision."
- Or, my favorite: Say to the decider, "If you like this proposal, may I suggest that we meet to plan how to present it to your boss? I can help you anticipate some of his probable questions and give you some answers that'll make you look smart. I've learned that without a good briefing, executives can be caught short and be embarrassed by the boss."

SUMMARY

High credibility gives the communicator several benefits.

- ☐ People listen to you for longer periods of time.
- ☐ The audience is more cooperative with you during your presentation.
- ☐ People believe what you say.

Credible people have three characteristics: (1) expertise, (2) trustworthiness, and (3) goodwill. Expertise and trustworthiness take time to build up; goodwill can be created during the presentation. Goodwill is established by the communicator's loving, generous intentions of good things for the listener. You must feel goodwill and project positive attitude.

You can build goodwill and credibility by projecting genuine respect and admiration for the audience. Use the *John-the-Baptist*© technique: Let other people cite your credentials and achievements for you.

7

Oral Communication

The Words You Say Are Less Than 10% of the Message

W hen it comes time to sell your big plan to the organization, what do you think is more important—your written reports or your oral presentation? Which type of communication will make you more influential, more respected in the organization—the reports and memos you write or the hundreds of casual hallway conversations and off-the-cuff remarks you make at meetings? In short, what type of communication do you think your boss, your co-workers, and your customers consider more valuable, oral or written communication?

The highly analytical among us may respond, "It depends on the organization and the person making the judgment." This analysis is right, of course, but "it depends" answers are the "can't read drive 'A' " messages on life's big computer.

Make no mistake, a well-written report or one-page summary is a powerful communications instrument. To be successful, you must master this skill. Oral communication is inherently more powerful than written, and, for many people, effective oral presentation is far easier to master than written. How often have you heard the meeting's chair, before asking for a vote, say "Is there any more reading we should do before we vote?" No, of course not, she always says, "Is there any more discussion before we vote?"

My experience and the experience of thousands of my graduate students and business associates shows that oral communication is more important than written in influencing business decisions. It is used more often, and executives make most of their decisions about people and plans based on oral communication.

ORAL AND WRITTEN STRATEGIES

If you write a report and then give an oral briefing on that report, you're dealing with two distinct sets of communication. You need to develop two distinct sets of communication strategies for your report and for your oral presentation.

Again, let me affirm that the ability to craft a solid report or tightly worded memo is indispensable—you must be able to write simply and directly. I decided that we could not teach both in a single book, however, and decided to emphasize the most important: oral communication. Even so, you'll find that the majority of techniques I recommend in this book apply to written communication, too.

This chapter first explores the essence and power of oral persuasion. Next, simple yet powerful message strategies are offered, then the chapter closes with tips and suggestions on how to deliver the oral message—all designed to make you more successful in business by being a better oral communicator.

Your attitude is everything in helping you become an effective, highly credible, and persuasive oral communicator.

BEFORE YOU SPEAK, SET YOUR ATTITUDE

Oral communication allows you to build a relationship with the audience. First, you build your credibility and so become more persuasive. Then, you actively share in the decision making as a group member, and finally, you emerge as the group's leader.

Your attitude is the power that drives the most important and powerful symbols you communicate. To be a great oral communicator, you must first manage your attitude. It's the way you say your words that makes you persuasive. In fact, the words you use in oral communication are only minor parts of the message your listeners receive.

Look at **Table 7.1, Oral Communications Mix.** According to communication researchers, 93% of the information that your audience receives comes from your tone of voice and the things they see (Raudsepp, 1993). **In Chapter 2, "Effective Communication: Symbolically Sharing Your**

TABLE 7.1 Oral Communications Mix

7%	words
38%	tone of voice
55%	visual

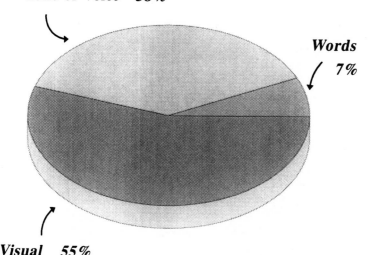

Tone of Voice 38%

Words 7%

Visual 55%

Tone of voice and nonverbal symbols comprise the majority of messages people receive from oral communication.

Personal Experience," we talked about the rich tapestry of symbols we use in communication. The way you look, your personal grooming, and your dress are some nonverbal symbols the audience initially sees. After their initial inspection, your listeners make a judgment about you and assign an initial credibility rating. Then, as they begin to listen to you and watch your movement and hear your vocal tone, they become enmeshed in your presentation.

Other communication modalities convey rich meaning to your listeners—such as your voice, the way you move, your inflection, emphasis, tone, pauses, and more. Your listeners can absorb more words than you can transmit. They can listen faster than you can talk (**Table 7.2, Oral Communication Bottleneck: Your Mouth,** gives you the data to prove it).

TABLE 7.2 Oral Communication Bottleneck: Your Mouth

(WPM = Words per Minute)	
Listener can receive	480 WPM
– You can transmit	120 WPM
[Oral Communication Deficit	360 WPM]

The communication gap: Your listener can receive more words per minute than you can transmit.

If you practiced and drilled to the point that you could spit out words at the rate of the Federal Express "Fast-Talking Guy" (created by Chicago's brilliant ad-maker, Joe Settelmeyer), your listeners would still gobble up the words and be hungry for more—360 words per minute (WPM) more.

When you were an infant, you learned to seek out information beyond the words people cooed at you. You actively looked for additional symbols from other people, seeking meaning to the world. You learned nonverbal communication first: the tone of your mother's voice, her facial expressions, and more. Nonverbal symbols rush in to fill the 360-WPM gap in oral communication. Obviously, your skill in manipulating nonverbal messages will be important to your success as a persuasive business communicator.

NONVERBAL COMMUNICATION

You've got five primary tools in oral communication. If you work to improve your skill in manipulating and using these instruments, you'll greatly enhance your effectiveness as a communicator. Here are your five tools in effective oral communication:

1. Tone of Voice
2. Facial Expression
3. Body Language
4. Word Selection
5. Delivery

Tone of Voice. All too many business communicators use a monotone voice when speaking. Your attitude, angry or elated, sad or confident, is communicated by your voice. Your meaning is conveyed by your vocal tone when people can't see you, for example, on the telephone. According to the North American Telecommunicators Association, 50% of phone calls made today are one-way (voice mail, answering machines). And messages are increasingly more brief. In 1982, only 22% of phone calls took less than one minute, today it's 52%. Consider the number of times you have to communicate important business information to others' voice mail boxes or in phone conversations.

Next time you're talking on the phone, use that opportunity to test the power of vocal tone in communication. Listen carefully to the person on the other end of the line. See if you can visualize the speaker's **facial expression.** You'll probably notice that you can tell when somebody is smiling, frowning, looking curious, and so on through the broad range of human facial expressions. The part of your brain that regulates vocal tone and the part that controls facial expression are located near each other. It makes sense that in the grand scheme of things these two powerful communication devices should be coordinated and work together.

If the other person is not using vocal inflection, you'll have trouble imagining his facial expression. His face will appear bland and uninterested in your mind.

TIP   When you're on the phone, you can give your communication effectiveness a big shot in the arm by changing your facial expression. I recommend smiling to convey power, love, and confidence.

TIP   Another way to regulate your vocal tone, much like facial expression, is through body language. Get up and move around when you speak; the added dynamism from your movement will translate into a more effective oral presentation.

LET YOUR BODY SPEAK FOR YOU

How to Stand Before an Audience. When you first stand before your audience, your initial posture and stance should be athletic—a more upright version of the stance used by tennis players waiting for a serve, football linebackers, and wrestlers: feet shoulder-width apart, hands above the waist, weight slightly forward on the balls of your feet. You want to stand upright and lean slightly toward your audience. This makes you look alert and dynamic. Because you've placed your feet in a good athletic position, you can easily move to your right, to your left, away from or toward your audience.

I've seen too many speakers try to project an attitude of casual confidence. Instead of filling his being totally with a feeling of positive confidence, a speaker can make the mistake of trying to use body posture to communicate an artificial attitude of casual confidence. This ill-fated speaker sets himself up to lose by draping his body across the table or leaning on the podium. At first he does look casual, at least until he feels the need to move. Now he's in trouble: He's stuck in place. His problem is that he has the urge to move during the difficult, high-metabolic stage fright phase at the beginning of the presentation (see **Chapter 5, "Managing Speech Anxiety: Action Steps You Can Take"**). He feels very self-conscious, and because he's frozen by muscle tension he has a hard time trying to be graceful when moving from what is an inherently awkward position. So the poor speaker finds himself stuck in that increasingly uncomfortable posture. He can't move. A look of great concern crosses his face and the audience begins to focus on his humorous position instead of on the words he is saying. Avoid this trap. Use the athletic stance during the awkward opening minutes—it's safe and looks great. After you're truly more relaxed, you can adopt any posture you feel is appropriate.

INITIAL COMMUNICATION:
STARTING THE ORAL PRESENTATION

The first information that your audience will use to judge you and your ideas is what it sees: you and the way you look. Personal grooming and the right business dress are important to your initial impression. I recommend that men begin the presentation with jacket buttoned and tie tightened. Women, too, would begin with a more formal business demeanor. If you want a more informal tone, you can communicate that later. A man can loosen his tie, take his jacket off; these gestures will communicate to his audience that he is shifting gears to a more casual and personal tone.

Word Selection. In Chapter 2, "Effective Communication: Symbolically Sharing Your Personal Experience," I had quite a bit to say about words as symbols and how to use words that evoke strong sensory memory in your listener. Later in this chapter I suggest some strategies for creating effective messages. The topic of using words to persuade is vast, one that

I'm saving for another book. I'm confident that as a well-trained, dynamic professional you will have many words you want to say. Your success will depend on how you **deliver** them. Let's focus on your delivery now.

Delivery is how you put it together: your superb vocal tones shaping your perfectly selected words, accented by wise and animated facial expressions, all housed in a powerful confident body posture and punctuated by strong, assured gestures. That's delivery. Does it sound hard? It's not. Making a great delivery is easy. Learning how to develop a skilled oral delivery manner is quite simple. You don't try. Don't even think about how you look, just focus on your message and your audience. Look into your memory and describe what you're seeing. Remember, successful presentations begin with your desire to deliver messages that you've mastered and have a passion to deliver. Those two factors are critical. With them, you'll soar and be known as a master communicator. Without passion to share or mastery of message, you'll be just another average executive working your way through the material, boring the audience, and communicating only half your ideas.

DURING A GREAT PRESENTATION, YOU DISAPPEAR

In a great presentation you don't even exist, you're not aware of yourself. You're too busy studying the faces in your audience; looking into their eyes and reading their reactions. Remember, communication is a two-way dance between speaker and listener moving together toward understanding and consensus. Your facial expression, vocal tone, body posture, and gestures are best regulated by your internal autopilot: **Your Attitude.** If you should make the mistake of actively trying to manage these illusive elements, that is, working hard to look dynamic and pasting contrived expressions on your face, you'll appear artificial and stilted. Your audience will know you're a phoney. Your credibility will crumble to dust and you'll fail to get what you want.

Meaning starts in your mind, flows to your body, then through symbols of gesture, tone, and expression, flows to your audience.

You can't force this process. You can—here is the good news—directly regulate these important communication tools. Vocal tone, facial expression, and body language are orchestrated by the interaction of your mind and your **attitude. Attitude is critical, it is your attitude that you must control.**

HERE'S WHAT GREAT ATTITUDE FEELS LIKE

When you've got a great attitude toward your topic and your listener, the feeling is distinct and very positive. You feel powerful and centered; while at the same time you feel like you're taking risks, you're hanging it out over the edge. You know that if you try to express an idea and fail to find the words, your audience will understand and they'll be drawn even more into your presentation as they work to find meaning with you. Because of your positive attitude, you don't have to deliver a flawless presentation. Actually, a slightly flawed presentation is preferred by the audience and is more credible.

As you speak, you become filled with feelings of joy and of pride for your ideas. You let your pride flow from you to your audience. It's your confidence that sells.

MOST MOTIVATING EMOTION = ENTHUSIASM

Of all the emotions that will move your audience to embrace your point of view, enthusiasm is the most important. It's the emotion that you should adopt as your primary tool in communication. Remember, persuasion is not just facts, it's emotional messages too.

CHEAP TRICKS FROM ADVERTISING

When I was working as an advertising executive, often the biggest challenge was to get the client to approve the commercial. I am ashamed to admit that more than once I succumbed to using the cheapest tactic in the advertising world: I'd put the client in the commercial. You see, unless the client approved the spot we could not run the commercial, and unless we ran the ad we didn't get paid. At the time I really needed the money. If I didn't sell, I didn't eat (quite different than my life today in the Ivory Tower). So, to get the spot on the air I'd say, "Now Harry, I've got a great idea, and don't tell me 'no' until you've heard me out. There is only one person in the world who can sell your product like you can, buyers want to meet the guy behind the company. You've got to appear in your

TABLE 7.3 Characteristics of the Enthusiastic Speaker

• Employs vocal variety	• Gains attention with voice
• Enjoys the topic	• Uses nonverbal communication
• Is excited about subject matter	○ body movements
• Uses voice to emphasize key words or concepts	○ gestures
	○ facial expression
	○ positive attitude

Enthusiastic speakers have these traits in common.

commercials." Well, as one might expect, old Harry would puff up and his eyes would get a misty gleam as he imagined his face splashed across the airwaves . . . and he'd agree in a heartbeat. So, now I'd have a bigger problem. I'd be faced with the challenge of taking an executive with little or no television acting experience and finding a way to coach, direct, push, and prod him into an acceptable broadcast performance.

Enthusiasm communicates your confidence and shows credibility: You appear more dynamic (one cornerstone of credibility). When you speak with enthusiasm you are more animated and dynamic, thus you communicate belief and honesty. The key to acting is to transmit honest, felt emotions to your audience. Time in and time out, I have found that enthusiasm is the easiest emotion for amateur talent to fake, and I heartily recommend it to you. If you have mastery of your message, a sincere desire to communicate, and you want the audience to like you, enthusiasm is your best choice (see Table 7.3).

Perhaps as you looked at **Table 7.3, Characteristics of the Enthusiastic Speaker,** you noticed that of all the factors listed that contribute to enthusiasm and, more important, to communicating your enthusiasm to your listener, *voice control* and *expressing your feelings through voice* appear quite often. Perhaps we should focus attention on voice control.

VOICE CONTROL

Great speakers share a common characteristic—they are masters at using their voices to express meaning. Let's talk about how you can learn to control and use your voice to communicate meaning, your feelings, and your attitude to your listener.

Don't Trust Your Ears—You Don't Sound Like That. We all have a common handicap when it comes to training our voices: Our ears give us lousy feedback. This is a major problem in improving your voice because you've got to have an accurate sense of how you sound if you're going to enhance your vocal skill. Remember the first time you listened to yourself on a tape recorder? Did you like the sound of your voice? Most people don't. We react with, "Is that me? I don't sound like that, do I?"

The reason we're all so stunned when we hear how flat and nasal our voices sound is because, as we are talking, we hear a different sound from our voices than do other people. Here is why: You know that sound is a vibration and your ears are organs that are designed to sense vibrations and translate them into acoustic information for consumption by your brain. The vibrations your listener hears come largely through the air. They travel a path from your mouth, through the air, and into your listener's ears. The sound vibrations that you get travel largely through your bones. That's right, you vibrate the bones in your head, throat, and chest. Your ears are mounted on the sides of your head and the hearing organs sit nestled in a cavity of skull bone. What you're hearing is the acoustic equivalent of singing in the shower. You know how great you sound in the shower? It's because your voice is vibrating the shower's tiles, amplifying your voice, giving it a wonderful resonance—a full, rich sound. Your listeners get only your unresonated sound. So, obviously the trick is to make sure that you deliver important business communication in the shower. Unfortunately, by the time you're so far up in the organization that you can order people to listen to you in the shower, you will not need this book. So, as an alternative, I'll show you how to increase your resonance by using more of your body when you speak.

BEND YOUR EARS

Learn to listen to yourself accurately through a technique called ear bending. Just like old-time radio announcers, cup your hand around your ear to scoop in more vibrating air, so your air vibration/bone vibration ratio changes. Of course you can't do this during a presentation, but you can when you practice. Practice is important, including practice using a tape recorder. I recommend that you tape your business conversations, including telephone calls, to see how well you're using your voice. How can you listen to yourself and work to change your vocal control when the feedback you get is highly distorted?

RADIO ANNOUNCER'S TIPS AND
EXERCISES TO IMPROVE YOUR VOCAL EXPRESSION

Years ago, when I earned my living by making the right noises into a microphone, I learned how important relaxation is to effective announcing. Speech and vocal resonance come largely from skillfully articulating and manipulating muscles in your mouth and throat. The vibration you need for speech comes from twin muscles located in your throat. As kids we called them vocal cords in the voice box. The scientific terms are *glottal folds* in the *larynx*. By flexing and squeezing a large, powerful, flat muscle—the diaphragm—that stretches across your abdomen, starting just below the center of your rib cage, you force a column of air up from your lungs, through your throat. As this swift rush of air passes over the *glottal folds,* they begin to vibrate. When you stretch and flex your *glottal folds* the air passing over them vibrates rapidly, making sounds that go up very high. When you relax your *glottal folds,* the air passing over them causes them to vibrate very slowly, making low, deeper sounds. Next, the vibrating air passes over the *articulators* in your mouth: your lips, tongue, and teeth. You use the articulators to shape that vibrating air into words. The articulated vibrations move from your mouth and through the air, until they contact your listener's ears. If the vibrations move very rapidly, they hit your listener's ears hard and sound loud. If you move the vibrations slowly, by whispering, the impact is very soft upon the ear and sounds quiet. When you whisper, you're hardly moving your *glottal folds* at all; most of the sound is air rushing past your articulators.

THE LAURA PETRIE EFFECT: *"Oohohohooh Rob"*

Now that you know a bit more about where speech comes from, you can better appreciate why relaxation is so very important. If you have tense muscles, they're too stiff to manipulate. The nuance of vibration and subtle movement of air eludes you. You can tell if somebody is tense just by listening—you can hear the tightness in his throat, the strain in her vocal chords. And we hate the feeling that we sound like Mary Tyler Moore's character, "Laura Petrie," on the *Dick Van Dyke Show*. When Laura was upset she'd get all nervous and in a quivering voice chirp out, "Oh, Rob" to her television husband played by Dick Van Dyke, starring in the *Dick Van Dyke Show*, starring Dick Van Dyke (or did I say that?). We would prefer it if we could conceal our nervousness from the audience. Relaxing and controlled breathing is the trick you must master so your voice will not betray you.

REDUCING THE VOCAL TENSION

Failing to relax affects your breathing, too. As you know from **Chapter 4, "When You're Afraid to Communicate: Understanding Anxiety and Fear,"** it's hard to take a deep breath when your upper body's "fighting muscles" are tense. When that region is held in spasm, you can't stretch the *intercostal muscles* between your ribs. Your ribs have to expand for you to take a deep breath. So you end up taking short, gasping breaths that increase the tension in your throat. Another problem with this "clavicle breathing" is that you can't move enough air past those very tight *glottal folds* to make them vibrate right, the way they vibrate during normal speech. When you're talking with a business associate you can tell when things are difficult for him by the tightness in his voice. This is because of generalized upper body tension that causes the delicate *glottal folds* to become very tight and makes it impossible for him to convey the rich, lush vibrations that communicate that the speaker is relaxed. So what do you want? You want to relax your speaking muscles: *glottal folds, abdomen,* and *intercostal muscles.* You should work to get rid of upper body tension (see "Relaxation Exercises" in **Chapter 5, "Managing Speech Anxiety: Action Steps You Can Take"**).

HUMMING AND OTHER VOCAL EXERCISES

Those relaxation exercises will help you take control of the larger muscles, but they will only indirectly reduce tension in your *glottal folds.* The following exercise will allow you to stretch and relax your vocal chords directly, without having to stick your hand down your throat. Relax your vocal cords directly by humming. When you hum slowly, especially tunes that have lots of low parts, like gospel music, you're giving your *glottal folds* a mini-massage with those pleasant vibrations. By humming a little tune you can stretch out the tension. And it's a lot easier than reaching down your throat and trying to massage them directly.

HUMMING PHRASES YOU CAN USE

First, hum. I recommend the old hymn *Rock of Ages,* it is excellent (I'm not kidding). Any song with lots of very slow, low parts is perfect. Humming will relax your vocal chords. Another good exercise is to sing-song the phrases listed below. Be sure to take as long as possible to say them. As a musician would say, keep the "sustain" on—really drag it out.

Here's how you do it. You sing the first word high then sing the second word low:

    king—kong
    ding—dong
    ping—pong

Avoid needless embarrassment: Find a place where you can do these exercises by yourself.

A WORD ON TAKING CHARGE
OF THE SPEAKING VENUE

When you're speaking before a group, at a special meeting, or in a job interview, you must assert yourself to get the few small things necessary to perform to your maximum ability. For example, I suggest that you leave the room before your talk. Go to the bathroom. I am serious. The natural excitement and tension will make your bladder feel fuller than it is. You must eliminate all possible sources of extraneous tension from your body. Your clothing must be comfortable and allow you to move well. Your shoes must support your performance movement. Make sure that your shoe soles are not so slick that you might slip when you move. This has happened to me and it's nasty—I've accidentally performed James Brown choreography and it hurts. I don't know how the "Godfather of Soul" does it.

Relax Your Whole Body by Stretching. While you're out of the room you can do some stretching exercises. Frequently, there is an empty room adjacent to the meeting room, or backstage if you're working in a conference facility or theater. There is an unwritten rule that the speaker is in charge of the room. The audience will comply with your reasonable wishes. If you want them to stretch and take a break, they will. If you want them to move forward to the front of the room, they will. If you want the lights on, they go on. It's your show. If you expect it to happen, it will. If you truly communicate what you want, your request will be honored.

TIP   When I was a younger man, I sold water conditioners door-to-door. While doing this difficult work, I learned several tricks on how to take charge of the sales venue when in somebody else's domain, like someone's house or office. The sales appointments were set in the evening so both husband and wife would be present to hear the pitch and could make the decision to buy. When I arrived at the prospect's home, frequently the family would be watching television. I knew that this distraction would interfere with my sales pitch and that I must get that set turned off. Here is what I learned: If I asked them, "Do you mind if I turn the TV off?" and then waited for an answer, the husband would look at the wife and they'd probably say, "Let's leave it on." But if I moved toward the set, as if to turn it off, and simultaneously asked, "Do you mind if I turn off the set?" they would always say, "Sure, no problem."

KEY   Be in motion, already doing what you want, when you ask permission. People will rarely stop you, nor will they resent you for doing it; it will seem natural and OK to your audience. So, when you say to the meeting chair, "Do you mind if I step out for a minute?" while you're getting up from your chair and heading for the door, she will answer, "Of course not, go right ahead." You must take time to prepare yourself; you owe it to yourself and to your audience.

You'll want to do some exercises to get your vocal instrument ready to speak.

MORE VOCAL EXERCISES

Stretch Your Speaking Instrument. Privately, before you go on to speak or before the meeting starts, take a few seconds and stretch your muscles as prescribed in **Chapter 5, "Managing Speech Anxiety: Action Steps You Can Take."** Then add these new, voice-specific exercises to your routine.

Do Ringo's Silent Scream. In the classic Hippie-era movie *The Magic Christian,* the Beatles' drummer, Ringo, while sitting in a Rolls Royce, mimed a series of isometric facial exercises at a traffic cop. Ringo was going for comedy, but I recommend that you do the same exercise to improve your vocal performance. Professional baseball players always stretch their game muscles as part of their pregame warmup, even the Cubs. As a speaker, your game muscles are your face, your abdomen, and your intercostal muscles. Open your mouth as wide as you can and while stretching your eyes wide, raise your eyebrows up high. You'll be doing the "Silent Scream," screaming without making any noise.

MAKE ROOM FOR MORE AIR:
STRETCH YOUR BELLOWS

Take a long, slow, huge, deep breath and hold it. You're inflating your chest and stomach like a giant weather balloon. While you're holding your engorged breath, you'll find that within a few seconds you can take in more air because your abdomen and the intercostal muscles between your ribs have stretched. Now suck in a few million extra air molecules. Slowly let the air out. Repeat this exercise a couple of times. Be careful: You're really loading tons of extra oxygen into your system. You could hyperventilate, get dizzy and disoriented; this is the last thing you want to do to your brain before you have to face your audience. So, take your time and don't rush these exercises. Stop just before you get slightly dizzy. You'll develop a far smoother, lower, more relaxed voice because you're not holding as much tension in your body. As a bonus, because you have a body full of oxygen, you'll get a wonderful feeling of well-being.

Now that you've got your instrument warmed up, let's practice some "vocal scales."

SPEAKING EXERCISES

If you've ever studied a musical instrument, you'll remember practicing "scales." You probably spent hours playing these nonmusical exercises to improve your technique. The next section gives you some vocal scales that will greatly improve your ability to articulate difficult sounds. After you've practiced these, you'll find that you've developed an enhanced vocal control. You'll take command of your audience with your increased vocal power. I can't promise that your listeners will march off a cliff like lemmings under the hypnotic spell of your voice, but they will gain greater meaning from your words, give you a higher credibility rating, and listen to you for a longer period.

When practicing the drills, first go for accuracy, then when you can say them perfectly, go for speed. Do not try to go fast at first. You're building new muscular coordination and establishing new neural networks in your brain, and this takes time. It's far better to practice a new skill perfectly, in small increments.

- **Instructions.** Say these aloud. At first, do these exercises in private. Then as you gain proficiency, ask someone to listen to you. (You'll find that doing these in front of somebody is a totally different experience than your solo performances.) Work on one sentence at a time. Slowly repeat it three times. Then, repeat and increase your pace.

  ◻ She says she shall sew a sheet.
  ◻ He saw six slim, sleek, slender saplings.
  ◻ We're your well-wishers.
  ◻ Toy boat.
  ◻ Some shun sunshine. Do you shun sunshine?
  ◻ Bugs' black blood.
  ◻ The sea ceaseth, and it sufficeth us. (Dr. Whalen's note: I've never been able to say this one, but maybe you can.)

TIP   Be sure to record your exercises and listen to the tape critically. Once you've made your tape, you can practice these exercises in your car—playing the tape back as you drive.

The above sentences are filled with sounds that shape words, that give a clearer articulation to your speech. For example, consonants have a crisp, sharp sound. Be sure to exaggerate your *t, h,* and *s* sounds.

TIP   Here is an old radio announcer's trick. Certain *s* sounds sound even better when you "buzz them" . . . put your teeth together and make a buzzing sound. For example, in "He saw six slim, sleek, slender saplings," when you say *saplings* buzz the last *s.* Practice by saying the word *Jazz* with and without the buzz sound. It gives your voice a clean, dynamic sound.

VOCAL TRAFFIC COP

Like a busy traffic cop, you want to direct your listener's attention to the parts of your ideas that deserve special emphasis. Some parts of your sentences are more important than others. Here is an exercise that will help you learn how to communicate your attitude by emphasizing different words to your listener.

Instructions. Read each sentence, placing expressive emphasis on a different word each time.

> I have some news for you.
> The return on portfolio "B" may become more attractive over time.
> That is the ugliest dog I have ever seen. (Dr. Whalen's note: This one is my favorite Emphasis Exercise; try it with a Southern accent.)

PROJECTING YOUR ATTITUDE TO YOUR AUDIENCE

Establishing Rapport With the Audience. Your first few minutes talking with a new group are very important. The group is scanning you very intently and deciding how credible you are (see **Chapter 6, "First, People Must Believe You: Managing Your Credibility"**). They are assessing many factors of expertise, trustworthiness, and goodwill. Simply, they are deciding if they like you and trust you. Now is the time to establish rapport and earn their respect. First rule: Don't try too hard to be impressive. I've noticed that some junior executives try to overcome their relative lack of rank, experience, and recognition by acting too formal and stiff, dropping their charm, sincerity, and humanity. Here are some tips on establishing rapport:

* *Be interested in them as people*

It's all too easy to think of your audience as a faceless blob. Perhaps you'll only think of the one or two key players in the audience who will be the leaders and deciders. Remember, these key listeners will form their opinion of you based on the rest of the audience's reaction to you. An audience is an organism with a life of its own. An audience is a group of individuals. If you are talking with an audience of 30 people, you're talking with 30 individuals, one at a time. Each audience member is different and will react uniquely to you. After you progress into your presentation, they will begin to form a common attitude and share the same feelings. First, you must establish rapport and interest in each person as an individual.

• *Be good-natured*

Try not to be so serious. Act like you enjoy what you're doing. Some subject matter may be more serious than others, but concentrate on a positive feeling. For example, if you're effective in establishing a conversational tone and relationship with your audience, they will talk back to you. When someone in your audience speaks to you by asking a question or making a remark, listen and react honestly. Anticipate that someone will attempt to make a joke as they talk with you. The audience will surely realize that she has made an attempt at humor, even if they don't laugh. If you don't react with some sense of amusement—if not joy—you'll seem out of sync, not tuned in, not really speaking with them.

• *Use humor*

I don't mean to imply that you should tell jokes. Unless you've got talent—don't make jokes. And if you are good enough to base your presentation on your gift for humor, I suggest that you seriously review your current career ambitions. You'll find that professional comedy pays lots more and is lots more fun. So, if you're like most of us, don't tell jokes. Use humor, wit, and observation as it flows from your interaction with the audience. It's best to attempt humor as you discuss your topic. It's even better if someone in your audience makes the humorous remarks and you do the laughing. It works wonders for your credibility. Typically, the funny audience member is beloved and respected. By recognizing her humor you will make yourself an honorary member of their group. Warning: Pay attention to the group's reaction to the audience member who makes humorous remarks . . . you may find that they resent this person and find him to be alien to their group. Don't affiliate with this person.

• *Use common experiences to establish common ground*

Work to find something that you share in common with your audience. Perhaps you hold the same beliefs as your audience, have the same hopes and aspirations. Maybe you have similar ambitions or have experienced the same things.

A surefire way of establishing rapport through common experience is by expressing sincere admiration. You can bet that members of a corporation hold certain people in high esteem; maybe the company's founder or the current CEO. Perhaps they have made technical advances or crafted new instruments or launched new products. If you truly appreciate and admire individuals, philosophies, or products, be sure to mention it.

You may need to prove your sincere appreciation to the audience. For example, if you sense that your audience of marketing and salespeople will not believe that you, the auditor, think that their travel and entertainment expenses are necessary and important expenditures—you many need to give two or three examples that show the depth and scope of your appreciation.

Express your familiarity and respect for people, things, and ideas that are highly respected by your audience.

• *Be straightforward*

I always recommend that you begin your presentation by futzing around a bit. This can establish your territory and gain poise. For example, moving the podium, adjusting your notes or the overhead projector, looking and speaking informally with the audience or certain front row members, gives you a sense of command and lets you settle down. You probably feel trapped (see **Chapter 4, "When You're Afraid to Communicate: Understanding Anxiety and Fear"**) and this will give you a feeling of freedom. Remember, time is limited, tell your audience what you want them to know right away (see **Chapter 9, "Strategies for Formatting Presentations: How You Say It"**).

• *Be direct*

Say exactly what you mean. Time will fly during your presentation so you don't have time to be elliptical. If you're too vague or "tease" your listeners by not coming right out and delivering your message, they will pay less attention to you and will fabricate their own message. You'll heighten the communication challenge. Time is short and your listeners' imaginations are rampant: Tell them clearly and simply what you want them to know. Make your message short and vivid.

• *Fill yourself with admiration and respect for your audience*

Your attitude and mental state are primary. You must convince yourself that you like your listeners. As you mentally prepare, try to convince yourself that you love them. Keep a positive feeling about you. It's not easy in such fear-provoking circumstances. You will win as a *Presenter*© and communicator when you train yourself to manage your own fear and project love to your listener.

• *Have fun*

By now, I bet that you fully understand why it's so important to have fun when you're presenting. If you're having fun, you project goodwill. Your sense of fun communicates confidence. Also, fun and enthusiasm are easy for an amateur actor to project and fun entertains your audience. If you're having fun, you open up communication into a two-way flow and encourage your audience to participate. And fun makes dry or difficult material more approachable.

• *Your audience is on your side*

Think about when you have an important communication to deliver. You visualize the negative outcomes; you're filled with fearful thoughts. It's only normal that you'd begin to think of your listeners as the enemy. They are causing you tons of anxiety, so how can they be anything else?

Look at it this way. The audience and you are on the same team and have the same objectives. You are all trapped in the presentation room for the uncounted minutes during the presentation. You're holding them prisoner. The doors are psychologically locked; they have to pretend to give at least minimal attention to your presentation and will have to think of a reaction, of something to say.

Your listeners have a selfish interest in your doing well. They are trapped with you for the next three minutes to one hour. Listeners are hungry to be entertained, informed, and enlightened. They want you to be interesting and lively. Have you ever attended a meeting and hoped it would be dull? When starting a new college class, did you ever say to yourself, "I hope this professor is dull as death"; "I hope the material is like slow death"? NO, of course you didn't. You're praying for a breath of life in your speaker, something interesting and important. When a speaker gives you a sense of joy and enthusiasm, it is hypnotic and intoxicating.

You've Got the Audience From the Beginning. Your listeners are with you from the start—during those first two to three minutes when you're insane with enhanced metabolism (see **Chapter 4, "When You're Afraid to Communicate: Understanding Anxiety and Fear"**), they are very forgiving. You've got them on your side, hanging on your every word—till you get dull and lose them. Keep it interesting, have fun, be young, drink Pepsi.

SUMMARY

Oral communication is more important than written in influencing business decisions.

Your audience receives 93% of its information from your tone of voice and the things they see. Your attitude drives the most important and powerful symbols you communicate orally. To be a great oral communicator you must first manage your attitude.

The optimal attitude begins with your passionate desire to deliver messages that you've mastered to an audience that you care about.

Delivery is how you put it together: your superb vocal tones shaping your perfectly selected words, accented by wise and animated facial expressions, all housed in powerful and confident body posture, punctuated by strong and assured gestures. Train your voice by practicing vocal exercises to build your skills in shaping sounds precisely—you want to speak very clearly to be understood. In a great presentation, you're not aware of yourself. As you speak, you become filled with feelings of joy and of pride for your ideas. You let your pride flow from you to your audience. It's your confidence that sells. Have fun—you can't bore your audience into following your recommendations. Remember, your listeners are on your side till you lose them.

8

Strategies for Developing Messages

What You're Going to Say

When you make a presentation, there are two things that make you successful: (1) What you say, and (2) how you say it. First, we'll talk about message content strategies. I'll share some ideas on how to construct powerful messages, the *What You Say*. Second, I'll show you how to design individual and team presentation strategies, the *When and How You Say It*. The third and last section of this chapter will give you a dozen tips on how to *Deliver Your Message*.

MESSAGE CONTENT STRATEGIES—WHAT YOU SAY

"The effective speaker has three characteristics: Logos, Pathos, Ethos."
Aristotle

The ancient Greeks had persuasion nailed. They were the best, perhaps because of their "town meeting" style of city-state government, where all adult male property owners met, face-to-face, for discussing and deciding public policy.

OLDIE, BUT A GOLDIE

Everything we modern scientists have learned over the past 50 years about what makes one person more persuasive than another—using our scientific designs, multivariate statistics, and mainframe computers—was

138

taught by Aristotle. He told his students that the ideal communicator is a "Man of Goodwill, possessing a good reputation and personality."

The Greeks discovered that the three pillars upon which persuasive communication is built are

- **Logos (Low-goes)**—logic and reasoning
- **Pathos (Path-ohs)**—emotional ideas, appeals to the human being
- **Ethos (Eeth-ohs)**—the speaker's reputation and personality

Your message must contain elements that communicate all three factors to your audience.

LOGOS

This one, I'm not worried about. Most professionals I have met are abundantly prepared to deliver facts. They can produce stacks of statistics, models, and conceptualizations to support their recommendations. I am sure that you have lots of facts at your command or can get them.

• *Facts are essential*
It is good that you are trained to be rational and factual. Intelligent managers and decision makers demand that you give them facts.

• *Facts are not sufficient*
You can't persuade someone with facts alone. By themselves, facts do not move people, do not change people. You have to use emotion to change people, to get them off center, to take risks—to buy into the new plan.

• *Numerical facts don't communicate through the aural sense*
Your listener has a hard time hearing facts: She hears your voice in her acoustic memory (see **Chapter 2, "Effective Communication: Symbolically Sharing Your Personal Experience"**).

• *We're spatially oriented*
Facts, particularly most statistics, exist on a one-dimensional plane; some advanced multifactorial statistics offer two or more dimensions—but these advanced forms are only rarely used outside the academic journal.

When is the last time your firm used conjoint analysis or even regression? Human visual sense needs two and three dimensions.

• *We can see geometry better than numbers*

That is why graphs and charts are so effective in communicating to businesspeople. They transform numbers into geometric shapes—wedges, rectangles, circles, and polygons. Our eyes and perceptual psychology are well equipped to see shapes. We survived in the jungle using a visual perception sense that can see the square bulky shape of the tiger against the tall linear shapes of the trees with superb clarity. This relic of our evolution is carried into business meetings today.

• *Audiences prefer that you send pictures into their minds*

Think of communication as sending pictures into people's minds; some of these pictures must be evocative and arousing. That is the role of *Pathos.*

PATHOS

Pathos is the part of your message that is designed to appeal to the human side of your audience: its pride, joy, fears, hopes, and ambitions. Remember that I suggested that Persuasion is *facts wrapped in emotion* (see **Chapter 2, "Effective Communication: Symbolically Sharing Your Personal Experience"**).

To be persuasive you must be passionate about your ideas: Passion persuades. You must be prepared to arouse your audience's emotions. This may take some work—I'll bet that if you're like most of my students, you would rather not use emotion. You may believe that emotion has no role in your work, in your profession, or in decision making. You may rely on "rational" decision making exclusively.

FACTS ARE LIMITED—INSTINCT IS VAST

In real-world business decision making, facts or hard data are used for only 15% to 20% of the data, or factors, that management considers. The other 80% to 85% of information is hunch, gut feeling, experience, qualitative information, conceptual models, emotion, and faith. Trust your instincts.

APPEALS TO EMOTION IN THE BUSINESS SETTING

One of my favorite moments as a business consultant comes when I get to show "rational" businesspeople who live in a "bottom-line driven" industry, how to use emotion in persuasive communication. For example: In our first meeting, Mr. Keith Hasty, President of Chicago's Best Foam Fabricators, told me that his customers were engineers and purchasing agents at serious companies—Thompson Consumer Electronics, Motorola, and Magnavox, among others. These stern buyers did not use emotion in their decision making. But, to his credit, Mr. Hasty gave me the benefit of the doubt and followed my recommendations to add some emotion to his sales team's presentations.

Keith Hasty is a living example of the American Dream. After taking his accounting degree at DePaul in the early to mid 1980s, he worked for what was then a Big-Eight accounting firm. After a couple of years, his entrepreneurial urges took hold. By pooling family money and recruiting his industrial engineer brother Steve and DePaul accountant alumna wife Diane, Mr. Hasty led the team as they took a bankrupt foam fabrication plant—purchased for $7,000—and turned it into an $8-million firm in less than eight years. I am proud to tell you that Mr. Hasty believes that adding a bit of emotion to Best Foam Fabricator's sales presentations was responsible, in part, for doubling his sales in the next year to $16 million.

MYTH: THERE IS NO EMOTION IN BUSINESS

To the naive outsider it may appear that there is no room for emotion in business. You'll hear people spouting these myths: *"Figures speak for themselves"; "The only thing that drives decisions here is the bottom line"; "In business, power is everything and power is cold."*

Let's take the wraps off the misconception that emotion has no role in business. All persuasive communication involves emotion to some degree. Over the years, my MBA students have built a list of emotions that they have observed in their business careers (see **Table 8.1, Emotions Used in Business Communication**).

Each of these emotions has been and can be used effectively in business. Frankly, the list is too long. I suggest that you will be better able to apply

TABLE 8.1 Emotions Used in Business Communication

anxiety	patriotism	delight
joy	hope	devotion
fear	euphoria	jubilation
pride	conceit	sadness
enthusiasm	shame	exhilaration
jealousy	cockiness	worry
excitement	happiness	dread
hate		

KGSB Students' list of emotions they've observed being used in business.

Professor Whalen's note: After reviewing the list, perhaps you can add to it. Please let me know. I'd be grateful if you'd drop a note telling me of any emotions that you've observed being applied in business settings.

emotion if you keep your strategic thinking simple. Under the pressure of business communication—when time is short and the ideas are flying fast and heavy, when you're feeling the pressure and may not be thinking as clearly as you might if you could relax and contemplate—you need to apply a simpler strategy. Here it is: There are two emotions that capture the entire list: Fear and Love. I believe that most people you deal with can be persuaded by using only two basic message strategies: Love and Fear. Look at **Table 8.2, Two Basic Business Emotions: Love & Fear.**

Love emotions are very powerful and can motivate people. You will want to use the positive, energizing force that is found in our various feelings of love. You can certainly love another person, and perhaps that is the type of love that comes quickly to your mind. Now think of the other types of things that can produce the positive feelings of love within you, such as

- Pride of accomplishment
- Joy at winning
- Excitement when solving a problem
- Happiness in receiving a promotion and raise
- Hope when beginning a new assignment

TABLE 8.2 Two Basic Business Emotions: Love & Fear

Love Emotions	Fear Emotions
exhilaration	anxiety
pride	hate
joy	jealousy
euphoria	shame
enthusiasm	cockiness
happiness	conceit
delight	sadness
jubilation	worry
devotion	dread
excitement	blame
patriotism	
hope	

All emotions can be classified as either Love Emotions or Fear Emotions. In this table you'll see some of the emotions people have told me they experience in making business decisions. I've categorized each emotion as either Love or Fear.

FEAR WORKS IN DISGUISE

You may not recognize fear because it masks itself. For example, anger is fear. Anger is a big, fierce front we put up when we're afraid. Most often we're afraid of losing something—like our position, money, face, the respect of others. Often we become angry and fearful if we are afraid that someone will say "No" in response to our requests. For example, how often have you seen people become angry when they try to present a complaint to a department store clerk. Perhaps all they want to do is return a shirt they have bought, but they approach the negotiation with a hidden fear that the clerk will not believe them and will say, "No—we can't take that back."

PERSUADING ANGRY PEOPLE

When you see someone being angry, you must realize that what you're witnessing is largely defensive behavior: Angry people are trying to protect themselves, they're afraid. Before you can persuade, you must get them to lower their defensive shields. They will not listen to you with their shields up. There is so much noise going on in their heads that they can't really think. In this defensive state they will filter everything you try to say to them through a thick fog of anger. There is no sense in trying to communicate your ideas to a person in this temporary psychological state. You'd be wasting your time and probably just make him more angry. But angry people can be managed.

• Here's how to manage people who are in fear

First, you must realize that fear transmits and spreads like a disease. The other person's fear is going to make you afraid. Different people have different ways of showing anger. Some people are quite demonstrative—they communicate their anger by talking loudly, speaking in an angry tone; their faces may be contorted into hateful expressions; their gestures may be choppy—they move their hands in fast, short thrusts.

Other people—particularly managers—try to hide their anger and may even deny to themselves that they are angry. This type of person may behave in a manner opposite from the angry person above. They will speak quite softly and not move at all. Their facial expression may be passive, but their eyes will contain a spark.

When dealing with the first, demonstrative type of person, you must manage your fear. Her raw emotional energy will tumble across the air space between you and make you fearful and perhaps angry. It's OK for you to feel it, but you must not communicate your rising fear to the other person. It will only pour gasoline on her raging fire. You must remain calm.

Step One: *Let him talk it out.* He may have a great fear, usually based on experience, that you will interrupt, disagree with him, and not let him talk. Most people do interrupt angry people. He may have fearful expectations that you are not going to listen to him. By listening, you remove that fear. Also, by listening and encouraging the other person to talk, you let him air his complaint. You may gain information that will help you find resolution. The angry person gets to hear himself speak and may realize, as he listens to himself, that the source of the fear is not quite so threatening. Don't interrupt except to help the person find the right words or to feed back to him that you're listening. People must talk it out to get a handle on their anger.

Step Two: *Show that she is safe with you.* You may be a threat to the fearful person. It's important that you do not present any threat. Keep your voice level, soft, and reasonable. Focus intently on the other person, show that you are listening to her.

Step Three: *Provide him with feeling words.* You may find that the person has difficulty expressing what he is thinking and feeling. Many people have a limited vocabulary of emotional words to describe how they feel. If you say, "You look angry" or "If I were you I'd feel very discouraged," then shut up and let the person talk, you may find that he will begin to bond with you and trust you a bit more. He may find that giving his feelings words helps him to understand the problem and be less fearful.

Step Four: *Communicate that it is natural and normal to feel as she does.* Part of the problem—that is, why she is angry—is that she is afraid that you'll think her foolish for acting angry. Some anger is fueled by shame and the person may be confused by that emotion. She may not feel comfortable being angry in a formal business setting. By saying things like, "If I were you I'd feel exactly as you do," you help by removing this source of shame and thus reduce the chance of further anger.

HANDLING ANGRY SUPERVISORS AND CUSTOMERS

All the above steps apply if you're handling an angry superior or customer. But a complaining customer or supervisor puts you in a more delicate position than when you're dealing with a peer, because your power over superiors and customers is limited. Your supervisor holds legitimate power over you. Your customer can freely take his business elsewhere and/or complain to your supervisor about you.

You can handle people who have authority and power over you by applying a little psychological judo. In judo, the person's superior force can be used against him. After you've gone through Steps One through Four and the person calms down, you continue to empathize with him. Using your imagination, try to think of all the negative ramifications and problems the situation has created for the person. Feed this information back to the angry person. As you describe the problem to him, he will begin to agree with you and perhaps take back the floor, wanting to talk more and continue with the complaint. That's great, this is just what you want him to do. Let him air it out. Soon you'll reach a point where the other person is satisfied with your understanding. Now, you continue to escalate and exaggerate your description of the problem and its impact, making it bigger and bigger until the other person says "No, it's not that bad," "You've done everything that could be done. It's OK." You keep describing the negative, fearful outcomes to the person until you exceed his perception of the situation. At that point he will shift his position—he will no longer be angry and will tell you, "It's OK, it's not that bad." As in all persuasive business communication, you must be sincere and honest in the things you say. If you try to blow smoke at a person who is in this state, and she realizes that you're patronizing her, you're dead meat. You must develop the ability to see things from the other person's perspective if you wish to be persuasive.

If you'd like to learn more about dealing with fearful people (and business is full of them), Dale Carnegie's excellent book *How to Win Friends and Influence People* offers reams of advice on handling angry people and winning them to your way of thinking.

USING POWERFUL EMOTIONS TO PERSUADE

I've found that the two most powerful emotions in business are people's desire for gain—their controlled greed—and their fear. Although people are afraid of many things, from death to disease to public speaking, the most common fear in business is fear of loss. Your message strategy must give managers something to decide against (Loss) and something to decide for (Gain). They must reject one course of action and select the other. For example, Kimberly is a market analyst working at Riccorp, a major, mythical Chicago corporation manufacturing and distributing athletic helmets used to protect bicyclists. Over the past three months she and her group have been assessing several possible acquisitions her firm could make. Kimberly believes that Riccorp should buy a competitor instead of acquiring a firm that markets products outside her firm's area of expertise: dog grooming products. Her message strategy is to paint the fearful picture of what will happen if they dilute their effort and seek to operate a firm outside Riccorp's area of experience: the pet care market.

- Lose market share to competition—due to inattention and fragmented use of resources (Fear message)
- Gain share, impede competition—by buying market share and creating a synergism with existing resources (Love message)

Another example of using both the fear and love message strategies comes from politics. Wise campaign strategists always design their campaign's advertising messages to give the electorate something to vote for and something to vote against. Unfortunately, some misguided candidates have recently placed greater emphasis on negative or attack advertising. It is not sufficient for the Fonsworth campaign to show that people should vote against Senator Tireair, for example, because of his overinflated promises. Fonsworth's media message gurus must find ways to show voters that they should vote for Fonsworth for many positive reasons. Too often a candidate will fail to offer both sides of the message: Love and Fear. The attacking candidate will rail against his opponent's evil incompetency (Fear message) without emphasizing his own strong, positive position (Love message).

USING FEAR TO PERSUADE

Compared with love messages, fear messages are far more powerful. People react far more extremely to fear messages. It makes sense that we would rather avoid harm than seek gain. Our primary instincts are directed at survival. Our brain is designed first to protect us from danger. Our cerebral cortex shuts down when our brain stem detects sufficient danger (see **Chapter 4, "When You're Afraid to Communicate: Understanding Anxiety and Fear"**).

In experiments, people have eagerly spent two and a half times as much money and effort to avoid fear than they would have spent to achieve a gain. Fear is two and a half times more motivating than gain.

FEAR MESSAGES CAN BACKFIRE—WATCH OUT

• *Fear appeals must be handled very carefully*
Research has shown a strong negative correlation between the effectiveness of a fear message and an audience's education and intelligence. Simply put, the higher the audience's education and intelligence, the less fear appeals work. Less educated people and children are very susceptible to a threatening message, but managers are not.

With management's higher education and intelligence (not compared to yours, certainly; I'm comparing managers to the general public), an ill-conceived fear message will be transparent—he'll realize that, "She's just trying to scare us." If you try to scare management into action and your appeal is seen as a ploy, it will backfire; you'll not be credible or persuasive.

That is not to say that fear appeals don't work with management, they do. The peril you predict must be plausible. **There must be a real danger, the potential for real loss.**

BUYER'S *FOUR BIG FEARS*©

Everyone has four basic fears when making a business decision or when making a personal purchase. The bigger the decision or purchase, the bigger the potential fear.

Fear One: *I won't get what you're promising.*

Persuaders are usually viewed skeptically by deciders—our desire to sell may cause us to exaggerate or, worse, lie to get our way. There is a great tradition of acceptable exaggeration in sales and advertising called *puffery,* and deciders are well aware of persuaders' tendencies to inflate their promises. For example, when you eat at Denny's, do the things you order ever taste as they look in the pictures on the menu?

Fear Two: *I'll pay too much for it.*

It's not just the potential for losing money that makes fear so big; we don't want to be a fool. Is there anything worse than making a major purchase, like a VCR or a Giant Screen TV, and then finding it on sale in next week's newspaper? The current cost-cutting strategies that are rampant throughout corporate America today make "paying too much" a form of fiscal treason. Beyond monetary cost, the listener may be concerned that she'll pay too much in terms of psychic energy, for example, having to take training before she can use your plan. Also consider the time cost, from your listener's point of view, for evaluation and installation time needed.

Fear Three: *My significant other(s) will say I was crazy to have bought it.*
Most people buy with someone real or imagined looking over their shoulder. Significant others include: supervisors, spouses, in-laws, professional associates, and even nosy neighbors and golf partners.

Job Interview Tip. Remember, when you interview for that next great job, that the person doing the hiring is afraid of making a mistake and having others in the firm, like the boss, say, "I can't believe you hired him."

TIP | Be sure to tell the interviewer how well your previous interviews went with others in the firm. "I've met some wonderful people at this firm; Ms. Hostile (the interviewer's supervisor) and I had a wonderful conversation."

Fear Four: *I won't like my self-image; it's not for people like me/firms like ours.*

Self-image may apply more to consumer products and the things we buy for ourselves than to corporate decisions. But companies have images, too. A corporation holds a market position and seeks to define and regulate its corporate culture. So your plans must be right, considering the firm's ethos. I recall an MBA candidate who wanted to sell a new computer system to his supervisors at an old and well-respected trust department on LaSalle Street. He asked for my advice in preparing his presentation. He planned to begin his pitch by emphasizing the computer's features that appealed to him: faster, the latest equipment, advanced high-tech performance. I pointed out that the attributes of his proposed computer system might frighten his conservative, risk-adverse supervisors. He was successful in getting his plan approved by emphasizing the system's fail-safe redundancy, its error-checking features, and how it would protect the customers—benefits that would appeal to his managers.

Another important message is: "This idea/product is used successfully by firms like yours/ours" (or firms you/we admire).

For each of the *Four Big Fears*© there are effective message strategies that will counter your listener's fears and allow you to be persuasive (see **Table 8.3, Message Strategies to Counter the *Four Big Fears*©**).

Fear One: *I won't get what you're promising.*

Message Strategy. Remind the buyer, subtly of course, of your credibility (expertise, trustworthiness, and goodwill). Credibility lets the listener believe what you predict and promise her. You can rely on your trust relationship with the listener (see **Chapter 6, "First, People Must Believe You: Managing Your Credibility"**). A more objective demonstration of your intent to fulfill promises is your lists of satisfied customers and

TABLE 8.3 Message Strategies to Counter the *Four Big Fears*©

Fear	Message Strategy
I won't get what you're promising.	•Credibility • Satisfied Customers • Performance Data
I'll pay too much for it.	• Value = $\frac{\text{Benefits}}{\$}$
My significant other(s) will say I was crazy to have bought it.	• Inoculation Theory • Build set of anticipated objections from others
I won't like my self-image; it's not for people like me/ firms like ours.	• We have satisfied customers just like you • Companies like ours, that we admire, use it

Strategies for countering the listener's *Four Big Fears*©

objective performance data. You can demonstrate that others have received what you now promise the listener. By offering objective data, you allow the customer to evaluate the potential outcomes without having to rely solely on your opinion.

Fear Two: *I'll pay too much for it.*

Your message strategy is a sales classic. When the buyer has objections about price (monetary, psychic effort, time, risk costs), your message is to sell value; that is, to increase the listener's perception of the good things he will gain. People want to maximize their return for the cost they pay. **Figure 8.1, Source of Value Calculation,** shows the two fundamental strategies you can use to increase value. Value is the benefit(s) the listener will gain by following your plan, divided by the cost(s) incurred to buy the benefit(s). To increase value and get the listener to adopt your recommendation, you can increase the benefit(s) or lower the cost(s).

Fear Three: *My significant other(s) will say I was crazy to have bought it.*

It's best to anticipate the players who may be in the "decision group," that is, the group of deciders, influencers, recommenders, gatekeepers, and evaluators who have some say in or influence over the decision to adopt

$$\frac{\text{Benefits}}{\$ \text{ Cost}} = \text{Value}$$

Figure 8.1. Source of Value Calculation
People buy the alternative idea or product that has the greatest level of value. *Value* is the benefit(s) the person will receive divided by the cost that must be paid. Persuaders can raise value by lowering the cost or by raising perception and awareness of the benefits.

your plan. Know what their needs, prejudices, and viewpoints are likely to be. I always recommend that you take time to establish a relationship with all members of the decision group. By making mini-presentations, you can establish a strong support base and learn in advance of any objections or problems they may have with the plan. With this intelligence, you can formulate your "Inoculation Strategy."

Inoculation Strategy. The idea behind an *Inoculation Strategy* is: If you know that your listener is going to hear negative comments about your plan, it is best to give the listener a dose of those negative opinions before he hears them from others. Like a medical inoculation, a *message inoculation* is a weakened strain that allows the listener to develop antibodies, in this case, counterarguments that will resist the negative influence others may have. You give the listener "what you may hear from others" or "some misconceptions that others may hold."

Be a Two-Edged Knife. One of the great 19th-century orators, U.S. Senator Theodore Gillmore Bilbo (a noted sleazeball), was called the Two-Edged Knife for his ability to debate any issue from either side with equal zest and skill. Bilbo was a shifty guy who did not stand for righteousness and good. I know that you do, however. You must know the reasonable person's (and the fearful person's) arguments against your ideas. It is important that you build a set of anticipated objections that other people may raise, and develop counterarguments. In your presentation, it is wise to touch on both sides of the issue. This makes your presentation more balanced and shows that you have considered other viewpoints as well as your own—that you've looked at the downside as well as the upside of your plan—and thus demonstrates the levelheaded decision making that people want and demand of business leaders.

Fear Four: *I won't like my self-image; it's not for people like me/firms like ours.*

The best solution is to offer evidence that, "We have satisfied customers just like you," that firms like the listener's, firms he admires, use and have benefited from this approach. That people he respects have embraced this idea.

Dr. Jekyll Becomes Mr. Hyde During Your Presentation. When the stakes are high and rational, levelheaded people are asked to make a decision, they frequently become a little nuts. **Figure 8.2, The** *Emotional Buyer,*© shows the psychological change that buyers undergo during the decision or buying process. The figure represents your listener's state of mind from the start of the persuasive process till the end, when he buys. Look at the left-hand side of the diagram (where your listener begins to evaluate your ideas) and compare it to the right-hand side (where he buys). You'll notice that at first you're dealing with a person who has lots of rational thoughts with only a small amount of emotion. But when it comes time to make a decision, you can see that the ratio of rational to emotional thoughts has reversed. You're now dealing with a very emotional and only slightly rational person. The nice, intelligent executive you first met has become a different person. He may not show his emotion by his actions or tone of voice. Business executives are great poker players who know how to maintain a blank face. A clue, however, is that now the things he says may not make sense. He suddenly decides that "it costs too much" when you've demonstrated the cost effectiveness, and earlier he had agreed that the price was right. He may say, "I've got to think it over." This makes no sense because all the facts are laid out, the thinking is over; it's time to do. You're now dealing with a fearful person. One or more of the big fears are probably at work.

STRATEGIES FOR PERSUADING MR. HYDE

Your first task is to help turn Mr. Hyde back into Dr. Jekyll—the diagram in **Figure 8.2, The** *Emotional Buyer,*© is axiomatic, it's got to happen. If

Change in Buyer's Mental State

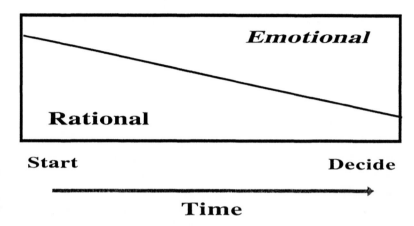

Emotional

Rational

Start   **Decide**

Time

Figure 8.2. Whalen's *Emotional Buyer*©
The Figure shows the change in the buyer's mental state from the time he begins to evaluate a product/idea to the time he decides to buy. The buyer passes from a mental state dominated by rational thought into an emotion-driven state of mind.

buyers doesn't get emotional, they don't buy. When you're asking an executive to make a decision that involves significant consideration and risk on her part, you must be prepared with persuasion and message strategies. On the Love Emotion Side, the listener must become excited at the prospect of attaining the benefits you're offering. No matter which way you cut it, fear or love, the decider will undergo some form of emotion that will reduce the mental space for rational thought. You have to prepare for this.

To turn Dr. Jekyll into Mr. Hyde you must reduce rational thoughts and raise emotion, the emotional thoughts that Dr. Jekyll is thinking. First, make more emotional (connotative) statements than rational (denotative) statements (see **Chapter 2, "Effective Communication: Symbolically Sharing Your Personal Experience"**).

Look for the Physical Signs. After the listener is excited and sees the benefits, you'll notice that he often begins to slow his thinking and his physical movements. Another sign that the listener is undergoing the shift from mostly rational thought to emotional thought is that he distracts himself. He may pick up something and read it. Or pick up the phone and make a call. Or change the subject abruptly. This type of behavior is an unconscious effort on the listener's part to reduce the uncomfortable mental state he is in. Remember, the perceived risks give rise to his fear. By this "non sequitur"-type behavior, he gains some form of relief from his fear.

TURN DOWN THE BUYER'S EMOTIONS

Now that your listener has become emotional, it may be necessary for you to reduce her emotional state and raise her rational thoughts. Keep telling her to accept the plan. Remind her of reasons why she wants the plan. Review and show rational facts that support the soundness of your idea. Use objective cost and performance data. Rely on your credibility and working relationship. Follow the recommendation of the master sales trainer Frank Bettger: Say to her, "If you were my own sister, I'd tell you what I'm about to tell you now: 'Adopt the plan; it's right for you.' " If you want to be more effective in persuading people from outside your department or outside your firm, read Bettger's *How I Raised Myself From Failure to Success in Selling.* It is a book that is worth every minute you spend reading it.

Manage Your Own Fear. Remember that fear transmits like a disease— you're likely to get it. Tell yourself: "Stay cool." Take a deep breath. Make an effort to relax as much as possible. Fill yourself with positive feelings. You can help the listener relax by having a calm, positive manner. Remember, when you get to the emotional part you're standing at the threshold of success. If you have carefully studied the listener's needs and believe to the best of your professional judgment that the plan is wise, you have a professional obligation to help the listener make the right decision.

THE PROFESSIONAL LOSER

There is a common but undesirable type of person in sales called the Professional Visitor. This salesperson is a nice, friendly, well-mannered individual who may be very knowledgeable about his products and how they can help prospective customers. This Professional Visitor does make some sales but not enough to be outstanding. His problem is that he can't deal with people when they become emotional. When it comes time for the buyer and the Professional Visitor to sign a contract, the Professional Visitor's emotions and fears rise, and he doesn't have the coping or self-management strategies that you will develop. He can take his prospective customers to the edge of the decision, but he is not equipped or trained to help them make the decision in the face of their own fears. The times he does sell, the buyer is unafraid or can make fearful decisions alone even though fearful.

Persuasion Ethics

I believe that a seller or persuader has two primary ethical obligations. First, she must be professionally trained to diagnose other's needs and to determine whether the prospective buyer does, indeed, need her product or service. Second, if she determines, in cooperation with the buyer, that the product or idea will benefit the buyer, she has a professional, ethical obligation to help the buyer overcome fear and make the decision to adopt her idea. It is not enough to make an effective presentation and "let the buyer decide." I believe that if the buyer is facing fear, you must help him through that difficult period.

Professional Emotional Management. You must work to regulate your emotions if you are to help your listener make a decision. You must be able to turn up your emotions to help the buyer become activated and excited, to anticipate and see the benefits your ideas offer. And you must be able to turn down your emotions so you can help the fearful buyer.

Deciding to Be Persuasive. After you read this book and begin to practice its ideas, you will be on your way to becoming more persuasive and thus more successful—if you want to be. Knowing how to persuade is not enough. You must have the courage to try to persuade other people—but you may not. Respectfully to you, my reader, I have seen countless intelligent, trained, charming, and dynamic businesspeople fail at persuasion because of one thing: They were not willing to take responsibility for the outcome of their own ideas. I believe that they were cut short in their careers because they did not have the courage and character to make a commitment to another person. To promise another person, based on strong faith, that their ideas will come true. You must commit yourself to helping deciders through the difficult, emotional process they have to undergo.

If you are willing to make that emotional, ethical commitment, and you continue to study and practice persuasion, you will find all the success you want. Only you can stop you from reaching your goals.

Can You Hear "No" but Accept Only "Yes"? For example, research and my own experience show that you may have to ask the decider to adopt your plan after she has said "No" three times. The fourth time you ask, she will probably say "Yes." The first three "Nos" were part of the decision process, part of thinking it over.

Feel Love; Feel Positive. The key to being persuasive with the *Emotional Buyer*© is your attitude: the feelings you have when you're persuading. If you feel love instead of fear—or more accurately, love in spite of the fear that is running through you—you'll win.

If You're a Guy, You May Have a Tougher Time. I've often noticed that men have a problem dealing with emotion. Their emotional circuits are too simple: Men are either "On" and experience anger or they're "Off" and are cool. Persuasion requires a more complex range of emotions than anger or cool.

For whatever genetic, biological, or social/learning reason, I've noticed that women are better at handling their emotions in difficult business discussions. I've seen a man frightened to his core, wanting to fight and go to court ("I'll sue the S.O.B."), when a woman steps in coolly and calmly, not projecting fear.

Perhaps this emotional sophistication has helped women take the lead in many sales categories, particularly in the sale of intangible goods like advertising, meeting and convention services, telecommunications, and public relations. These fields were largely dominated by men until women entered. Women have rapidly risen to the position of market dominance in these sales categories.

I believe that because women manage emotion better than men, they have succeeded in selling complex products and plans. I also believe that men can learn to deal well, be persuasive, and lead others during emotional conflict, but generally need more training to do so.

KEY | Emotional management is a vital skill for successful persuasive communication.

|SUMMARY

To be persuasive, facts are not enough: You must have emotion. To be persuasive, you must be passionate about your ideas: Passion persuades. You can rely on two basic business emotions: Love and Fear. Love emotions are very powerful and can motivate people. Fear is anger; angry people are afraid. Our primary fear is fear of loss.

You can persuade angry people by first dealing with their fear before you "solve their problem."

Persuasive messages must have both Fear and Love, that is, promise of potential loss if the plan is not followed and of gain if it is. Fear of loss is two and a half times more powerful a persuader than is gain.

When they have to make a decision, people move from largely rational thought into an emotion-driven state of mind. The more important the decision, or the greater the risk to the listener, the greater is this shift in emotion.

The techniques offered in this book will make you more persuasive. But you have to apply them earnestly and with a good, loving heart. If you chose not to apply them, you are choosing not to be persuasive. The persuader must have the strength of character to accept responsibility for the outcome of his or her recommendations.

9

Strategies for Formatting Presentations

How You Say It

ROCK AROUND THE CLOCK FORMAT

If you walked into one of this nation's 10,000 radio studios, you'd likely notice a multicolored, pie-shaped chart pinned strategically to the wall. This ubiquitous little device is called the *Clock Format*. The disc jockey knows exactly what to do at each part of the hour during her show by following the instructions printed on the *Clock Format*. Each slice of the pie calls for a different type of record (Oldie Goldie, Top 10, Motown, House Music, etc.), or when to play a commercial. It will even tell her when to read the weather or a public service announcement. The disc jockey also knows to say the station's call letters first when "coming out of a record" and last when "going into a song"; formats call for countless other prescribed patterns of performance.

Now, you may think that the *Clock Format* is too restrictive, but it's not. Rather than being a straitjacket, the *Clock Format* allows the jock great freedom. For example, if the jock is a bit tired, not feeling well, or especially "spark-plug" creative, he can lay back and just do the format and have a fairly good show. The listener may not even be able to tell. When he feels great, he can go beyond the format and soar. The station management is assured of a strong level of minimal programming quality thanks to the *Clock Format*.

Clock Format Presentations. I recommend that you learn some "Presentation Clock Formats" that will allow you to make good presentations when you feel rotten or, more likely, don't have sufficient time to prepare. Then when you're feeling tops and have time to work on your presentation, you too can soar, climbing the heights of persuasive success.

These formats are golden, and I'll bet that you've probably heard one or two of them before. I promise you this: For years I've used these formats myself as a salesman, advertising executive, political consultant, and even teacher. I've taught thousands of people how to use them successfully. They will work for you, too.

The first presentation element that you must format is your opening.

OPENING THE PRESENTATION

Taking charge and making the right impression during the opening of your presentation is critical (please see **Chapter 7, "Oral Communication: The Words You Say Are Less Than 10% of the Message"**). The listeners are forming opinions about you, and simultaneously, you're probably going through a psychological and metabolic sleigh ride with some level of stage fright. As you take center stage, be it in a theater or at the head of a conference table, you have three primary and immediate tasks:

Task One	Capture the listeners' attention.
Task Two	Take control of the meeting and the room.
Task Three	Build a good feeling of rapport with your listeners for yourself, and if you're on a team, for your teammates.

I suggest that you don't risk being too cute or clever. Save that for later when your metabolism has settled down and you're calmer. Play it nice and friendly, but straight.

Opening the Presentation. Start each presentation by introducing yourself (your teammates), or if you're well known to the group or have just been given an adequate introduction by the meeting's chair, you can introduce yourself by the task you've undertaken or the purpose of your talk:

> Mel, Cindy, and I were asked to analyze market growth rates for five SBUs and make some recommendations. We hope that as you leave this meeting you agree that we have one SBU that deserves our support and that we must prune two SBUs to fund our winner.

In less formal meetings, a great way to take control is to formally and clearly, with some gravity to your demeanor, state the purpose of the meeting or your portion of the meeting.

Be sure to make a prediction for the audience. Tell the audience right up front what it is about to hear . . . what you want it to believe or know at the end of your talk.

THE *QUESTION OPENING*©

A wonderful way to capture your audience's attention instantly is to ask a question. There are two tricks that make the *Question Opening*© work: (1) You must ask your audience a question that you really want them to answer—either aloud or mentally, and (2) you must wait for the answer. If you ask the question with the pose of an intellectual lecturer's rhetorical question—"What could the Bard have been thinking when he wrote 'Double, double, toil and trouble'?"—you'll signal to your audience to "Shut-up, sit there, and listen," and "Let me do the talking." You'll shut down communication at a point where your goal should be to open communication up. You must be patient and wait. Give your audience plenty of time to think—remember *Einstein's Time Shift*©. As your listeners are thinking, look at their individual faces, smile and nod, encouraging them to think. Most of the time, some of the audience will answer aloud. When that happens, you know you've got them hooked.

Ask a question that causes listeners to go into their memory and search for an answer. You will cause your listeners to focus their attention on seeking the answer to your question. You've thus created a group-mind: The audience's shared vision is what great presenters seek. You now have the audience's attention and you've directed its thinking to the task at hand.

Checklist for successfully executing the *Question Opening*©:

- ☐ Ask a question that you want answered.
- ☐ Pick a topic for your question that will cause your listeners to consider the issues at hand.

☐ Pick a question that causes your listeners to use their sensory memory to find an answer.

☐ Expect your listeners to answer—wait, give them time to think.

Later, in **Chapter 10, "Message Delivery: Performing the Presentation,"** in the section titled "The Psychology of Questions—The Power of Brainwashing," you'll learn more about managing your audience by using questions.

BUSINESS PRESENTATIONS
ARE NOT STORYTELLING

When people are put in new social settings, they tend to revert to their core personality traits. For example, a person who has learned to use humor will tend to make jokes. A critical person will tend to criticize. This normal human trait becomes even more evident when you are under pressure—such as having to make a business presentation. Most people have few opportunities to speak before groups and they have little time and even less training, so they tend to rely on their core sets of behavior and experience.

Presentations Learned at the Dinner Table. So they "revert to type," they make their presentation using techniques and strategies that they have used or have seen used in the past. This can be a big mistake. Without even realizing it, you may mimic presenters you have seen—maybe not even because they were good presenters, but because they reside in your unthinking mind and are available to you. The few times most people have spoken to groups in the past were to tell a story. For example, most people have their first speaking experience before a group at the family dinner table. Mom says to him, "So, Billy, what did you do at school today?" Billy then begins a reluctant, rambling narrative of his day. He may relate the events chronologically or hit highlights, if he can think of any.

Adolescent Raconteur. Later in life, during your early teens, you logged lots of speaking experience before groups; for example, when you were at a party or out with friends. You would take turns sharing stories of your experience:

You think your Dad's lame? Wait'll I tell you what my old man did. We've got this plastic pool in our backyard, you know, and its always got this green stuff growing in it, you know. So, Dad goes, "I'll get it clean." So he uses Drano . . .

The techniques that make for a good "social presentation" are not optimally effective in the business setting. They force your listener to sift through your needless, low-information buildup till you give the punch line. A business-style packaging of the same story would be: "My Dad's so lame he used Drano to clean my wading pool." Then you'd provide the details.

BUSINESS PRESENTATIONS
VERSUS SOCIAL PRESENTATIONS

The primary goal in a business presentation is efficient persuasion. Time is very limited. In a social presentation, time is not limited and the goal is to provide your companions with entertainment and develop a relationship. The key difference between the two is that the social presenter holds her audience in suspense until she reveals the punch line: "So, the Drano eats a hole in the bottom of the pool . . . duh!" or "So, the dog says, 'I've never had $20 before.' " You hold your audience's attention, working to build up to the big punch line or story ending. Along the way to your story's ending you may offer some interesting sidelights—"So Dad's wearing his usual weekend outfit, cutoff jeans and a wasted Jimmy Buffet T-shirt"—but your primary goal is to build up to the big ending: Usually the ending is the big news, the weirdest, funniest, most surprising part of the story.

Business Gives the Punch Line First. Dynamite business presentations are just the opposite: You give away the punch line right up front; the first thing you say is the punch line. That is, you state the purpose of your presentation and what you want the audience to believe. Then you give them facts and illustrations that support the conclusions you want them to adopt.

Your social storytelling usually unfolds in chronological order.

So, I got up that morning and decided to go to the mall. So, I called Kathleen, and said, "Do you wanna go to the mall," and she sez, "OK." So, I picked her up, but first I put $5 worth of gas in my car. You know that car of mine is making a funny noise, kinda of a chugga-chugga at stoplights. Whatta you think that is? Anyway, so I pick Kath up and we get to the mall . . .

ad nauseam.

Business Presentations "Cut-to-the-Chase" Early. A business presentation is more streamlined: It begins,

> Our team believes that this firm can increase market share by one and a half percent and increase ROI by three points by adding sales coverage in the Western markets. And now to show you why we believe this, here is Bob who will show our regional sales figures for 1994 and the 1995 projections.

Bim-bam-boom, right to the point. Set up the listeners with your conclusions right up front, then show them why you came to those conclusions. This method is the fastest (you've only got a few minutes), it grabs and holds the audience's attention, and it is persuasion dynamite.

Tell 'Em What You Learned, Not How You Learned It. All too often, businesspeople revert to their social experience for their presentation formats and strategies. They relate how they arrived at their conclusions chronologically, like this,

> Thank you for giving us some time to speak with you about our research project and plans for 1995. Our team first looked at the present sales figures in all the regions and compared them with each other. And, frankly it wasn't easy to get the figures from the East Coast; I think their software blew up or something. Right when they were trying to fax it to us all they could send was garbage. It caused quite a stir in our offices, let me tell you. Anyway, we knew that if we looked at sales expenses as a function of sales revenue for comparison . . .

Of course, the underlying message that the speaker is trying to convey is, *"I am very smart and worked very, very hard on this."*

This type of presentation is like slow death. The *Presenter*© is challenging the audience to pay attention. The audience must be maximally disciplined to sit through this all-too-common type of presentation. Though the key information will eventually be presented, the audience is forced to extract the data it needs: The *Presenter*© is hiding the information from his audience by burying it in his rambling, unnecessary narrative.

The solution is to use the classic *Tell 'em*³© presentation.

A CLASSIC PRESENTATION FORMAT—*TELL 'EM*³©

*Tell 'em*¹ Tell 'em what you're gonna tell 'em

*Tell 'em*² Tell 'em

*Tell 'em*³ Tell 'em what you just told 'em

I'll bet you've heard of this format before. You will want to use this magnificent, simple, and yet powerful presentation format in all your presentations. It works every time. I'll bet that you may think to yourself, "But, doesn't it get boring?"; "Don't they know what's coming and tune out?" The answer is no. The opposite is true. Storytelling is boring, unless you're Mark Twain. Businesspeople's attention spans are getting shorter every year, because every year managers' responsibilities increase and their resources (staff and money) shrink. In addition, they have more to think about and remember. You must respond to this more challenging communications environment with short, tightly organized presentations.

THE MAGIC NUMBER IS THREE

Thanks to the work of the great psychologist Herbert Kelman, we've known since the early 1960s that people remember best what you want them to know if you tell them three times. Repeating your ideas twice is not enough and four times may be too many. Three is just right, Baby Bear. When you use this format your listeners are sure to hear your conclusion, the thing you want them to know, believe, and/or do, a minimum of three times (or did I say that?).

***Tell 'em*¹**: *Tell 'em what you're gonna tell 'em*
In clear, right-to-the-point words, tell them what you want them to know, believe, and/or do because of your presentation. Do this right away, as soon

as you can, at the beginning of your presentation. Open with a short, sharp, clear conclusion.

Tell 'em[2]: Tell 'em
Using facts, figures, reasoning, models, evidence, and description, show them why you believe what you're presenting. *Important:* Be sure to tie your evidence and reasoning directly to your conclusions. Don't assume that your audience is drinking in your every word. They may be only half listening to critical points. You must be specific, perhaps even redundant.

Tell 'em[3]: Tell 'em what you just told 'em
Frequently, speakers find that ending a presentation is the most difficult part. Perhaps you've heard speakers who opened their presentation with fire, spoke brilliantly and clearly, then seemed to run out of energy at the end and closed with a series of rambling bursts of nonsense: *"Well I guess that's all, are there, uh . . . any . . . uh . . . questions? Well I guess not . . . so, ah . . . thank you."* The last impression you leave your audience with is the most powerful. In longer presentations, your final message (*recency effect*) lasts even longer in your listener's memory than your initial impression (*primacy effect*). It is important that you plan both your opening and closing. You may even want to script them in advance.

The Cold Closing©—A Solid Gold, Works-Every-Time Closing. The first and last impressions you give an audience are the most powerful and the most remembered (*primacy* and *recency*). A surefire closing follows this recipe:

1. Quickly summarize what you've told them, then
2. Make a strong, positive prediction of the good things that will happen in the future if your listeners follow your ideas.

Remember that leadership flows to the person who has a vision of the future. Your listeners will ascribe that characteristic to you if you use this closing.

No Thanks, Please. Don't say "Thank you" to signal to the audience that you're finished and it's time for them to applaud. That is for amateurs.

Think of it this way: If your presentation is any good, you've just delivered a well-conceived, carefully planned, beautifully delivered set of ideas. You've worked very hard. Your audience should thank you. **And they will if you let them.**

But what usually happens is that the inexperienced *Presenter*© panics at the end. He may end with a clear summary and strong statement of his vision for the future: " . . . and I believe that with reengineering, retooling, and a newly lit fire in our bellies, RunCo Manufacturing will enjoy growth and profitability for many years to come." Then *Einstein's Time Shift*© kicks in. Remember, time moves far slower for the audience than for you. The *Presenter*© feels like it has been 15 minutes since he said "many years to come" and the listeners are just staring at him . . . he panics and says, "Thank you, thank you very much," and he gets his applause.

In reality it was only two or three seconds. The audience members were moving in SLOW-MO and just beginning to realize that he was done. Their bodies were just starting to feel the surge of emotion and energy that his last words had created, and in one more second they were going to applaud wildly and passionately. But he stepped on their natural reaction. If he had just had a bit more courage, looked back at his audience with a strong, confident smile, nodded slightly and waited for that eternity, the loud, warm wave of thanks would have washed over him.

> **KEY** To execute the *Cold Closing*©, wait for your applause; it takes a couple of seconds for the audience to react.

End Your Presentation Like a Grammy-Winning Rock Star. Too many amateur business presentations do a slow, clumsy "board fade" ending. A board fade is when a record ends with the band continuing to play and the recording engineer slowly turning down the volume. This is an OK way to end a record, but a far better ending is the "cold" ending where the band writes a strong concluding set of chords or a powerful, clean drum riff to end their song. A *Cold Closing*© is a strong statement that sticks in the listener's mind. A *board fade* is just that, boring.

In watching thousands of business and student presentations, I've too often seen a good presenting team kill their final impression with a rambling, weak finish. You can leave a strong, positive impression with a *Cold Closing*©.

A PERFECT STRATEGY:
THE *NICHOLS' TWO THINGS*© PRESENTATION

Critical Decision: "How Much Data to Present?" This is the most important and the easiest decision you have to make. In fact, I'll give you the answer right here: Your goal is to communicate *two ideas* to your audience. You know that in oral presentation, the volume of facts that can be transmitted is quite limited (but the mass of nonverbal and attitudinal information is massive). If you try to get your listener to remember three things, she'll forget everything you told her. But, if you tell your listener: *"There are two things you'll want to take with you"* or *"There are two major things that are working here: A & B,"* the chance that she'll remember them is 90%. Brief oral presentations are best, so you say just enough to support and illustrate your two visions.

You can help your listener remember more than the two major ideas by tying other facts directly to your major points.

Any set of data, no matter how complex, can be reduced to one or two major themes. For example, consider the classic and much used themes of Good and Evil. A theologian can summarize Moslem, Jewish, and Christian philosophy in terms of good and evil. Historians can do the same with good and evil in reporting World War II (Allies = Good; Axis = Bad). Investment strategies can be framed as good and evil, too (see **Table 9.1, Reducing Massive Constructs to *Two Big Ideas*©**).

GIVE YOUR LISTENER A PREVIEW,
THEN GUIDEPOSTS ALONG THE WAY

Dr. Don Nichols, an international expert on message packaging and communication and the inventor of the *Nichols' Two Things*© Presentation, suggests that you start your verbal presentation with a preview of what you're going to say; the other ideas and facts you present are guideposts that your audience expects to find along the way. Your audience will hang on your every word and remember what you say. You'll be amazed how much more persuasive you'll be when people listen to you, accurately hear what you're saying, and then remember what you said. If your ideas are sound and your evidence is tightly and logically linked to your conclusions (*Big Ideas*©), you'll persuade.

TABLE 9.1 Reducing Massive Constructs to *Two Big Ideas*©

Massive Construct	Big Idea One	Big Idea Two
Love and marriage	Honeymoon	Making it work
Raising children	Nurturing them	Letting them go
Voice mail	No-hassle messages	Hard to reach people
Marketing strategy	Finding out what customers want	Giving it to them
Financial strategy	Big risks = Big gains	Big risks = Big losses

Each *Massive Construct* can be reduced to two *Big Ideas*© that summarize and create a theme. It is this theme, the *Big Idea*©, that listeners remember.

THE *FIVE-MINUTE PRESENTATION PREPARATION*©

You can write any presentation in five minutes, guaranteed, using *The Nichols' Two Things*© *Presentation*. During the late 1960s and early 1970s, Dr. Nichols earned a national reputation as a winning debate coach. His Texas Junior College teams consistently won national championships against Ivy League debate powerhouses. Dr. Nichols's secret was: (1) exhaustive preparation of facts—his teams were more knowledgeable and better prepared, and (2) his secret weapon: *The Nichols' Two Things*© Presentation. While other teams were executing their strategy of over-whelming the judges with a mountain of facts, the Nichols-coached Texas teams were concentrating their facts into *Two Big Ideas*©. Here is Dr. Nichols's elegant system for organizing a massive set of facts and ideas— *The Nichols' Two Things*© *Presentation*. This elegant message development and delivery system uses three principles:

Principle One   *Repetition* of *Big Ideas*© or Themes.

Principle Two   *Making Links* among the evidence and facts you offer and the *Big Ideas*© or Themes.

Principle Three   *Visualization*. Your *Big Ideas*© and evidence should use sensory modality, particularly your listener's visual senses.

Remember: Effective communication is sending pictures into your listener's mind.

I		*II*	
a		a	
	1		1
	2		2
b		b	
	1		1
	2		2

Figure 9.1. The *Nichols' Two Things*© Presentation

Don Nichols showed his debaters how to take a piece of paper and make the classic outline structure you see in **Figure 9.1,** *Nichols' Two Things Presentation*©. The first step is to write down the two things or themes that seem to summarize the issue. These two big themes go next to Roman numerals I and II.

For example, let's prepare a presentation on something stupid like Peanut Butter. My major themes, the *Big Ideas*© are: I. Peanut butter is fun to eat, and II. It can be dangerous.

I. Peanut butter is fun to eat   II. It can be dangerous

Next, I think of two things that will support each of my *Two Big Ideas*©. These supporting premises will become sub-A and sub-B under Roman numerals I and II.

I. Peanut butter is fun to eat   II. It can be dangerous
   A. Tastes great   A. Eat too much
   B. Kid's food   B. High in fat

Finally, two supportive pieces of evidence are marshaled under each sub-a and sub-b.

I. Peanut butter is fun to eat   II. It can be dangerous
   A. Tastes great   A. Eat too much
      1. Nutty flavor   1. Dense food
      2. Crunchy and smooth   2. Loaded with calories

B. Kid's food
  1. PB & J sandwiches
    at school

  2. Recapture feelings
    of childhood

B. High in fat
  1. As much as butter

  2. Heart disease

Sample Presentation

Let's think about a great, fun food: peanut butter. Perhaps you've not given this All-American food much thought lately . . . but, if you think of it, I'll bet that two major ideas pop into your head: Peanut butter is fun to eat, but it can be dangerous. Before we consider peanut butter's potential danger, let's talk about how much fun peanut butter is to eat.

There are two big reasons that peanut butter is fun to eat. It tastes great and it's a kid's food. Why does it taste great? Most people tell us it's peanut butter's great nutty taste, "it tastes like fresh roasted peanuts" as the commercials say. It's the flavor of peanuts at the ball park. Peanut butter tastes great because of its texture, or what food scientists call "mouth feel."

Peanut butter comes with a choice of mouth feels: crunchy or smooth. What is your favorite? That is why peanut butter is fun: It tastes great.

But there are more reasons why peanut butter is a great, fun food. It rekindles memories of your childhood, because peanut butter is kids' official food. The PB and J . . . or peanut butter and jelly sandwich . . . is by far kids' favorite lunchtime food (a close second is "tooney-fish"). I'll bet that PB and J was one of your favorites as a kid, too. Am I right? That is why, today, peanut butter is a fun food; it lets you recapture your feelings of childhood.

With all the stress, pressure, shrinking resources at work, the crime and chaos in the streets, it's only natural that we should, for a few brief moments, retreat to memories and feelings of childhood. Look at the growth of cookie sales as Boomers and Generation X-ers alike rekindle the milk and cookies after school experience. Peanut butter is another great way to have some fun as you did as a child.

But, it's not all good news for peanut butter. Peanut butter can be dangerous. While we agree that peanut butter is fun, we must consider its darker side (etc., etc., etc.).

Themes Emerge. As you work your way through this outline you may discover that other *Big Ideas*® emerge. For example, perhaps you'll find that one of your sub-A points is a better major theme than the idea you have under Roman numeral II. If you have mastered your subject matter, you'll find that this structure is a wellspring of inspiration and organization that will help you quickly and easily organize your ideas into a surefire oral presentation.

KEY | *Repetition:* **Your listeners will hear each idea the magic number of three times (or more).**

KEY | *Making Links:* **It is critical that you tie your evidence into your major themes each time—you cannot depend on your listeners making the connection unless you show them how it fits.**

KEY | *Visualization:* **Put a picture in your listeners' minds—this they will remember.**

THE FINAL FORMAT— PRESENTING AS A TEAM MEMBER

For decades, advertising people, engineers, architects, and sales people have made formal presentations to clients and senior management in teams. Today, reengineering, TQA (Total Quality Assurance), TQM (Total Quality Manufacturing), and ISO 9000 programs have brought together teams of workers and managers to make plans, diagnose problems, and make recommendations. Teams may be composed of people from customer service, quality control, accounting, purchasing, engineering, and marketing. Together they present their ideas and plans to the company and sometimes to senior management.

I imagine that you've had the opportunity to make a presentation as a member of a team. If not yet, I predict that you will soon.

BENEFITS OF TEAM PRESENTATIONS

A team presentation is different from a solo act in one important way: In a well-designed team presentation, each person plays a specialized role. Three benefits spring from this strategy: (1) The audience has a strong, clear perception of each individual player, thus promoting and facilitating communication; (2) there is a synergy from the heightened "sense of team" that is transmitted to the audience; and (3) as with any specialist, the individual team member can concentrate on her own role and responsibilities and deliver a better message with superior skill.

SPECIALTY ROLES

Host[©]. In advertising and sales presentations, the *Host*[©] role is usually assigned to the senior executive, who is often the best *Presenter*[©]. Her job is to project the positive, warm attitude of a winner to the audience. The volume of data that is presented by the *Host*[©] is actually quite small. The *Host*[©] demonstrates confidence in her team by letting the "junior members" take responsibility for the presentation. Here is the Host's list of duties, in the order they are performed:

First: State the goal/purpose of presentation: *"As the result of what you hear today, we believe that you'll agree that teal is the right color for your team's logo and uniforms."*

Second: Introduce the team using the *John-the-Baptist*[©] technique (see **Chapter 6, "First, People Must Believe You: Managing Your Credibility"**). *"One of the smartest people in advertising came up with the breakthrough insight that led to the solution we're recommending today, Diane Tinsley . . ."*

Third: Share the *Big Idea,*[©] metaphors, or two ideas (theme): "You need to project an image of THE GREAT OUTDOORS as well as TROPICAL imagery."

The Hand-Off[©]: Finally, the *Host,*[©] with pride and joy, hands-off to the first *Presenter*[©]: *"Now, Bill Burrell will take you through the color palette used by other players in your industry . . . Bill."*

The *Hand-Off*[©] makes the pace of the presentation faster. By making a quick introduction of the next *Presenter*[©], that speaker is immediately free to begin her presentation. Without *The Hand-Off*[©], the speaker would have to introduce herself, "Hi, I'm Sarah Rego, and I am in charge of financial analysis. I've looked at your financial reports for the first three years and . . ." This slows the presentation. Most business presentations are brief (or should be brief). The precious time saved may be small, only 20 to 30 seconds, but the psychological impact on the audience's perception of time is significant. The presentation seems faster.

When making short presentations (less than 45 minutes), I recommend that the *Host*[©] does not present data or evidence; she must leave that to her teammates. If you have decided that the *Host*[©] must present evidence, perhaps due to her superior expertise or the fact that the team has only two members—let the *Host*© hand-off to the first *Presenter*©, then return later as a *Presenter*©. If the *Host*© performs the Host's duties and then launches into presenting the data, the pace of the presentation really slows. In longer presentations, however (one hour to full-day), you may want a slower pace. Here, the *Host*© might give the introductory message, then proceed to presenting evidence.

John-the-Baptist© IN TEAM PRESENTATIONS

The *Host*© introduces the *Presenters*© (who carry forward the bulk of the persuasive messages to the audience) in glowing terms, building their credibility like *John-the-Baptist*©. When it's your turn to be the *Host*©, you'll build credibility by introducing your teammates with glowing affection and respect; you'll cite their credentials (expertise, trustworthiness, and caring). The idea is to let them sell the ideas; you sell the team. Incidentally, through the *halo effect,* your teammates' heightened credibility will reflect back on you and through the *association effect,* because you're on the same team, your credibility rises with theirs. So, you'll get the benefit of high credibility without having to say a single word on your own behalf.

Presenter(s). The Presenter's job is to execute effectively the team's communication mission. You have asked for important people's scarce time because you have important ideas that they must hear. The team's communication strategy is to sell two big ideas persuasively (see *Nichols' Two Things*© presentation, above).

Each *Presenter*© begins by clearly and cleverly stating the major idea being supported. The *Host*© has already introduced the *big idea,* now it's the Presenter's job to deliver the supporting evidence and visual information.

The *Presenter*© illustrates the *Big Ideas*©, metaphors, or two ideas (theme) with data, examples, and visual storytelling.

Important. As *Presenter*©, you must tie the evidence, data, examples, and stories to the big idea, metaphors, or two ideas (theme). The listeners will not make the link unless you literally show them how the data and themes fit together. The manner in which you make the link can be subtle and brief, or it can be oblique, but it must be done.

Finally, the *Presenter*© hands off to the next *Presenter*© or, if at the end, to the *Host*©.

Host© **Closes.** The *Host*© closes the presentation using the *Tell-Em*[3©] technique. Please see the Step Three—Tell 'Em What You Just Told 'Em, and Solid Gold—Works-Every-Time Closing sections above for suggestions on ending the presentation.

Lucy—Key Team Member. The team member with the most critical role during the presentation is *Lucy*—the projectionist. *Lucy* operates the overhead projector and pulls the slides for his teammates (as in the *Peanuts* comic strip, where "Lucy" pulls the football from "Charlie Brown"). Although computer-generated slides, LED computer projection devices, and television projectors are available and are beginning to appear in some business presentations, by far the vast majority of presentations in business today are supported by overhead projectors. Tear sheets on easels, photographic slide projectors, black-/whiteboards, and mimes (using gestures) are used by a few. For example, at the Chicago office of the great advertising agency, Foote Cone Belding, the "New Business Team" uses prepared cards, hand-lettered by agency artists, to provide visual evidence. This practice, however, is not common.

Lucy Is the Conductor. Like a symphony's conductor, *Lucy* must know the entire presentation far better than anyone else on the team because she will control the pace and timing by moving faster or slower through the slides. Of course, the *Presenter*© may indicate with a nod or a quick word to *Lucy* when she is ready for the next slide.

Equipment function is Lucy's responsibility, too. He must check out the overhead projector and make sure that an extra bulb is available. ***Important:*** If you don't have an extra bulb, you can be sure that the one in the machine will blow out. Overhead projectors can be evil: They can sense when the presentation is important and if there is no replacement bulb in the room. I personally believe that this is just their way of asserting importance. Show your overhead projector some respect by checking it out.

Lucy **will center the transparencies** by first centering the beam of light, without any transparency on the machine. *Lucy* makes sure that the projected spot of light fills every edge of the screen to the maximum, without spilling over onto the wall. As an experienced projectionist, *Lucy* knows that he must make sure that the slide being projected is centered on the screen by looking at the projected image, not by looking down at the actual slide on the machine. Often, the machine must be set out of parallel with the screen to project a centered image. If you align the slide on the machine, it may be projected crooked onto the screen.

TIP | Use both hands to center and adjust a transparency—it's faster and more sure than using one hand. One-handed adjustments make you look too fumbly.

The critical information on the slide must be projected on the upper two thirds of the screen, or above the center line. People sitting at the back of the room may have their view blocked by other audience members or by the projector itself.

Be Invisible. A final word on the considerable *Lucy*. For all her responsibilities, *Lucy* is best when unnoticed. She should sit behind the projector, so as not to block the audience's view. The audience should be aware only of the presenters and the visual evidence that is projected on the screen.

| SUMMARY

If you format your presentations, you'll be sure to get a consistent level of quality. Your format should include a design for your opening, the packaging of your ideas, and your closing.

The three tasks of the opening are

Task One	Capture listeners' attention.
Task Two	Take control of the meeting and the room.
Task Three	Build a good feeling of rapport with your listeners.

The key to the successful *Question Opening*© is to pause and wait for an answer. The question should be "on topic." Use sensory messages to trigger the audience's sense memory.

A classic presentation format: ***Tell 'em***[30]

☐ *Tell 'em*[1]—what you're going to tell them (give them the conclusion)

☐ *Tell 'em*[2]—make your presentation

☐ *Tell 'em*[3]—summarize your recommendations

Remember to create a strong closing: We recommend the *Cold Closing.*[©]

1. Quickly summarize your ideas.
2. Predict things for the future.
3. Don't say "Thank you."
4. Smile confidently and wait for the applause.

A wonderful format for all kinds of presentations is the *Nichols' Two Things*[©] Presentation format. The secret is to boil your ideas down into *Two Big Ideas.*[©] The *Nichols' Two Things*[©] Presentation will work for you if you remember the principles:

Principle One   *Repetition* of *Big Ideas*[©] or Themes

Principle Two   *Making links* among the evidence and facts you offer and the *Big Ideas*[©] or Themes

Principle Three   *Visualization* of your *Big Ideas*[©] and evidence should use sensory modality, particularly your listener's visual senses.

10

Message Delivery

Performing the Presentation

I t's now time to talk about how to act during a presentation. I'll bet that this is the part of the book that you've been looking forward to reading. Most of the people I train in effective communication are very concerned about how they appear when they stand before an audience and present their ideas (me, too). Worrying about how you appear to an audience can be a major cause of Speech Anxiety and Stage Fright (see **Chapter 4, "When You're Afraid to Communicate: Understanding Anxiety and Fear"**). Now you're ready to consider which behaviors and attitudes make for a superior presentation.

Have Fun. Here is my first piece of advice: Don't worry about making a fool of yourself (even though I know you probably do—it's only natural to feel that way). Of the thousands of businesspeople I've coached, 99.9% are concerned about acting like a dimwit or "saying something stupid." I am not concerned for a minute that you'll come off like a fool. I am far more worried that you'll be too stuffy, create a distance between your listeners and yourself, and bore people. Your challenge in preparing your mental state before a presentation is to loosen up, to have fun. Think about the great business presenters you've seen, the business gurus like Tom Peters, or the president of your company, or the leaders you admire in your industry. I'll bet that they have a sense of humanity, of fun and enjoyment, when they are speaking. Deep inside you is a sense of playfulness and fun that all great speakers share. Our task is to help you get the kid inside you, out.

TABLE 10.1 The Persuasion Chain-Effect

Entertainment	=	Attention
Attention	=	Memory
Memory	=	Benefit Salience
Benefit Salience	=	Buy Your Ideas

First you must entertain your audience, before they walk through the sequence of thoughts and experience that result in "Buying Your Ideas."

YOU'RE IN SHOWBIZ

Your goal is to persuade the audience. To persuade you must first entertain your audience. Please see **Table 10.1, The Persuasion Chain-Effect.** Let's walk backwards through the *Persuasion Chain-Effect* so you can see why you must entertain your listener. Before a person can *Buy Your Ideas,* she must understand how they will satisfy her needs (personal advancement, altruism, company growth, financial security, sense of appreciation by others, etc.). This understanding of need satisfaction happens when the listener sees the benefits your ideas offer as salient: that is, "These benefits are meaningful to me," or *Benefit Salience.*

Before your listener can realize *Benefit Salience,* she must process your ideas in her mind; both the emotion and evidence must be considered— your ideas must be in her *working memory* and interacting with her prior experience housed in short-term (STM) and long-term memory (LTM).

Before your ideas enter the listener's *memory* she must pay *attention* to you, and to gain *attention* you must *entertain.* You are competing for your listener's attention with a variety of very influential and commanding sources.

POWER OF SELECTIVE ATTENTION

Your audience is automatically thinking about something else every 30 seconds, even if your presentation is fantastic. It doesn't tune you out because it's undisciplined or because you're not fascinating and your ideas are not important—it's just human nature and circumstances beyond your control. For example, you might be speaking to a tired audience, or individual members might have other items on their personal and business agendas that will intrude into their thoughts while you are presenting.

If you don't work hard to be lively, interesting, and entertaining, your listeners will find that the back of the person's head seated in front of them is far more fascinating than you are. You must compete with the hundreds of intrusive thoughts that are poised on the edge of a listener's consciousness. These invading thoughts will march in and take over your listener's mind unless you act to keep his attention. The invasion is poised to launch an attack every 30 seconds.

Fight Back—Work to Refresh Listener Attention Frequently. When I began in radio, my mentors told me to talk about any one subject for a maximum of **10 seconds**—after that, listeners would push the button on their radios to another station. Every 10 seconds I had to vary my tone, tempo, or vocal style or deliver another piece of information or entertainment to keep their attention.

You must do the same thing. Although your business audience will have a longer attention span than my radio listeners, don't depend too much on your audience's discipline and hunger for your ideas. A better strategy is for you to submit evidence frequently, offer new examples, and change the focus.

Move 'Em Around. Every 30 seconds or so give a pictorial example. Every three to five minutes give a bit of interesting information or entertainment. Tell a story, vary your tone of voice, vary your tempo, change the rate of your delivery. Walk to the other side of the room; walk to the back of the room. Look into another listener's eyes.

You must entertain and be lively if you are to persuade. Remember, one characteristic of a credible communicator is *dynamism.* Make your presentation dynamic, and you will win your audience over to your ideas.

A wonderful technique is to use *questions* to keep your audience tuned in to your presentation.

THE PSYCHOLOGY OF QUESTIONS

An excellent method for keeping your audience involved in your presentation is to ask questions. Not rhetorical-type questions like professors ask: *"What could Hamlet be thinking at this point?"* The difference between your question and an English professor's question is that you want an answer—he doesn't. If your audience really thinks that you want it to consider your question and try to answer, some magical brainwashing happens.

The Power of Brainwashing. When you ask a question, and you are effective in convincing your listener that you really want an answer, a wonderful sequence happens in your listener's mind. First, your question sets his mind to zero. Whatever he was thinking before you asked your question is gone. He stops thinking his own thoughts and goes to short-term memory (STM) and long-term memory (LTM) to get the data he needs to answer your question. These memories are loaded into working memory (the part of our minds that we're aware of—where our active thoughts live). You've effectively brainwashed your listener. Along with the rational thoughts come emotional memories and sensory memory (scenes and feelings from his experience).

If you've designed your question correctly and asked your listener to consider factors that have some emotional quality for her, you can begin to create a mood or attitude in your listener (*"Remember when you had your first job interview? Remember how you felt?"* or, *"Who is going to tell these workers that they are fired?" "What do they tell their families?"* or, *"What do you think our customers will say when they see this price increase?"*).

Questions can also provide the method of analysis you want your listener to employ when she thinks about your ideas (*"I suggest that past market performance may be the best predictor of this plan's success . . . and how do you think the market has performed?"*).

By asking your audience questions, you draw it into your presentation and produce higher involvement on its part with your ideas. Questions can produce a higher activation and emotion in your listeners—study after study shows that a moderate level of listener activation produces greater attitude change: You become more persuasive.

HOW TO STRUCTURE YOUR
PRESENTATION WITH QUESTIONS

First, think about how your audience sees things. Your own point of view may be different from your listeners'. You should ask questions that come from the audience's point of view; after all, it's your listeners' memories that you're attempting to tap into, not your own.

Next, think of the logical sequence of thoughts that must be undertaken to analyze your plan or come to the conclusions that you want your listeners to embrace. Think of the questions that they would ask or should ask. Then, structure your questions to follow that logical sequence of thought. As a listener answers each of your little questions, he will take another step down the path toward your idea. You, with your fine, well-trained mind came to those conclusions, so your listener probably will, too. Your questions can lead the listener down the path of reasoning to your conclusion.

BEFORE YOU ARE INTRODUCED, CHECK TO SEE IF YOUR AUDIENCE HAS A PULSE

Be aware of the **mood the group will be in** when you begin making your presentation. Is it tired from listening to other presentations? Perhaps it is restless from sitting too long in one position and needs a minute to stretch. Do you think that the group might be interested in hearing a unique presentation—unlike those of the other speakers on the agenda? Or, is the group fresh because this presentation comes early in the agenda?

TIP | If you're not first on the agenda, other speakers may have worn the audience out. If people have been sitting for more than one hour—ask them to stand and stretch.

PREPARE FOR THE DISASTER THAT WILL NEVER COME

As you prepare your presentation, one thing you must ask yourself is, *"What is (are) the worst thing(s) that could happen?"* By now you're well aware of how too much of this type of thinking can lead to excessive Speech Anxiety. Yet the assiduous application of worst-case-scenario thinking to your preparations will pay big dividends. You can prepare by considering what you might do in response. You should also think about the best thing(s) that might happen.

Ten Tips and Rules of
Persuasive Presentations

TIP 1   Keep your communication mission simple. Too large a payload and your craft will crash. Sell no more than two ideas in your presentation.

TIP 2   Get on and get off fast. Promise you will talk for only 10 minutes, then get off after seven minutes. They will love you for it. Should you go on for 12, you're spending hard-earned relationship capital that could go to persuasion rather than tolerance.

        Remember: Great presentations seem short to the audience—either because the Presenter's brilliance makes time fly or because the team (or Presenter) gets on and off quickly. I recommend that you do both: Deliver a sparkling, beautifully packaged message and do it briefly.

TIP 3   Use the power of silence . . . enjoy pauses. When you ask your listeners a question, pause and let them think about it. It's the pause that's the difference between an empty "rhetorical question" and powerful communication.

        Picture your audience's mind as sand on the beach and your ideas as water in a bucket. You present your ideas by pouring the water onto the sand. If you pour too rapidly, the sand cannot absorb the water and it runs off the surface. If you pour at just the right rate, the sand can drink in the water. Pauses allow your audience to drink in your ideas.

TIP 4   Don't fill the silences with empty mouth noises. Silence is far better. For example, as you select your next thought, don't say "uh" . . . "uhmmmm" . . . "er" . . . "ya know." Just remain silent, that's far more powerful.

TIP 5   If your teammate goes blank, fill in, provide the key word. As you discovered in the chapters on Speech Anxiety (see Chapters 4 and 5), we often go mentally blank and fail to find the right word or to make the leap to our next thought. In a presentation, the illusion that time is compressed may cause your teammate to panic. There is no need to let your teammate twist slowly in the wind while you sit there as if there were an invisible pane of glass between you. Speak up calmly and naturally. Complete the thought for your teammate and he'll pick up right where he left off.

In fact, there is no reason two or more teammates should not share the stage, making verbal and nonverbal *Hand-Offs*[©] to each other. It's a technique that I love to use when working with more talented and experienced Presenters, after we have learned to work together.

TIP 6

Don't read your talk. If you have a kind and generous spirit, and you want your listeners to catch up on sleep or to practice their doodling—or perhaps enjoy some daydreams—be sure to read to them.

But if you're more selfish and want the audience members to listen—if you insist that they hear your ideas and consider your point of view—speak from an outline. Reading is sleep-inducing, unless you're very talented, trained, and have rehearsed your script. Few of us have that ability. Don't read a scripted address. Have your opening and closing well prepared, even memorized, but ad-lib, speak extemporaneously from an outline of key phrases and words.

Now, having said bad things about reading, sometimes you have to read a script to your listeners: (1) If you're part of a televised program and that format is expected; (2) if your statement is likely to be legally inflammatory or risky; (3) if you are part of a large, scripted, multimedia-driven meeting—on these occasions you should agree to read your address. Then you have the onerous job of making it seem natural. Hire a coach—when you reach the point in your career where you must read a presentation, you can afford one and can't afford not to get professional help.

You'll sound like you're doing the Pledge of Allegiance in grade school. Memorizing your presentation is not a good strategy, either. When you deliver a text that you've memorized, it tends to force a sing-song delivery tone in your voice. That tone of voice signals the audience that you're not speaking directly with it. The result? It tunes you out.

TIP 7

Don't bore the listener with the saga of how you came to your conclusions. Your listener wants your ideas, your conclusions. She is not as interested in learning how hard you worked or the steps in collecting your data. It is a natural mistake to spend our listener's precious attention asking him to hear how hard we worked, *"We first examined all available secondary data with ADI C/D ROM—we did not find much, but a single article really gave us insight. Next, we called all our primary suppliers and asked them to send us a record of costs related to . . ."* Getting sleepy?

KEY

Your listeners are interested in benefits—what they will gain from your information, from your insight.

TIP 8 Don't upstage your teammate(s). This fascinating bit of theater minutia has use for you beyond giving you another tidbit for cocktail conversation. Master actors know that the upstage position (behind your teammates) is very powerful. Even though the downstage actor is nearer the audience, an actor who is standing upstage can easily distract the audience's attention by making small movements. The lesson is: Even when you're not actively presenting, if the audience can see you, you're still "on." So, if you choose to stay in audience view, instead of stepping offstage and taking a seat while your teammates present, you must maintain your concentration and listen to what they're saying. This can be tough because you're probably not listening, you're rehearsing your talk if you're waiting to go on, and if you have already presented you're thinking about how it went.

A Bit of Theater History. According to theater lore, the actor's terms *upstage* and *downstage* are said to come from the ancient Greek theater. Unlike today's theater—where the audience sits on a raked plane and the stage is flat—the Greek theater placed the actors on an inclined plane and the audience sat on level ground (see **Figure 10.1, Greek Theater**). The players typically stood in a semicircular line called the "chorus." When a member of the chorus had a line to speak, he moved toward the audience, or literally *downstage*. The members of the chorus were *upstage* from that actor. Today this terminology is used in the theater. An actor who is closer to the audience is downstage from any actor or set piece (a piece of furniture) that is farther away from the audience.

You can use the upstage power to make nonverbal contact with audience members as they look at you. First, give them a bit of your positive vibrations' charm, then look back in earnest to the other Presenters . . . you'll find that they follow your eyes and begin to attune to the speaker.

TIP 9 Handling props. From time to time you'll want to use props to illustrate your ideas. For example, a stack of printouts, law books, or the client's product are frequently used. *Warning:* Your props can upstage you. They can dominate the stage, so if you don't want the audience to focus on a prop, keep it out of sight. Keep the prop behind the podium until you need it. After you're through with it, put it away. Your audience will be distracted by looking at the prop even after you've moved on to other topics.

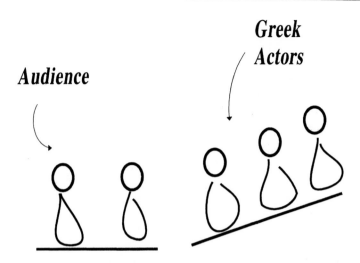

Figure 10.1 Greek Theater

In ancient Greek Theater, the audience sat on a flat plane while the actors stood on a raked stage. Today's theater uses the opposite design, in which the audience sits on an angled plane while the actors perform on a flat stage.

TIP 10 Handling the company's/client's product. When you hold the product—show your respect, handle it with care. Pretend you are holding valuable crown jewels. You must communicate the product's value even if it's a machined hunk of steel. When the client hands you his product (or brochure, etc.) take it as if you were accepting his newborn child. It's probably no less precious in his eyes.

Handling Audience Questions

Start By Actively Listening to the Question and Questioner. The audience will judge you and your credibility by how you handle audience interaction, particularly how you listen to and answer its questions.

Of course, most of the time you want to be attentive to and respectful of your listeners. Audience members identify with the questioner and will feel slighted if you patronize or insult the person. On the other hand, if the questioner is a hostile idiot or a group outlier whom the audience hates anyway, you can damage yourself by affiliating with or giving the questioner too much recognition or sympathy. Similarly, you can advance your cause by standing up to stupidity, bullies, and errors. You must have an iron fist inside a velvet glove. When handling questions, you must put your antennae out to the audience and sense its reaction. I recommend that if you sense a question is stupid, hostile, or difficult, you first scan your audience for its reaction. Often, if you've set up the right type of rapport with your audience, certain audience members will pick up the cue from your eye-scan and answer the question themselves or tell the person to "shut up—that's not relevant here."

- Sometimes questioners are quite earnest, asking questions that will help clarify your talk, but have trouble expressing themselves. You'll want to step in gently and provide phrases and terms to help form the question.
- Help the questioner: Do not treat questions as annoyances or interruptions. If you've mastered your topic, you can handle any question. You want a conversation with your listeners, not a speech directed at them. Remember, your credibility comes from showing that you understand.

Keys to Good Listening. While the audience member is asking the question, give him lots of nonverbal feedback: nod, change expression (with listener's statements), lean forward, shift posture with flow of conversation, tilt your head to show interest.

KEY   Listen actively.

When You're Stuck, Buy Some Time. If you're stuck for an immediate answer, use silence—wait, he'll start talking again, giving you more time to think. To give yourself time, repeat the question and ask the listener, "Do I understand your question?" Usually by this time the right answer has composed itself in your head.

How to Handle Obnoxious or Hostile Questions. First, relax, do not show fear. It's easy to become afraid; fear transmits. Remember, the hostile person is in a state of fear, and you might catch it. Remember, you have superior power. You may be caught off guard by the attacking tone: It's rare that an audience member will be rude, so it can be surprising. Buy time, restate the question. This gives you more time and you can strategically restate the question in less confrontational terms. Ask the listener, "Is that your question?" She will probably agree with your watered-down version of her attack, and now you can go on to answer it.

Give a moderate but meaningful answer. Most of the audience will agree with a more moderate point and will probably be embarrassed by the hostile questioner.

Consider Using the Group to Control a Hostile Person. If the questioner seeks to dominate by making a speech instead of asking a question, or, after you've answered one question continues to ask other, hostile questions, trying to box you in, say, "We have other questions" or "The other people have come to hear more than your interesting question." You may wish to offer to meet the questioner after the presentation for further discussion. Remember, the hostile questioner often only wants your audience's attention; when confronted with the prospect of talking just with you and not enjoying your spotlight, she'll decline the offer.

If You Don't Know, Admit It. Tell the person that you'll find out and get back in touch—or ask the audience, perhaps someone else knows.

Meeting the Audience; Moving About the Room. It's important that you speak within the communication space of each person in the audience—this is not easy and is often impossible. Think of an area with a 10-foot radius around you. People within that distance receive a more detailed and powerful message than do those more than 10 feet away.

The difference is not the words you say, it's the information from your facial expressions. Your eyes and mouth deliver volumes of information. Think of your eyes and mouth as a *Communication Triangle.* The small muscles around your eyes and mouth transmit volumes of expression. We read the triangle-shaped area around the eyes and mouth for nonverbal data. Prove it to yourself. Take note in informal conversation—notice what features people look at on other people's faces.

Be sure to move about the room. Work to get in the *communication space* of each audience member. Remember the technique I recommended to reduce speech anxiety: Get to the room early and welcome each person as they come in. This momentary contact makes you seem like a "real person" to the audience members, as well as reducing your anxiety.

Problem: Deciders May Sit at the Back of the Room. Often the key person in the audience, for example, the boss, sits at the back with a phalanx of subordinates between you and her. Even a little bit of contact helps. One technique is to give each person a handout. This will give you the excuse (or motivation, as actors say) to move to the back and communicate with the boss in her *Personal Communication Space.*

Dr. Whalen—All your ideas sound great, BUT
"I have to present like my boss," or
"My firm is very conservative—they just want me to present the financial report without adding any comments."

I've heard dozens of students (out of the thousands I've trained) voice these concerns.

Here is how I answer:

- "That's too bad—it will be worse for you having to sit through those dull, low-communication presentations."
- "Do it your way and see what happens, take some risk. Perhaps your firm does not know any other way to present."
- "Try to adopt some of the more unobtrusive techniques."
- "You don't have to present like Dr. Whalen to be successful; there are many other methods of presentation that work well."
- "Take the lead, tell your boss about your training with Dr. Whalen and offer to show him how."

SUMMARY

Have fun. Don't worry that your listener will think that you're a fool; worry that she'll think you're stuffy and dull.

Work to refresh the listener's attention:

☐ Every 30 seconds or so, give a pictorial example.

☐ Every three to five minutes, give a bit of interesting information or entertainment.

Ask questions to lead your listener through a sequence of decisions, leading to your conclusion. Break your conclusion into a series of rational steps.

CHECKLIST OF PERSUASIVE PRESENTATIONS TIPS

☐ Get on and get off fast.

☐ Use the power of silence . . . enjoy pauses.

☐ Don't fill the silences with empty mouth noises.

☐ If your teammate goes blank, fill in, provide the key word.

☐ Don't read your talk.

☐ Don't bore the listener with the saga of how you came to your conclusions.

CHECKLIST FOR HANDLING AUDIENCE QUESTIONS

☐ Repeat the question and ask, "Have I stated your question correctly?" If not, learn what the question is.

☐ Respect the questioner.

☐ Defuse obnoxious or hostile questions by rewording them.

☐ Use the group to control any angry or hostile questioner.

☐ If you don't know, admit it . . . and promise to find out. Ask the audience, perhaps someone will know the answer.

11

Visual Tools for Presentation

KEY | If numbers are important to your presentation—show the number (overhead projector, card, tear sheet).

You must have visual support for presentations. Visual evidence greatly increases the persuasive impact of your presentation: People really do think that "seeing is believing." If you don't have the opportunity to prepare projectable illustrations, you can have a teammate write what you're saying (key words and figures) on a blackboard, tear sheet, or a blank overhead transparency.

Pictures of numbers are vastly better communicators than digits are, even with quantitatively oriented audiences. For instance, show a picture of those numbers as a pie chart or a big guy next to a little guy.

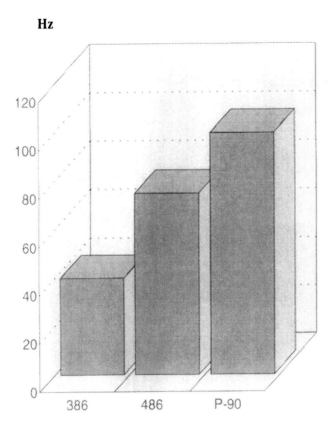

Figure 11.1. Bar Graph

HOW TO MAKE TABLES/GRAPHS:
GRAPH AND CHART TYPES

Bar: The most commonly used chart. Excellent for comparing magnitude among phenomena, for example, "which is bigger." **Caution:** More than three comparisons in a single chart become increasingly harder for the viewer to comprehend and analyze—the clock speed in hertz among three different computer processor chips; the income of college graduates (with bachelor's degree) and those with MBAs.

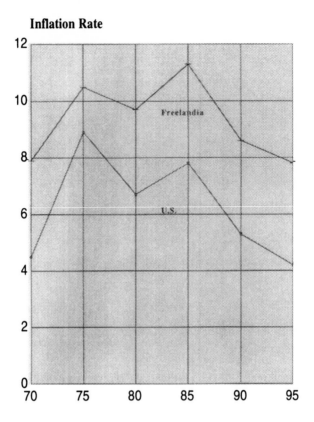

Figure 11.2 Line Graph

Line: Excellent for showing change over time. Use when you have multiple observations over time. May be used to show the change in a single variable over time. For example, the annual inflation rate in the United States over 10 years. May also be used to compare two or more variables. For example, to show the salary trends for male MBA holders and female MBA holders over 10 years.

Attend to drink beer

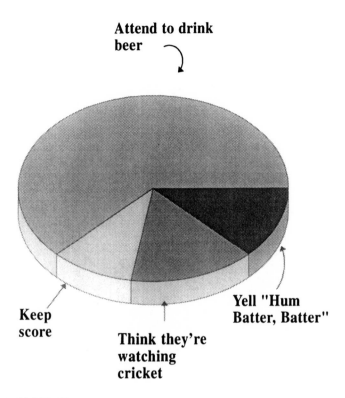

Keep score

Think they're watching cricket

Yell "Hum Batter, Batter"

Figure 11.3 Pie Chart

Pie: Use only to illustrate the relative magnitude of all component parts of a complete set or universe. For example, the percentages of men and women in a group; the market share of all competitors in a category. Pie charts are rarely used.

When you select a key statistic, such as the age distribution of people in a target audience, you'll want to report at least three numbers.

Why Use Three Numbers? The reason you pick the top three *index numbers,* although you're actually using only the biggest one, is because the two smaller numbers help sell the bigger number.

The other two numbers serve as reference points that allow the client (or your boss, or the loan committee, or whomever you're trying to persuade) to gauge the relative magnitude of the data. In psychology, it's called

TABLE 11.1 Consumption Index of Golf Club Buyers by Age

Age	Index
18-24	156
35-49	105
65 +	82

Younger golfers (Age = 18-24) tend to buy more golf clubs (Index = 156) than do older golfers.

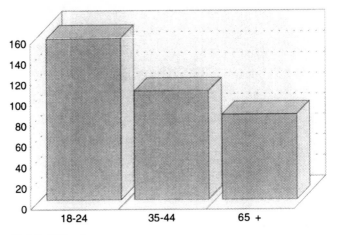

Figure 11.4 Golf Graph

Perception of Contrast. You can't see a white cat eating a dish of vanilla ice cream in a blizzard—everything's white, nothing stands out. But when you sprinkle some chocolate chips on top of the ice cream, those chips really jump out. The smaller numbers allow your chosen *index number* to jump out.

Sometimes the top two or three numbers are very close together (constricted range). In this case, your chart will not have the visual contrast you require. So to get the smaller, contrasting number you may have to include four or more corresponding categories in your chart. Of course, in this case you'll be reporting more than the usual three statistics. When possible, it's important that your chart or graph show some big numbers and some smaller numbers to deliver a clear, persuasive presentation. See **Table 11.4, Consumption Index of Golf Club Buyers by Age** and **Figure 11.4, Golf Club Buyers,** for examples.

TYPE SIZE

Make sure that your visual can be read from the back of the room. That is often where the decision maker sits, so you'll want to use 18- to 24-point type (or larger). The bigger the point size, the bigger the type.

This is an example of 18-point type

This is an example of 24-point type

TYPESTYLE

Use proportional serif type. The text you're reading now is written in proportional serif type (see **Chapter 12, "Writing Memos With High Communication Factor,"** for examples of serif and sans-serif type).

Margins. Use wide margins—a minimum of 1.25" top and bottom, with right and left margins of 1.25". If you use small margins, your slide may run over the area projected on the screen.

KEEP PUNCTUATION TO A MINIMUM

For maximum readability avoid

- Slashes: as in "black/white"
- Parenthetical expressions separated by an em-dash: such as "is definitely—hypothetically speaking"
- Exclamation points (!): They look like the letter I when projected.

HOW MUCH INFORMATION TO PUT ON A SLIDE

There are no firm rules on how much data to put on a slide, but here is a rule of thumb. Use a maximum of seven (7) words per line and five (5) lines per page.

TABLE 11.2 Using Color to Increase Readability

Slide Element	Recommended Color
Background	Blue
Foreground (Letters & Numbers)	White
Accent Color	Red

Certain colors work well with our eye's physiology and our mind's psychology to communicate better.

COMMUNICATE WITH COLOR

Advertising research has shown that a full-color ad draws twice as many readers as the same ad in just black and white. When using color, for the greatest readability make the background blue and the foreground (letters, lines, symbols) white. Use red only as an accent color (see **Table 11.2, Using Color to Increase Readability**).

Here is why. Blue's wavelength falls just before and just behind our eye's focal plane. As a result, the color blue looks a bit out of focus to us. Notice how blue things are a bit softer to the eye than things of other colors. Blue makes the perfect background to nest letters in. The light waves of white-colored objects, on the other hand, fall perfectly on our eye's focal plane. White things look sharp. When you put sharp-colored white letters and numbers on a soft blue field, the characters jump off the screen.

Blue's the Favorite Color. Another reason to use blue for your background is that, when polled, most people say that blue is their favorite color. The background will be the largest element in your slide, so you'll be giving listeners lots of their favorite color.

COMMUNICATING IDEAS VISUALLY—
LABEL ALL VISUAL ELEMENTS

You want your audience to think about the ideas behind your numbers . . . not about the numbers themselves. So, when designing your graph or figure, ensure that your listener or reader does not have to guess what the illustration is trying to say. Make sure that tables and graphs are clearly labeled, including

- axes (X = horizontal, Y = vertical)
- wedges, bars
- title
- measurement scale
- each number, so it is quickly understood
- a title for the table or graph; this is vital

Each element in your slide should be clearly labeled or be self-explanatory.

PRESENTING WITH VISUALS

When reading the words on the screen to your audience, use the very same words. Substitution can cause confusion.

Don't let your visuals upstage you. When you are talking about the visual's data or words, point or turn around about three fourths of the way and look at the screen with your audience. Give your audience a clear line of sight to the visual. Don't block the view.

TIP | Keep the amount of "butt meat" you show the audience to a minimum.

Rehearse Your Visuals. Become comfortable and skilled in handling visuals. If you can, rehearse in the room where the actual presentation will be made.

WHEN TO HAND OUT MATERIALS

The old school of presentation is all about controlling the pace, rate, and order in which the audience receives information. Most communication trainers mandate that you show the visual just when you're ready to talk about it. The reason for this is that the audience will start to look/read and will not be listening to you. The same advice is given for handing listeners anything, such as handouts, brochures, the product, and so forth.

Let Your Audience Self-Feed the Information. I recommend the latest thinking in regulating the flow of information. Different people have different needs for information. Some people read more quickly than others. Some parts of the presentation will be more interesting or will require more study than other parts. For example, your financial people may linger over the spreadsheets, whereas marketing people like connect-the-dots and coloring sections (just kidding). I recommend that you remain flexible and let your audience consume the information at its own pace. If listeners want you to jump ahead or return to earlier parts of the presentation, I suggest that you do. This presentation strategy returns control to the audience members and makes them more confident, because they feel like they're more in control and will thus be more able to accept your ideas. By restricting the flow of information, you take their power and control away. Managers like power.

Sample Presentation Visuals

You may find that most presentations will have a minimum of four slides, containing the following information:

1. **Title Slide**
   - ❑ Presentation's Title or Topic
   - ❑ Team Name (if any)
   - ❑ Participants
2. **Statement of Purpose** (*Big Ideas*©)
   Short statement of what you want your audience to believe at the end of your presentation. For example, your purpose could be to share one or two *Big Ideas*© with your audience.
3. *Big Ideas*©, **Two Ideas, Metaphor, Conclusion(s)**
4. **Outline of Presentation, Key points**

This series may require several slides. Your presentation should be structured by using bullets.

Note on Using Numbers or Bullets. If there is a numbered sequence of steps or a ranked hierarchy, use numbers to order your key words. If there is no natural hierarchy and therefore no meaning to the numbers, use bullets. You'll typically use more bullets than numbers on your slides.

If there is a written report to accompany your presentation, the key words may be similar or identical to the subheads in your report. This shows your audience the logical flow of the presentation.

TIP | Here's an efficient way to make visuals for an oral presentation of your written report. First, read your report looking for key phrases, subheads, and short sections that seem to summarize or capture your ideas. Use a yellow highlighter to mark them. Then, using your word processor, edit out all extraneous text, leaving the key words. You'll find that you have highlighted the essence of a good presentation.

| SUMMARY

Checklist for making presentation visuals

☐ Use 18- to 24-point type (or bigger) in your visuals; 36-point and 24-point are even better and more readable.

☐ Use proportional serif type—it's the easiest to read.

☐ Use margins of 1.25" for overheads.

☐ Keep punctuation to a minimum.

☐ Use a maximum of seven (7) words per line and five (5) lines per page.

☐ Use color. For the greatest readability, make the background blue and the foreground (letters, lines, symbols) white. Use red only as an accent color.

☐ Clearly label all important parts of your graph:
   ◻ axes (X & Y)
   ◻ wedges, bars
   ◻ title
   ◻ measurement scale

TIPS FOR PRESENTING VISUALS

☐ Give your audience a clear line of sight to the visual. Don't block the view.

☐ Don't let your visuals upstage you—point or turn about three fourths and look at the screen with your audience.

☐ Keep the amount of "butt meat" you show the audience to a minimum.

12

Writing Memos With
High Communication Factor

I f your memo is in response to a request and is expected and generally known to the reader, write a brief summary sentence or paragraph previewing your memo's main ideas.

OPENING THE MEMO

Sometimes your reader is not expecting to receive your memo or may not be familiar with the ideas you have expressed, so he's not particularly motivated to read it. You must motivate your reader to invest time in reading your memo. Write a sentence or two . . . right at the very start of the memo (below the memo masthead) to motivate the reader.

MOTIVATING THE READER TO LEND YOU AN EYE

Open with a short paragraph designed to motivate the reader. Just put yourself in the reader's shoes and write to her motivations. Some suggested approaches follow.

- Talk directly about the benefits the reader will receive.
- Ask a question to draw the reader in.
- **News**—offer the latest information; report changes in the environment; share ideas for change.
  - ❑ Who—will it affect; who says so/who's the information from?
  - ❑ What—describe and define.

◻ When—what is the time frame; what's the data's date; running out of time?

◻ Why—why is it important; what are the causal factors?

◻ Where—location; scope; relevance?

◻ How—process; with what impact?

- Impact upon the reader

  ◻ How will it **affect the reader?**

  ◻ How will it **help the reader** reach his goals (personal/professional)?

- Show how you're *responding to his request.*

- Summarize **what she can expect to learn/find out** by reading your memo.

Memo-Writing Rules

1. Memos range from one to three pages, single spaced.
2. The data must be presented in narrative form; tables are optional. Use the required format for including numerical data in your text (see **Chapter 14, "Writing With High Communication Factor,"** section titled "More Interesting to Your Reader").
3. If you have data, be sure to use a table or graph.
4. Write a subhead for each section and subsection.
5. Make your subhead a headline for the text that follows; it should be information rich, summarize the text, and convey an attitude.

An example of a suggested memo masthead is shown below. Note that the masthead is bolded and followed by a line to give it a crisp look.

TO:	**D. Joel Whalen, Ph.D., Assoc. Prof. of Mkting**
FROM:	**Ms./Mr. Your Name, Title or Department**
DATE:	**June 14, 19XX (Date Assignment Is Due)**
RE:	**(Topic of Your Memo)**

Note that the memo masthead is bolded, followed by a line, to give a crisp look

Selecting the Right Typestyle

• For maximum readability, use a 12 point proportional type with serifs. For example: Times Roman, Times, or Roman typefaces are proportional type faces with serifs.

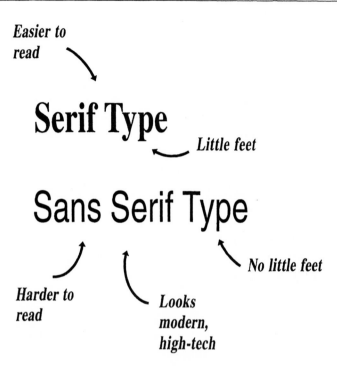

Figure 12.1 Serif and Sans Serif Type

Most books, newspapers, and magazines are printed in serif, proportional type. Our brain's pattern recognition capability has been trained to recognize the more familiar serif type quickly. As a result, the brain's decoding process happens far faster when reading serif type than sans serif type—because we have seen far more of the widely used serif proportional type than the less popular sans serif.

This is a sample of 12 point Times Roman

This is a sample of 14 point Times Roman

• There are occasions for using sans serif type. Sans serif type looks more "modern" or "high-tech"—use it when you want that space-age effect: For example, when presenting technological innovations or writing promotional copy for engineering firms. Do not use it when you want the reader to plow through more than a half-page of text, however. It will seem tedious—even for engineers (see **Figure 12.1, Serif Versus Sans Serif Type**).

I SEE WHAT YOU MEAN

• Proportional type is easier for people to read than non-proportional type. Here is why: Each individual word appears more readily because there is more white space between the words than between the letters. This white space acts like a frame around a painting. Each word stands out on the page.

Non-proportional type puts too much white space within the word. The reader must spend extra milliseconds seeking out the word. Over thousands of words, this becomes fatiguing and requires more effort on the reader's part.

For example, notice the difference between the two sentences below. The first is in proportional type, the second is in a harder to read non-proportional type.

Times Roman 12 point
Education is vital to success in today's rapidly evolving, high-tech business world.

```
Courier 12 point
Education is vital to success in today's
    rapidly evolving, high-tech business
    world.
```

As you can see from this example, proportional type is easier to read and takes up less space than non-proportional type. See how the second, identical sentence, set in Courier type, takes up more space—the proportional type packs more information into less space and is easier to read.

• Another point on selecting typestyle: Avoid using reverse type—that is, white letters set on a black background. People find this very hard to read. It will stand out and grab attention (because it's so seldom used it will be an attractive oddity), but your text will not be read because it is too hard to decode.

DRAWING ATTENTION TO KEY WORDS

You may wish to emphasize certain words, sentences, or paragraphs; the typographic element you choose can either increase readability or slow the reader down.

For maximum readability, use boldface or italics to direct the reader's attention to a particular word or to add emphasis. Avoid using underlining, as it adds to the visual clutter, making it harder for the reader's eye to sort out the words from the background noise. You may underline entire sentences or paragraphs with minimal reduction of readability. Never underline single words or phrases, however.

For example, notice how your eye processes the following paragraphs:

> For maximum readability, use boldface or italics to direct the reader's attention to a word or to add emphasis. <u>Avoid using underlining</u>, as it adds to the visual clutter <u>making it harder</u> for the reader's eye to sort out the words from the background noise. You may underline entire sentences or paragraphs with minimal reduction of readability. <u>Never underline single words or phrases, however.</u>

> For maximum readability, use boldface or italics to direct the reader's attention to a word or to add emphasis. **Avoid using underlining,** as it adds to the visual clutter **making it harder** for the reader's eye to sort out the words from the background noise. You may underline entire sentences or paragraphs with minimal reduction of readability. *Never underline single words or phrases, however.*

Increasing Scannability

Today, executives are buried under mountains of memos, electronic mail, and reports. They tell us that they have a hard time getting through all their reading material, including *Fortune,* the *Wall Street Journal, Business Week,* and the *Harvard Business Review.*

The solution selected by executives to combat the paper landfill on their desks is: scan and speed read. You can better communicate with the scanning manager by using *subheads.* Subheads add to the scannability of your copy.

Your memo should include subheads. The subhead should be interesting and should communicate the essence of the information contained in the text that follows. Use subheads to convey your attitude or special, personal spin.

REQUIRED FORMAT FOR SUBHEADS

- Subheads are rarely longer than one half to two thirds of a line of text (two to five words long).
- The first letter of the first word and the first letter of proper nouns in the subhead are uppercased.
- The entire subhead is bolded.
- Two lines of space are placed above the subhead and one line of space below. Actually, in my personal writing I like to use even more lines of space to make the subhead really stand out and catch my reader's eye.

SUBHEADS

Subheads tell the reader, in two or three words, the essence of the paragraph that follows.

Subheads should be upper and lower case and set flush left. An example of a Subhead (First-Level) follows:

EXAMPLE:

Demographic Profile

The automobile consumer is primarily female (Index = 110), age 25-49 (Index = 145). She is well placed as a professional (Index = 178) and can provide a significant contribution to her family's income (Income = $50,000 +; Index = 167).

HINTS ON COMPOSING SUBHEADS

Subheads should summarize the section that follows. Construct the subhead so it communicates with the reader—think first of what the reader is looking for in your report, then consider what your section contains. Write a brief subhead that tells readers what they are about to read and what information and perspective they are to gain, presented from a mutual frame of reference shared by you and your readers.

When you start a new idea, for example, a new paragraph or set of paragraphs, (it) they should be preceded by a subhead.

SECOND-LEVEL SUBHEADS

Subheads (Second-Level) are upper and lower case and are italicized.
An **EXAMPLE** of a Subhead (Second-Level) follows:

Peter Pan peanut butter

Subheads (Second-Level) are rarely used in memos or short reports (less
than 10-15 pages). They can make the report appear too "busy," cluttering
up the page and confusing the reader. They are more appropriate for longer,
more complex reports. The decision to use (or not to use) Subheads
(Second-Level) is based on the complexity and organization of your report,
not solely on length.

SPACING AROUND THE SUBHEAD
AND SECOND-LEVEL SUBHEAD

Use two line spaces between the preceding copy and the subhead. Use
one line space between the subhead and the copy that follows.
An example of how to space around subheads follows:
EXAMPLE:

. . . and so it is recommended that the desired levels of increased product
usage may be attained by adding chocolate morsels to the peanut butter.

Anticipated problems

Although the addition of chocolate morsels to peanut butter will find
rapid acceptance among the consumers (Kids), the buyer (Mom) may
entertain the perception that chocolate enhanced peanut butter may
be a "treat food" rather than a "meal food" or . . .

SPACING WITH APPLE (AND OTHER) COMPUTERS

If you use a word processing package other than WordPerfect (WP)
5.0-6.0, you may find that it automatically produces a larger typestyle and

more space between lines, creating more white space. WP 5.0-6.0 uses pica type (10 characters per inch) and a line height of 0.167 inch. You'll want to adjust the document's spacing standards to give your memo or report the right layout and presentation look.

No matter what software you select, your report must have 200% more space between the preceding copy and the subhead, and a single line of space between the subhead and the following body copy. By using white space, you make your subhead stand out on the page and be logically and visually linked with the paragraph it introduces.

SUMMARY

If the reader is expecting the memo—open with a summary. If the reader is *not expecting* the memo, write a sentence or two motivating her to read it.

To motivate your reader pitch the benefits accruing to the reader, announce some news, or show how the memo's information impacts the reader.

Keep memos short (one to three pages). Use subheads like headlines to lead your reader and set his expectations.

CHECKLIST FOR USING SUBHEADS

☐ Make no longer than one half to two thirds of a line of text (two to five words long).

☐ Uppercase first letter of first word and of all proper nouns.

☐ Make the entire subhead boldface and set flush left.

☐ Place two lines of space above the subhead and one line of space below.

☐ Use a 12 point proportional type with serifs. For example: Times Roman, Times, or Roman.

☐ Don't underline to emphasize words or phrases: Use **boldface** or *italic* type.

13

Writing Reports With
High Communication Factor

- Only typewritten reports are acceptable today.
  - Use a word processor—because you'll want to write and rewrite (iteration).
  - If you decide to use Apple Computer word processing, you'll have to adjust the spacing requirements to that format. Apple tends to have larger type and a greater line height than DOS/WP. The goal is to have a consistent and pleasing balance between the white space and text/figure information (see "Spacing With Apple (and Other) Computers" in **Chapter 12, "Writing Memos With High Communication Factor"**).
- When making a master copy, do not use erasable bond paper. Use laser-jet quality copier paper. Although textured paper, that is, paper with a high rag content, makes a good impression, it drinks in the ink, giving your text a soft look. It does not reproduce well.
- Special covers add to your report's credibility.
- If the report is not bound, staple papers in the upper left-hand corner. Do not use paper clips—they will slip and lose sheets or, when in a stack of papers, grab onto the nearest page/piece of paper and make it part of your report.

Product & Competitive Analysis

of

Retention Memory Systems

prepared for

Mr. Matt Altschuler

President
Cotton Expressions, Ltd.

by

D. Joel Whalen, Ph.D.

Kellstadt Graduate School of Business
DePaul University

September 12, 2001

Figure 13.1. A Title Page Format

MAJOR   1. Title page
SECTIONS   2. Introduction
            3. Body (e.g., Problem; Situational
               Analysis; Recommendations)

TITLE PAGE

A suggested Title Page format for formal reports and proposals is offered in **Figure 13.1, A Title Page Format.** Please note that it is centered both horizontally and vertically and bolded.

Executive Summary

The Executive Summary section is highly desirable in the business world. It should

- be one page long, no longer
- begin with a summary of the most important things (ideas, facts) your report has to offer
- provide the basic and important facts that the executive must know to understand the overview and the results (impact, effects) that are predicted by your report

The Executive Summary is designed to give senior personnel a quick read and an overview of the report. All key facts must be included. Typically, Senior Executives will rely upon the judgment of their Junior Executive for the details of most technical business decisions.

The Senior Executive will read the Executive Summary to judge the report's impact upon the firm and the firm's direction in the marketplace. The Junior Executive will read all the details in your report—and usually ask for more. The Senior Executive may read only the Executive Summary.

Introduction Section

In longer, formal, or research reports use an Introduction Section with the following elements: Statement of Purpose, Summary, and Structure Statement. These elements will greatly aid your reader by giving him a "road map" of your report. They will prepare the reader's mind in advance, making his journey seem easier and more predictable.

The Introduction Section should contain the following elements.

STATEMENT OF PURPOSE

The first sentence should be a **Statement of Purpose**—a clear, direct, declarative sentence that tells the reader the report's topic. Here is an example of a Statement of Purpose:

This report presents an Aspinwall's analysis of women's shampoo.

SUMMARY

Next, write a **Summarization** of the report's key findings and recommendations.

For technical reports, when you want to be highly formal and/or objective, tell the reader the major data sources and viewpoint the report uses.

STRUCTURE STATEMENT

The last paragraph in your **Summary** is called the **Structure Statement.** This is an example of a Structure Statement:

The report will first offer a demographic/psychographic profile of the brand's main consumer. Next, a subjective analysis of the consumer's motivation to purchase will be made. Finally, the selling strategy or "pitch" of each competing brand will be analyzed.

The Structure Statement (above) uses "Framing Words," for example: *first, next,* and *finally.* Other examples of framing words are: *second, third, then,* and *followed by.*

The Structure Statement should look like part of the Introduction. *Do not use a Header or Subhead titled "Structure Statement."*

Layout Instructions

• Use Times Roman Serif type, 12 point or larger. Executives more than 40 years old appreciate 14 point type.

USE PLENTY OF MARGIN (WHITE SPACE)
TO GUIDE YOUR READER

White space makes your presentations more readable. The reader will be more inclined to continue reading if your report or proposal has "eye-appeal."

Minimum margins for maximum communication:

Top margin, first page	1.5"
Top margin, other pages	1.0"
Left & right margins	1.0"
Bottom margin	1.0"

All reports are single spaced. Double space between paragraphs (do not indent paragraphs).

Put plenty of space around tables, graphs, and bullet-pointed sections. As a guideline, use a minimum of three lines of space between indented, tabbed, and bulleted copy and the preceding and following text.

HEADS

Use "Mini-Headlines" to give your report high scannability. You can lead the reader through your report. These brief, information-dense section headings work with your reader's memory. As a result, your report seems easier to read, so the executive will have a better attitude toward your work. Heads should be set in a larger type size or capitalized; all heads should be centered, and if the type is capitalized, **bolded.** This is an example of a Head:

EXAMPLE:

INTRODUCTION

or

Introduction

This report presents a competitive market analysis of the automobile industry.

Heads introduce the reader to your major sections. Examples of frequently used heads follow.

- **EXECUTIVE SUMMARY**
- **PROBLEM**
- **SITUATIONAL ANALYSIS**
- **STRATEGIC BUSINESS UNITS**
- **RECOMMENDATIONS**
- **SUMMARY**

SPACING FOR THE HEAD

If the Head is the first element on the page, it should be placed no less than 1.5 inches from the top. If the Head appears after Body Copy, there should be at least four lines of space between the preceding Body Copy and the Head.

Use two lines of space between Heads and the following Body Copy.
EXAMPLE:

MARKET ANALYSIS

The Peanut Butter category is clearly divided into two distinct categories: those brands selling to the buyer (Mom) and those primarily pitching to the consumers (Kids).

SUMMARY

MAJOR REPORT SECTIONS

1. Title Page
2. Introduction
3. Body (e.g., Problem; Situational
   Analysis; Recommendations)

The Executive Summary is designed to give senior personnel a quick read and an overview of the report. It should

- be one page long, no longer
- begin with a summary of the most important things (ideas, facts) your report has to offer and provide the basic and important facts that give an overview and the results (impact, effects)

CHECKLIST FOR HIGH
COMMUNICATION FACTOR REPORTS

☐ Use Times Roman Serif type, 12 point or larger.

☐ Executives more than 40 years old appreciate 14 point type.

☐ Use plenty of margin (white space).

☐ Minimum margins for maximum communication:

  ▫ Top first page   1.5"
  ▫ Top other pages   1.0"
  ▫ Left & right   1.0"
  ▫ Bottom   1.0"

☐ Single space all reports.

☐ Double space between paragraphs (do not indent paragraphs).

☐ Put a minimum of three lines of space around tables, graphs, and bullet-pointed sections.

☐ **Heads** should be set in a larger type size or else capitalized; all heads should be centered, and if the type is all capitals, **bolded.**

☐ If the Head is the first element on the page, it should be placed no less than 1.5" from the top.

☐ If the Head appears after Body Copy, there should be at least four lines of space between the preceding Body Copy and the Head.

☐ Use two lines of space between a Head and the following Body Copy.

☐ Consider using 14 point type or larger if your reader is more than 40 years old.

14

Writing With High Communication Factor

LOW KEY, "NO SELL" SELLING

If you want to appear objective, not trying to sell, write in the passive objective voice; do not use personal pronouns—for example, *I, you, she, he.*

EXAMPLE:

For example, rather than write
"We recommend that . . ."

you'd write
"It is recommended that . . ."

COMMON GRAMMATICAL ERRORS

Pay close attention to grammar, spelling, and sentence structure. Common grammatical errors include

- using the word *which* when the proper choice is *that* (*which* is used only "parenthetically"; the word *which* must appear between two commas—in a nonrestrictive clause)
- dangling prepositions
- lack of subject/verb agreement

MORE INTERESTING TO YOUR READER

You can lull your readers into a dull-minded state. Wake them up:

- Offer a variety of words; use words like a cook uses spices. Do not reuse the same key words (i.e., verbs, adjectives, and descriptive nouns). Edit out repetitive words or phrases.
- Vary the length and structure of your sentences. Check the content of paragraphs and see if long paragraphs can be broken down into smaller, more readable paragraphs.
- Spell out numbers nine and lower; use digits for numbers 10 and higher. This is how most newspapers do it—it's the Associated Press Style.

EXAMPLE:

. . . of the 15 major automotive tire brands, four are made in the United States.

- You can present supportive statistics (index numbers, ratios) within the narrative text without interrupting the flow by placing the digits within parentheses.

EXAMPLE:

Gender does not provide sufficient segmentation; men (Index = 105) and women (Index = 109) tend to consume vacation cruises equally.

- ◻ Draw conclusions. Bravely take a stand and defend it confidently. Remember, in business you state your case, make your recommendation, make a promise or prediction, then proceed to back it up with facts and reasoning.
- ◻ Type your paper; construct your tables and figures with superior attention to detail. Remember, presentation counts. Form is as important as content.
- ◻ **Get to the point.** *Business report writing is not storytelling.* You don't want to keep the client or your firm's senior people in suspense while you build up to a big surprise ending. You may win a prize for literature, but you'll never be promoted on the strength of your report writing.
- ◻ **The shorter the better.** It's far harder to write briefly. Distill your thoughts through three iterations.

EDITING TIPS

TIP Write your memo or report over a minimum of three sessions. Consider each version a rough draft; work to make it better each time.

TIP Proofread your paper so you won't have any Heads or Subheads that are Widows or Orphans.

TIP Follow the page format instructions given in this document exactly. You'll give your paper strong "eye appeal."

TIP Eliminate or reduce the number of prepositions (*in, to, into, through, about, on, between, beside, down, during, from, over, toward, until, up, with*) and/or conjunctions (*and, but, for*) in your writing.

Here's Why. If you are a skilled verbal communicator, you probably use lots of prepositions. When you examine your first draft you'll find that it is littered with prepositions. Prepositions place objects in semantic space. They allow you to communicate with greater facility, because you're tapping into your audience's visual sense. Yet the same number of prepositions in a written sentence causes confusion. In oral communication, prepositions give the listener a visual grip on what you're saying; in writing, they just clutter up your sentences and make them too complex.

The same is true of conjunctions. These words are used to string phrases and simple sentences together. Edit out excessive prepositions and conjunctions.

Prescription for Better Communication. To avoid confusing and fatiguing your reader, reduce the number of prepositions and conjunctions in your copy. First, circle all the prepositions and conjunctions in your text. Then, work to edit out as many as you can by restructuring your sentences and breaking long sentences into two or three shorter ones.

TIP Try to say the same thing with fewer words. Make sure that each word contributes to your message's clarity and meaning. If a word fails to add meaning, drop it.

TIP Read your copy aloud—this will give you the benefit of a more objective reading and, most important, increase the conversational tone and move away from a dull, formal voice.

SUMMARY

Checklist for Writing With *High Communication Factor*

☐ If you want to appear objective, use the passive objective voice; do not use personal pronouns (e.g., *I, You, She, He*).

COMMON GRAMMATICAL ERRORS

☐ use of the word *which* when the proper choice is *that*. (*Which* is used only "parenthetically"; the word *which* must appear between two commas—in a nonrestrictive clause.)

☐ dangling prepositions

☐ lack of subject/verb agreement

GRABBING YOUR READER'S ATTENTION

☐ Offer your reader a variety of words; use words like a cook uses spices.

☐ Do not reuse the same verbs, adjectives, and descriptive nouns within the same paragraph.

☐ Edit out repetitive words or phrases.

☐ Vary the length and structure of your sentences.

☐ Break long paragraphs into smaller, more readable paragraphs.

☐ Spell out numbers nine and lower; use digits for numbers 10 and higher.

☐ Draw conclusions. Bravely take a stand and defend it.

☐ Type your paper and draw your tables with superior attention to detail.

☐ Remember, presentation counts. Form is as important as content.

☐ Get to the point. The shorter the better.

EDITING TIPS

TIP   Write your paper over a minimum of three sessions.

TIP   Proof your paper so you don't have any Heads or Subheads that are
       Widows or Orphans.

TIP   Reduce the number of prepositions (*in, to, into, through, about, on,
       between, beside, down, during, from, over, toward, until, up, with*)
       and/or conjunctions (*and, but, for*) in your writing.

15

Becoming the Great Communicator

Some Special Words to Participants in Dr. Whalen's
Effective Communication Classes and Workshops

THE PROCESS OF BECOMING A BETTER COMMUNICATOR
IS CONSTANT SELF-IMPROVEMENT

Desire to Change. If you've spent a few years in business, I believe that
you have all the motivation you need to sharpen your communication skills.
You know that success comes from superior communication ability—and
if you've been in a position of having to persuade others to follow your
ideas, you know the meaning of frustration. Motivation is not a problem.
Moreover, this quarter you'll be making presentations before your fellow
students and the KGSB faculty—so you have plenty of motivation.

Hear New Skill Explained. First, before you try a new technique, it will
be explained by me or one of the other instructors. Many of the techniques
you'll learn are also presented in this book.

See New Skill Demonstrated. Much of effective oral communication
comes from the speaker's attitude toward his or her message and listener(s).
The audience reads your attitude through the subtle gestures, facial expressions, movements, and vocal tones you make. Written or oral description
can't capture and fully communicate attitude. To learn, you have to watch
somebody who is skilled in communicating attitude. Learning by modeling

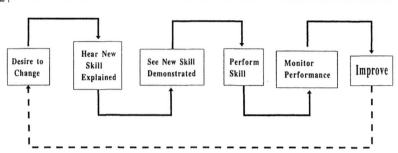

Figure 15.1 Steps to Building Communication Skill
[Illustrated here is the Joel Whalen, Ph.D. Effective Communication process of training business managers to become better influential communicators: Constant Self Improvement. It's the learning approach we use in our workshops and at the Kellstadt Graduate School of Business at DePaul.

is the key. You'll see each technique demonstrated and you'll learn by watching what you will later do.

The process you'll follow in this class is illustrated in **Figure 15.1, Steps to Better Communication.**

Perform Skill. An important principle of persuasion is that *behavior* is the most powerful agent of change. Your persuasive strategy must include active, physical participation by the audience. You must get people *doing* before they can change. This is true of knowledge sets, and it's especially true of skills. You can't learn how to swim by hearing a lecture, watching somebody diagram the strokes on a blackboard, and sitting on the side of the pool watching others cut smoothly through the water.

You'll become a better communicator by trying, then practicing the new skills.

Monitor Performance (Receive Feedback). A very painful and important part of learning is listening to caring, accurate, and helpful feedback from your teammates and studying yourself on videotape. I watched myself recently on tape giving a seminar to a group of business people. Ouch, I'm no Sean Connery. Actually, I'm no Vern either. When we see ourselves on tape we are too hard on ourselves, we're hypercritical. Repeatedly, you'll see that your teammates are far less critical of you than you are. We have far higher personal standards for public speaking and small-group presentations than we do for the rest of our lives. If we all applied the same standards of performance to our driving, the accident rate would be far lower.

Improve. The result of your training, experience, and work in communication gives you greater ability and confidence based on that new, higher level of skill.

Naturally, the next step is iterative—you return to the beginning of the process, with more motivation to learn more. Communication can be an endless study of constant self-improvement. After 30 years in public communication, I still live my life by the model of Constant Self-Improvement.

You can speed your training in effective persuasive communication through Enlightened Self-Awareness

Introspection, self-analysis, and personal critique of your performance are key elements in building your communication skills. Enlightened Self-Awareness is a technique used by social scientists to gain more subtle information on the phenomena they are studying. For example, sociologists look into themselves, as "laboratories," to gain insight into the theories, hypotheses, and observations that they make.

Using Enlightened Self-Awareness, you can depend upon yourself to provide volumes of useful data on you as a communicator. **Caution:** Most people tend to be hypercritical of themselves; some even descend to bashing themselves with false negative messages about inadequacy and failure. To counter the tendency to flagellate yourself needlessly, the class encourages open feedback among students. Over time, you'll learn to trust this feedback. Often, students will hear the positive feedback on their performance and filter out this praise. They tend to hear only the negative, the suggestions for improvement. This type of student thinks that the others in class are "only trying to be nice." These poor people are prepared to accept only harsh negative feedback that confirms their fears.

You'll learn to use Enlightened Self-Awareness accurately; not for self-bashing, but for self-training and to speed your growth as a communicator.

People can receive maximal training benefit and become better communicators by taking personal risks in a predictable, safe, supportive atmosphere

To grow you must take risks, and this is especially true of communication training. You'll feel tons of risk just getting up before a group and speaking, or by sharing your views in a small group. Speaking before a college class is one of the more difficult venues you'll encounter. It's easier to take a risk when you truly know that your listeners are on your side. In class, we all adopt a positive, nurturing attitude toward each other, especially toward the person who is in the spotlight, seeking to build her or his communication skills.

Effective persuasive communication is a vast body of knowledge. It can only be effectively studied atomistically—by taking little chunks at a time

Some exercises and learning experiences are abstract—we will ask you to learn and to practice skills that are essential to effective communication but are things that you'd never do in a business setting.

Although you won't duplicate that presentation back at work, you will gain intense insight into critical elements of communication.

Your training will be a blend of abstract exercises designed to enhance particular aspects of you as a communicator, and real-life, real-time presentations that you can put to work.

Not the World's Most
Perfect Approach to
Effective Business Communication

Please understand the meaning behind my overt and perhaps blind enthusiasm for this set of training methods. Our intense focus makes us look like zealots. As you read this book and speak with me in class or in a Joel Whalen, Ph.D. Effective Communication Workshop, you may get the impression that I think I have the answer for everything related to persuasive business communication. I know that I don't have all the answers. We have, however, developed a significant set of knowledge and training exercises that have worked beautifully for hundreds and hundreds of Kellstadt Graduate School of Business students and in private seminars.

Dr. Whalen's Persuasive Business Communication is just one approach

There are many other effective communication training methods. The set of knowledge about human behavior and psychology is vast. If we do our job, you'll spend the rest of your professional life learning how to sharpen your understanding of persuasive business communication.

The Whalen approach works beautifully with graduate-level business students and other businesspeople. We use it because it has been refined and tested with hundreds of businesspeople. We know it works.

We try to be open to new ideas and techniques

This book and class are in a constant state of evolution. I've used the power of desktop publishing and the philosophy of Constant Process Improvement to "reengineer" this class with each teaching. Some ideas contained in this book come from ideas shared by students and developed in class meetings. There are eight earlier versions of this book, in workbooks and Beta Editions. That is much iteration and process improvement in two years. Students from the first class would recognize little of what takes place in today's class.

There are many effective presentation techniques that are not covered in this class

There are many excellent approaches to communication training: Toastmasters, Dale Carnegie Courses, Fred Pryor Seminars, and dozens of private communications consultants and trainers. Each has something important that you can learn.

Presentation is an individual art that can be aided by scientific knowledge—make it your own

To be a credible, effective communicator you must use your own personality, style, and approach to dealing with people. We do not seek to train a battalion of Whalen/KGSB automatons who present in unison. These techniques are designed to set you free to become yourself when speaking before other people. That is the true power of Persuasive Business Communication.

The techniques and approaches used in this class work. Use this class as an opportunity to master them. Then, take with you what you like. Adapt, copy, or use what you prefer.

We ask that you give these techniques a fair trial. A passive wait-and-see approach will not help you. You must commit yourself to them. Like the sailor with one foot on the dock and the other foot in the boat, you'd best get on board or you'll get wet.

After a while you'll make these techniques and attitudes your own. After you've completed your Effective Communication training, take and use what you like and discard any ideas that don't ring true for you.

Evaluating Presentations

You and your teammates are graded on application of techniques taught in this class—not on your personality or level of charisma

Personality and charm are indispensable elements in effective communication. You brought these assets with you to class. You will not be issued a sack of charisma as part of your training materials—nor will we seek to develop new personality assets for you. The Persuasive Business Communication techniques you learn will free you to use the human relations skills you already have. You may find that your attitude toward people changes a bit, making you more facile in human relationships—this will make you a better communicator, too.

Judgment of your performance will be made on the basis of how well you execute objective, observable behaviors (as we say in the social sciences). Persuasive Business Communication consists of a set of objective criteria. You will learn to see these behaviors, as will your teammates—you will assess each other's behavior based on those criteria. This is not a personality contest.

Your communication will be evaluated during this class by the other participants in this class

You will enjoy the supportive, positive atmosphere and the constructive feedback you get from your fellow students. You're all in the same boat, working to learn the same things. You'll probably find that you are learning about yourself as a presenter as you watch, listen, and evaluate your fellow students as they make presentations from their point of view.

Much of what you bring to your presentation is important but not evaluated—only key techniques are used in grading

Though personality and charm are not graded, they are an indispensable part of you and your effectiveness as a communicator. By not grading these important intangible factors, we don't mean to downplay their role in communication. Instead, we seek to grade communication techniques that are more objective and that you probably did not already have the first day of class. We seek to help you become a better communicator, not just confirm how wonderful you already are.

This is a very difficult class to grade

You're going to find out how hard it is to assign grades, because you'll be responsible for assigning evaluations (grades) to your teammates. You'll see that much of effective communication is intangible and hard to quantify and judge objectively. "I know what a good presentation is, but I can't tell you why one presentation is better than another." That is why we stick to objective, observable criteria.

Another important reason that this is a very difficult class to grade is that your feelings and ego are on the line more than in any other class you'll take at the KGSB. We're talking about things that go to the core of your soul. You'll be evaluated on how well you share and communicate the things you believe. People can feel vulnerable and exposed. As we said earlier, you're taking varying degrees of risks in this class.

For those reasons, we ask that you are kind to each other in your verbal critique and when assigning scores to your teammates' performance. We will actively seek to help each other improve; to find things we can improve as communicators. It is more important to point out what people do well so they can enhance these behaviors and depend upon these skills, than it is to make someone aware of any shortcomings.

SUMMARY

THE WHALEN APPROACH
TO COMMUNICATION TRAINING

A communicator's generous, nurturing spirit and playful, entertaining attitude make the speaker and message more approachable and interesting for the audience. To persuade, rational logical statements are not sufficient. You have to arouse an audience's emotions.

Persuasion can take time and is very similar to the educational process. Planning, applied persuasion psychology, sensory communication, and simple models are the most powerful communication tools.

We seek to add a layer of skill to your core personality. We will avoid coaching you on "appropriate gestures" and "eye contact" or "picturing your audience naked."

People can receive maximal training benefit and become better communicators by taking personal risks in a predictable, safe, supportive atmosphere.

EVALUATING PRESENTATIONS

You're graded on the application of techniques taught in this class—not on your personality or level of charisma, but on how well you execute objective, observable behaviors. Many people will give you feedback on your performance—your teammates and instructors.

16

A Message to DePaul Kellstadt
Graduate School of Business Students

Effective Communication (KGSB 499)

Why Must I Take This Course First?

The sage overseers who direct your MBA studies—the kind and wise senior faculty and administrators who selected the sequence of courses, knowledge, and agony that you must pass through and master to be deemed an MBA—believe that you must first have effective communication skills before you experience any other classes. Why? For practical reasons: Much of what you'll learn in the Kellstadt School will come through informal class discussion, analysis of cases and problems, and formal presentations. We believe that you'll become a better communicator if you practice the communication skills and knowledge you learn in this class in conjunction with a set of real-life factors, for example, accounting models or marketing strategy or financial analysis taught in other classes. We believe that your graduate program will be a wholly different experience: You'll learn more in other classes if you practice your communication skills.

BUT I'M ALREADY A
VERY EFFECTIVE COMMUNICATOR

Respectfully, to you and your considerable experience and maturity, you may be a super communicator, but many of your classmates are not. (Average

age range of KGSB students is 27 to 31 years; average business experience range, five to eight years). In today's competitive business arena, particularly with the advent of e-mail and work teams, you must have superior communication skills.

IS THE MBA THE KEY TO SUCCESS IN BUSINESS?

The MBA has become the popular power credential among businesspeople, and for good reason. Though the mythical sixty-thousand dollar a year starting salary and BMW complete with vanity plates may not instantly appear in the parking lot when you receive your degree—the knowledge and experience gained during MBA studies will give you significant, cutting-edge competitive advantage. In addition, the contacts you make among your fellow students, alumni, and faculty are invaluable.

Still, the romance between business and the MBA has cooled down a bit from the hot passions of the 1980s. The number of managers holding the MBA (and other graduate business degrees, e.g., Master's in Taxation, Master's in Finance) has made the credential less than unique.

SUPERIOR ANALYSIS AND PLANNING

Even though some of the flash and glamour that surrounded the MBA have faded, the solid core of deliverable skills and knowledge that formed that degree's reputation remains. MBA degree holders can predict, explain, and therefore control business phenomena to a remarkable degree. Business rewards these skills.

SO, IS THERE A PROBLEM?

Yes, there is a problem. Superior ability in analysis and planning alone will not assure that you'll be successful. Look at the top businesspeople you've met or read about. Their attainment did not come from their analytic skills alone. Their ascent to leadership came through their ability to communicate their vision, their plans—and to convince others to follow them.

THE PITCH

Consider the probable future of two freshly minted MBAs.

Jane holds a B average from a solid but lesser-known business school. Yet when she speaks, others listen. She communicates brilliantly, speaking with clarity and fire; her reports and written communications are brief, clear, and persuasive. People like and trust her. They believe that Jane understands them and has their best interests at heart. They follow her vision.

Bob is an A + scholar from a top graduate school. His brilliant brain generates so much static electricity that his hair stands on end and sends off sparks. He pins the meter on all achievement tests. He sets the curve on all exams. In his case discussion classes, however, he is silent. Bob is hindered by fear and an overwhelming sense of inhibition. When he does speak, it's dull and, frankly, others are confused by his tangled, redundant, abstract presentation. Bob is boring. His ideas make sense but lack the persuasive thrust necessary to push them over the top. He is more comfortable expressing his ideas in mathematical models and tedious but accurate reports.

WHICH MBA WOULD YOU HIRE?

You might hire Bob rather than Jane, assuming that your firm has a position for a brilliant analyst and is so large that you can afford to hide Bob from clients and customers. But, for which student do you predict the brightest future? Which one will likely become the leader, the innovator, the next entrepreneur? Which one will you read about in *Business Week* 10 years hence? The smart money's on Jane.

Brilliant analysis bottled up inside a brilliant mind is useless. Ideas are only useful to business if they can be communicated, embraced, and acted on passionately by others on the business team. Ideas must be communicated accurately, in detail, and with persuasive impact. Ideas must be sold.

Ask any business leader, any top executive, "Do you think that communication skills are important?" What answers do you think you'll get? Frankly, it's not a question you need to ask. You already know the answer, don't you? "It's very important." A better question is: "Why isn't this critical skill taught in all MBA programs?" At the KGSB it is.

RECONCEPTUALIZING THE *CUSTOMER*

You may think that you're the customer—and to some degree you're right. After all, you pay tuition, you do the hard work under the faculty's direction, and as a result you receive the educational and intellectual growth. We disagree—you're not the primary customer, the one we strive to satisfy. You have come to the KGSB so management will hire you, respect your ideas, promote and reward you. You subscribe to the notion that the MBA will help you attain those worthy goals. The customer, the person we seek to satisfy, is your current or potential employer. Please forgive the inherent harshness of this manufacturing metaphor, but to us you are the raw material that we process into a form attractive and useful to our customer: the employer. You and the KGSB faculty are working hard to satisfy the same customer, your boss. We do this by producing the best quality product on the market—you, or who you will be when you successfully complete your MBA.

LISTENING TO OUR CUSTOMER'S VOICE

Taking a page out of our own marketing classes, we went to our customers and asked them what type of products they wanted us to produce, what they wanted to buy.

DePaul is blessed with superb guidance from our Advisory Boards (with members drawn from the leading business, governmental, and social institutions in Chicago and beyond). We asked these leaders (who, I might add, make attractive employers) what we could do to improve our graduates' training. Many meetings were held to assess this issue. We conducted market surveys. Here is what we learned.

GENESIS OF THIS COURSE: CUSTOMER COMPLAINTS

The faculty was a bit surprised. The continuing criticism of our MBA graduates by the Business Advisory Boards was not of their understanding and application of analytic models, but of their weak communication, teamwork, and leadership skills. This criticism touches an important area. In most business settings within the larger number of corporations, brilliant analysis and planning ability are not sufficient to guarantee success.

Traditionally, successful managers must be able to effectively communicate, lead, empower, and inspire.

THE COURSE'S STRUCTURE

This course drew from three great, traditional sources of knowledge—**(1) Speech and Rhetoric, (2) U.S. Business Conventions,** and **(3) Persuasion Psychology**—and merged them into a single course.

Speech and Rhetoric as studied and taught in a college or department of communication. Much of what is taught in traditional speech classes will be used in this class and explored in this book—and much will not. If you have a background or training in speech making, you'll find that this course will encourage you to amplify and reinforce some of the skills you've gained and recommend strongly that you may want to abandon others. Frankly, some posturing and "speechifying" typically taught in college and public communication seminars actually creates barriers to effective business communication and makes the speaker appear pompous, artificial, and less effective.

U.S. Business Conventions. We believe that business communication is unique. You communicate differently as a businessperson than you do when at home with family, when socializing (*hopefully*), or when you engage in other types of communication. The rules that guide and determine communication are different from venue to venue, from love and family to business.

In the United States, business communication is built on a long tradition of conventional rituals that have, over the decades, formed into an efficient, effective code of behavior and symbols. The highly efficient machine that is the American Way of Business is due in part to highly codified, predictable, and observable Rules of Conduct. You'll learn the conventions of business communication as it is used in the boardroom, in the conference room, and on the sales floor.

People from around the globe believe that the United States leads the world in business education. They send their best and brightest people to graduate schools in this country to learn how we analyze, plan, and conduct business. As a member of the KGSB, you'll be proud to know that DePaul is taking the leadership position in business communication training through this course and through the Master's in International Marketing and Finance (MIMF). Persuasive Business Communication is considered a cornerstone class, required in the first quarter for the MIMF students.

Persuasion Psychology. Effective communication can be taught. Advances in persuasion psychology give us keen insight into human behavior in business. By following a learnable set of rules, an MBA is taught to predict, explain, and to a real degree, to control other people's attitudes and behavior—just as MBAs can be taught to predict, explain, and control the behavior of markets . . . probably with greater reliability. These discoveries give us very effective models of human behavior. When you study and master these principles and apply these techniques, you can influence others.

DO YOU REALLY WANT GREATNESS?

Frankly, these techniques work. The question you must answer for yourself is: *"Do I really want to be more successful in business by influencing and leading others?"* Many people, even holders of the MBA degree, would rather follow than lead. During your time with us, you will find many opportunities to explore what you want. Over the next two to three years you'll find out just how hard you're willing to work, how much you'll grow and change to get what you want. When you graduate, you'll have been exposed to all the ideas, all the knowledge you need. You'll have had ample opportunity to practice your skills. If you want to be a great business leader, it's yours for the taking. You will design, either actively or passively or through benign neglect of opportunity, the boundaries of your career.

Some Things We Believe About
Persuasive Communication at the KGSB

• *Superior persuasion strategies and skills are more important to business success than superior analysis and planning. Effective Analysis and Planning is necessary but not sufficient.*

Follow this three-step chain of logic:

1. To be *used,* the plan must be *understood* by all team members.
2. To be *understood,* the plan must be *communicated effectively.*
3. To be *implemented,* the plan must be *understood by people outside the team.*

    To attempt the new, to change the organization, to grow, expand, or undertake risk, faith and confidence must be present in adequate quantities to move the group. A group's faith in the unknown is the result of effective persuasion by leaders.

• *People trust and follow skilled speakers.*

There is ample evidence, in study after study, that shows superior communicators are judged to be more intelligent, more attractive, and better leaders than those who don't communicate as well. Leadership flows to those who speak well.

• *Students benefit more when they build skills.*

Reading this book and attending class will not make you a better communicator—you will know **how** to be a better communicator, but you will not actually **be** a better speaker, message packager, or leader.

Only by doing, acting, practicing, and engaging in actual communication will you build skills.

We believe that you need more than knowledge, you need skills to be successful.

• *Personality and charisma are important to communication but we don't know how to teach these valuable attributes—yet.*

We cannot teach you how to be more charismatic—nor will we evaluate you on your personality.

There is, however, a distinct set of behaviors, attitudes, and skills that we will teach you to make you a skilled communicator. And some of these behaviors, attitudes, and skills are the very same ones used by highly personable and charismatic communicators.

If you wish, by applying these techniques and adopting these attitudes, you'll become more personable and charismatic. But that will not be due solely to what we teach, it will come from what you desire to become.

Appendix

"Preparing to Present" Audience Checklist

To enjoy successful, persuasive presentations, **Audience Analysis** is essential. You must customize your message and delivery for the audience.

KEY   The more you know about the audience . . . the more powerful your presentation.

Use the following checklist when *preparing to present.* When you have the answers to these questions, you'll have valuable insight into your audience and will be in a better position to deliver a superior presentation.

- ☐ How many do I expect in the audience? _____
- ☐ What topics should I avoid? _____
- ☐ What topics must I cover? _____
- ☐ Who are the group's leaders? _____
- ☐ What is/are the group leader's positions on my topic? _____
- ☐ What is the range of expertise (low to high) on my topic? _____

What is the mix of:

- ☐ men and women? _____
- ☐ age ranges? _____
- ☐ socioeconomic and ethnic groups? _____
- ☐ job titles? _____
- ☐ occupations? _____
- ☐ educational backgrounds? _____
- ☐ regions of the country? _____

236

Roles in the Decision Process

☐ Decider   ☐ Analyst

☐ Specifier   ☐ User

☐ Recommender   ☐ Gatekeeper

☐ Do audience members identify with any particular political, religious, or professional group?

☐ Why are the audience members attending the presentation?

☐ What is there about this subject that will interest the audience?

☐ How much do audience members know about the subject? Do they all have about the same level of knowledge?

☐ What is the audience's attitude toward the subject?

☐ What will impress this group and what best communicates my ideas:

     ☐ technical data?

     ☐ statistical comparisons?

     ☐ cost figures?

     ☐ historical information?

     ☐ generalizations?

     ☐ demonstrations?

☐ What do I want the audience members to feel, believe, or do as a result of this presentation?

☐ How do the audience members feel about my **purpose** in making this presentation?

☐ What is the audience's attitude toward me and/or my company?

☐ What is the **status** of audience members compared with mine?

☐ How does this audience usually react to speakers?

If You'd Like To Learn More

Recommended Reading

Bettger, Frank. *How I Raised Myself From Failure to Success in Selling.* Englewood Cliffs, NJ: Prentice Hall, 1986.

Carnegie, Dale. *How to Win Friends and Influence People.* New York: Simon & Schuster, 1981.

Cialdini, Robert. *Influence: The New Psychology of Modern Persuasion.* New York: Quill, 1990.

Craig, James. *Designing With Type.* New York: Watson-Guptill, 1980.

Duncan, Tom, and Sandra Moriarity. *How to Create and Deliver Winning Advertising Presentations.* Chicago: Crain Books, 1991.

Kato, Hiroki, and Joan Kato. *Understanding and Working With the Japanese Business World.* Englewood Cliffs, NJ: Prentice Hall, 1992.

Littlejohn, Stephen W. *Theories of Human Communication,* 3rd Ed. Belmont, CA: Wadsworth, 1989.

McCormack, Mark H. *What They Don't Teach You at Harvard Business School: Notes From a Street-Smart Executive.* New York: Bantam, 1984.

Ogilvy, David. *Ogilvy on Advertising.* New York: Vintage, 1985.

Settle, Robert B., and Pamela Alrech. *Why They Buy: American Consumers Inside and Out.* New York: John Wiley, 1984.

Tufte, Edward R. *The Visual Display of Quantitative Information.* Cheshire, CT: Graphics Press, 1983.

Tufte, Edward R. *Envisioning Information.* Cheshire, CT: Graphics Press, 1990.

Take These Training Courses

Dale Carnegie Effective Human Relations
Fred Pryor Seminars *Successful Presentation Skills*
Toastmasters International

Bibliography

Andersen, Kenneth, and Theodore Clevenger, Jr. "Summary of Experimental Research in Ethos." *Speech Monographs,* Vol. 30, 1963, pp. 59-78.

Aronson, Elliot, and Burton W. Golden. "The Effect of Relevant and Irrelevant Aspects of Communicator Credibility on Opinion Change." *Journal of Personality,* Vol. 30, 1962, pp. 135-146.

Baker, Michael J., and Gilbert A. Churchill, Jr. "The Impact of Physically Attractive Models on Advertising Evaluations." *Journal of Marketing Research,* Vol. 14, November 1977, pp. 538-555.

Bell, Gerald D. "Self-Confidence and Persuasion in Car Buying." *Journal of Marketing Research,* Vol. 4, February 1967, pp. 46-52.

Bem, Daryl J. "Self-Perception Theory." In *Advances in Experimental Social Psychology,* Vol. 6, edited by L. Berkowitz, pp. 1-62. New York: Academic Press, 1972.

Berlo, David K., James B. Lemert, and Robert J. Mertz. "Dimensions for Evaluating the Acceptability of Message Sources." *Public Opinion Quarterly,* Vol. 33, 1969-1970, pp. 563-576.

Berscheid, Ellen, and Elaine Walster. "Physical Attractiveness." In *Advances in Experimental Social Psychology,* Vol. 7, edited by L. Berkowitz, pp. 157-215. New York: Academic Press, 1973.

Bettger, Frank. *How I Raised Myself From Failure to Success by Selling.* Englewood Cliffs, NJ: Prentice Hall, 1986.

Bither, Stewart W., and Peter L. Wright. "The Effect of Distraction and Self-Esteem on Mass Media Persuasibility." Pennsylvania State University Working Series in Marketing Research, January, 1971.

Bloom, Paul N. "Effective Marketing for Professional Services." *Harvard Business Review,* September-October 1984, pp. 202-210.

Bone, Paula, Ellen Fitzgerald, Pam Scholder, Richard W. Easley, and Samuel E. McNeely. "A Comment on 'Relationship Between Source Expertise and Source Similarity in an Advertising Context.' " *Journal of Advertising,* Vol. 15, 1986, pp. 47-48.

Brandon, Karen. "We May Reach Out, But We Don't Touch Much." *Chicago Tribune,* September 25, 1994, sec. 1, pp. 1, 20.

Carnegie, Dale. *How to Win Friends and Influence People.* New York: Simon & Schuster, 1981.

Chaiken, Shelly. "Communicator Physical Attractiveness and Persuasion." *Journal of Personality and Social Psychology,* Vol. 37, 1979, pp. 1387-1397.

Chaiken, Shelly. "Heuristics Versus Systematic Information Processing and the Use of Source Versus Message Cues in Persuasion." *Journal of Personality and Social Psychology,* Vol. 39, 1980, pp. 752-766.

Chaiken, Shelly, and Alice H. Eagly. "Communication Modality as a Determinant of Message Persuasiveness and Message Comprehensibility." *Journal of Personality and Social Psychology,* Vol. 34, 1976, pp. 605-614.

Chaiken, Shelly, and Alice H. Eagly. "Communication Modality as a Determinant of Persuasion: The Role of Communicator Salience." *Journal of Personality and Social Psychology,* Vol. 45, 1983, pp. 241-256.

Cialdini, Robert B. "Full-Cycle Social Psychology." In *Persuasion and Ethics,* pp. 21-47. New York: Quill, 1989.

Cialdini, Robert. B. *Influence: The New Psychology of Modern Persuasion.* New York: Quill, 1990.

Cialdini, Robert B., Richard E. Perry, and John T. Cacioppo. "Attitude and Attitude Change." *Annual Review of Psychology,* Vol. 32, 1981, pp. 357-404.

Clevenger, Theodore, Jr., John T. Lazier, Gilbert A. Clark, and Margaret Leitner. "Measurement of Corporate Images by Semantic Differential." *Journal of Marketing Research,* Vol. 1, February 1965, pp. 80-82.

Cohen, Arthur R. "Some Implications of Self-Esteem for Social Influence." In *Personality and Persuasibility,* edited by Carl I. Hovland and Irving L. Janis, pp. 102-120. New Haven, CT: Yale University Press, 1959.

Cooper, Joel, and Robert T. Croyle. "Attitude and Attitude Change." *Annual Review of Psychology,* Vol. 35, 1984, pp. 395-426.

Craig, James. *Designing With Type.* New York: Watson-Guptill, 1980.

Cronkhite, Gary, and Jo Liska. "A Critique of Factor Analytic Approaches to the Study of Credibility." *Communication Monographs,* Vol. 43, June 1976, pp. 91-107.

Dance, Frank E. X. "The Concept of Communication." *Journal of Communication,* Vol. 20, 1970, pp. 204, 208.

Deaux, Kay. "Anticipatory Attitude Change: A Direct Test of the Self-Esteem Hypothesis." *Journal of Experimental Social Psychology,* Vol. 8, 1972, pp. 143-155.

Delia, Jesse G. "A Constructivist Analysis of the Concept of Credibility." *Quarterly Journal of Speech,* Vol. 62, December 1976, pp. 364-374.

Delia, Jesse G. "Constructivism and the Study of Human Communication." *Quarterly Journal of Speech,* Vol. 63, February 1977, pp. 66-83.

Dholakia, Ruby Roy, and Brian Sternthal. "Highly Credible Sources: Persuasive Facilitators of Persuasive Liabilities?" *Journal of Consumer Research,* Vol. 3, March 1977, pp. 223-232.

Dinner, Sherry H., Bernard E. Lewkowicz, and Joel Cooper. "Anticipatory Attitude Change as a Function of Self-Esteem and Issue Familiarity." *Journal of Personality and Social Psychology,* Vol. 24, 1972, pp. 407-412.

Eagly, Alice H. "Involvement as a Determinant of Response to Favorable and Unfavorable Information." *Journal of Personality and Social Psychology,* Vol. 7, November 1967, pp. 1-14.

Eagly, Alice H. "Sex Differences in the Relationship Between Self-Esteem and Susceptibility to Social Influence." *Journal of Personality,* Vol. 37, 1969, pp. 581-591.

Eagly, Alice H. "Recipient Characteristics as Determinants of Responses to Persuasion." In *Cognitive Responses in Persuasion,* edited by R. E. Petty, T. M. Ostrom, and T. C. Brock, pp. 173-195. Hillsdale, NJ: Lawrence Erlbaum, 1981.

Eagly, Alice H., and Shelly Chaiken. "An Attribution Analysis of the Effect of Communicator Characteristics on Opinion Change: The Case of Communicator Attractiveness." *Journal of Personality and Social Psychology,* Vol. 32, 1975, pp. 136-144.

Eagly, Alice H., and Shelly Chaiken. "Why Would Anyone Say That? Causal Attribution of Statements About the Watergate Scandal." *Sociometry,* Vol. 39, 1976, pp. 236-243.

Eagly, Alice H., and George I. Whitehead III. "Effect of Choice on Receptivity to Favorable and Unfavorable Evaluations of Oneself." *Journal of Personality and Social Psychology,* Vol. 22, 1972, pp. 223-230.

Eagly, Alice H., Wendy Wood, and Shelly Chaiken. "Causal Inferences About Communicators and Their Effect on Opinion Change." *Journal of Personality and Social Psychology,* Vol. 36, 1978, pp. 424-435.

Festinger, Leon, and James M. Carlsmith. "Cognitive Consequences of Forced Compliance." *Journal of Abnormal and Social Psychology,* Vol. 58, 1959, pp. 203-210.

Friedman, Hershey H., and Linda Friedman. "Endorser Effectiveness by Product Type." *Journal of Advertising Research,* Vol. 19, October 1979, pp. 63-71.

Gendlin, Eugene. *Let Your Body Interpret Your Dreams.* Wilmette, IL: Chiron Publications, 1986.

Giller, Earl, Jr., Bruce Perry, Steven Southwick, Rachel Yehuda, Victor Wahby, Thomas Kosten, and John Mason. "Psychoendocrinology of Posttraumatic Stress Disorder." In *Post-Traumatic Stress Disorder: Etiology, Phenomenology, and Treatment,* edited by Marion Wolf and Aron Mosnaim. Washington, DC: American Psychiatric Press, 1990.

Golden, Linda L. "Attribution Theory Implications for Advertisement Claim Credibility." *Journal of Marketing Research,* Vol. 14, February 1977, pp. 115-117.

Greenberg, Bradley S., and Gerald R. Miller. "The Effects of Low-Credible Sources on Message Acceptance." *Speech Monographs,* Vol. 33, 1965, pp. 127-136.

Haiman, Franklyn S. "An Experimental Study of the Effects of Ethos in Public Speaking." *Speech Monographs,* Vol. 16, September 1949, pp. 190-202.

Harvey, John H., and Gifford Weary. "Current Issues in Attribution Theory and Research." *Annual Review of Psychology,* Vol. 35, 1984, pp. 427-459.

Heider, Fritz. "Social Perception and Phenomenal Causality." *Psychological Review,* Vol. 51, 1944, pp. 358-374.

Heider, Fritz. *The Psychology of Interpersonal Relations.* New York: John Wiley, 1958.

The Holy Bible. King James version.

Hovland, Carl I., Irving L. Janis, and Harold H. Kelley. *Communication and Persuasion.* New Haven, CT: Yale University Press, 1966.

Hovland, Carl I., and Walter Weiss. "The Influence of Source Credibility on Communication Effectiveness." *Public Opinion Quarterly,* Vol. 15, 1951, pp. 635-650.

Infante, Dominic A., and Jeanne Y. Fisher. "Anticipated Credibility and Message Strategy Intentions as Predictors of Trait and State Speech Anxiety." *Central States Speech Journal,* Vol. 29, Spring 1978, pp. 1-10.

Jaccard, James. "Toward Theories of Persuasion and Belief Change." *Journal of Personality and Social Psychology,* Vol. 40, 1981, pp. 260-269.

Janis, Irving L. "Personality Correlates of Susceptibility to Persuasion." *Journal of Personality,* Vol. 22, 1954, pp. 504-518.

Janis, Irving L. "Anxiety Indices Related to Susceptibility to Persuasion." *Journal of Abnormal and Social Psychology,* Vol. 51, 1955, pp. 663-667.

Janis, Irving L., and Peter B. Field. "Sex Differences and Personality Factors Related to Persuasibility." *Journal of Personality,* 1959, 55-68.

Janis, Irving L., and Donald Rife. "Persuasibility and Emotional Disorder." In *Personality and Persuasibility,* edited by Carl I. Hovland and Irving L. Janis, pp. 121-137. New Haven, CT: Yale University Press, 1959.

Jones, Edward E., and Keith E. Davis. "From Acts to Dispositions: The Attribution Process in Person Perception." In *Advance Experimental Social Psychology,* Vol. 2, edited by L. Berkowitz, pp. 219-265. New York: Academic Press, 1965.

Kaplan, Stuart J. "Attribution Processes in the Evaluation of Message Sources." *Western Speech Communication,* Vol. 40, Summer 1976, pp. 189-195.

Kaplan, Stuart J., and Harry W. Sharp, Jr. "The Effect of Responsibility Attributions on Message Source Evaluation." *Speech Monographs,* Vol. 41, November 1974, pp. 364-370.

Kato, Hiroki, and Joan Kato. *Understanding and Working With the Japanese Business World.* Englewood Cliffs, NJ: Prentice Hall, 1992.

Kelley, Harold H. "Attribution Theory in Social Psychology." *Nebraska Symposium on Motivation,* Vol. 14, pp. 192-240. Lincoln: University of Nebraska, 1967.

Kelley, Harold H. "The Processes of Causal Attribution." *American Psychologist,* February 1973, pp. 107-128.

Kelley, Harold H., and John L. Michela. "Attribution Theory and Research." *Annual Review of Psychology,* Vol. 31, 1980, pp. 457-501.

Kelman, Herbert C. "Processes of Opinion Change." *Public Opinion Quarterly,* Vol. 25, 1961, pp. 55-78.

Lesser, Gerald S., and Robert P. Abelson. "Personality Correlates of Persuasibility in Children." In *Personality and Persuasibility,* pp. 187-206. New Haven, CT: Yale University Press, 1959.

Leventhal, Howard, and Sidney I. Perloe. "A Relationship Between Self-Esteem and Persuasibility." *Journal of Abnormal and Social Psychology,* Vol. 64, 1962, pp. 385-388.

Linton, Harriet, and Elaine Graham. "Personality Correlates of Persuasibility." In *Personality and Persuasibility,* pp. 71-101. New Haven, CT: Yale University Press, 1959.

Liska, Jo. "Situational and Topical Variations in Credibility Criteria." *Communication Monographs,* Vol. 45, March 1978, pp. 85-92.

Littlejohn, Stephen W. *Theories of Human Communication,* 4th Ed. Belmont, CA: Wadsworth, 1992.

Lumsden, Donald L. "An Experimental Study of Source-Message Interaction in a Personality Impression Task." *Communication Monographs,* Vol. 44, June 1977, pp. 121-129.

Lutz, William. *Doublespeak*. New York: Harper & Row, 1989.

Mathieu-Coughlan, P., and M. H. Klein. "Experiential Psycho-Therapy: Key Events in Client-Therapist Interaction." In *Patterns of Change,* edited by L. N. Rice & L. S. Greenberger. New York: Guilford, 1984.

McArthur, Leslie Ann. "The How and What of Why: Some Determinants and Consequences of Causal Attribution." *Journal of Personality and Social Psychology,* Vol. 22, 1972, pp. 171-193.

McGuinnis, E., and C. D. Ward. "Better Liked Than Right: Trustworthiness and Expertise as Factors in Credibility." *Personality and Social Psychology Bulletin,* Vol. 6, 1980, pp. 467-472.

McGuire, William J. "Personality and Susceptibility to Social Influence." In *Handbook of Personality Theory and Research,* edited by E. F. Borgatta and W. W. Lambert, pp. 1130-1187. Chicago: Rand McNally, 1968.

McCormack, Mark H. *What They Don't Teach You at Harvard Business School: Notes From a Street-Smart Executive.* New York: Bantam, 1984.

McCroskey, James C. "A Summary of Experimental Research on the Effects of Evidence in Persuasive Communication." *Quarterly Journal of Speech,* Vol. 55, 1969, pp. 169-176.

Milgram, S. "Behavioral Study of Obedience." *Journal of Abnormal and Social Psychology,* Vol. 67, pp. 371-378, 1963.

Miller, Gerald R., and John Baseheart. "Source Trustworthiness, Opinionated Statements, and Response to Persuasive Communication." *Speech Monographs,* Vol. 36, March 1969, pp. 1-7.

Minick, Wayne C. *The Art of Persuasion.* Boston: Houghton Mifflin, 1968.

Mizerski, Robert W. "Attribution Theory and Consumer Processing of Unfavorable Information About Products." Unpublished Doctoral Dissertation, University of Florida, 1974.

Mizerski, Robert W. "Causal Complexity: A Measure of Consumer Causal Attribution." *Journal of Marketing Research,* Vol. 15, May 1978, pp. 220-228.

Mizerski, Robert W., Linda L. Golden, and Jerome B. Kernan. "The Attribution Process in Consumer Decision Making." *Journal of Consumer Research,* Vol. 6, September 1979, pp. 123-140.

Munch, James M., and John L. Swasy. "An Examination of Information Processing Traits: General Social Confidence and Information Processing Confidence." Pennsylvania State University Working Series in Marketing Research, September 1980.

Nisbett, Richard E., and Andrew Gordon. "Self-Esteem and Susceptibility to Social Influence." *Journal of Personality and Social Psychology,* Vol. 5, 1967, pp. 268-276.

Ogilvy, David. *Ogilvy on Advertising.* New York: Vintage, 1985.

O'Keefe, Robert D., and D. Joel Whalen. "The Relationship Between Gender and Information Processing Strategies: A Validation Study." In *Strategic Issues in a Dynamic Marketing Environment: Proceedings of the Southern Marketing Association: Buyer Behavior Track,* edited by John H. Summey and Paul J. Hensel, pp. 153-156. Atlanta: Southern Marketing Association, 1988.

Orvis, Bruce R., John D. Cunningham, and Harold H. Kelley. "A Closer Examination of Causal Inference: The Roles of Consensus, Distinctiveness, and Consistency Information." *Journal of Personality and Social Psychology,* Vol. 32, 1975, pp. 605-616.

Osgood, Charles E., and Percy H. Tannenbaum. "The Principle of Congruity in the Prediction of Attitude Change." *Psychology Review,* Vol. 62, 1955, pp. 42-55.

Parkinson, Thomas L. "The Influence of Perceived Risk and Self-Confidence on the Use of Neutral Sources of Information in Consumer Decision-Making." In *Proceedings of the Southern Marketing Association,* edited by Barnett A. Greenberg. Atlanta: Southern Marketing Association, 1974.

Petty, Richard E., and John T. Cacioppo. "The Effects of Involvement on Responses to Argument Quantity and Quality: Central and Peripheral Routes to Persuasion." *Journal of Personality and Social Psychology,* Vol. 46, 1984, pp. 69-81.

Pitts, Robert E., and Eric R. Reidenbach. "Not All CEOs Are Created Equal as Advertising Spokespersons: Evaluating the Effective CEO Spokesperson." *Journal of Advertising,* Vol. 15, 1986, pp. 30-46.

Pitts, Robert E., John K. Wong, and D. Joel Whalen. "Exploring the Structure of Ethical Attributions as a Component of the Consumer Decision Model: The Vicarious Versus Personal Perspective." *Journal of Business Ethics,* Vol. 10, 1990, pp. 43-51.

Plax, Timothy, and Lawrence B. Rosenfeld. "Individual Differences in the Credibility and Attitude Change Relationship." *Journal of Social Psychology,* Vol. 3 1980, pp. 79-89.

Raudsepp, E. "Body Language Speaks Louder." *Machine Design,* Vol. 65, 1993, pp. 85-88.

Rosenfeld, Lawrence B., and Timothy G. Plax. "The Relationship of Listener Personality to Perceptions of Three Dimensions of Credibility." *Central States Speech Journal,* Vol. 26, 1975, pp. 274-278.

Sattler, William M. "Conceptions of Ethos in Ancient Rhetoric." *Speech Monographs,* Vol. 14, 1947, pp. 55-65.

Settle, Robert B. "Attribution Theory and Acceptance of Information." *Journal of Marketing Research,* Vol. 9, February 1972, pp. 85-88.

Settle, Robert B., and Pamela Alrech. *Why They Buy: American Consumers Inside and Out.* New York: John Wiley, 1984.

Settle, Robert B., John H. Faricy, and Glenn T. Warren. "Consumer Information Processing: Attributing Effects to Causes." *Association for Advertising Research: Proceedings of the Annual Conference,* 1971, pp. 278-288.

Settle, Robert B., and L. Bruce Gibby. "The Measurement of Attributed Image." *California Management Review,* Vol. 3, 1976, pp. 70-74.

Settle, Robert B., and Linda L. Golden. "Attribution Theory and Advertiser Credibility." *Journal of Marketing Research,* Vol. 11, May 1974, pp. 181-185.

Sherif, C. W., M. Sherif, and R. E. Nebergall. "Attitude and Attitude Change: The Social Judgement-Involvement Approach." In *The Process of Social Influence,* edited by T. Beisecker and D. Parsons. Englewood Cliffs, NJ: Prentice Hall, 1972.

Silverman, Irwin. "Differential Effects of Ego Threat Upon Persuasibility for High and Low Self-Esteem Subjects." *Journal of Abnormal and Social Psychology,* Vol. 69, 1964, pp. 567-572.

Silverman, Irwin, Leroy H. Ford, Jr., and John B. Morganti. "Inter-Related Effects of Social Desirability, Sex, Self-Esteem, and Complexity of Argument on Persuasibility." *Journal of Personality,* Vol. 34, 1966, pp. 555-568.

Smith, Robert E., and Shelby D. Hunt. "Attributional Processes and Effects in Promotional Situations." *Journal of Consumer Research,* Vol. 5, December 1978, pp. 149-158.

Stanley, Thomas J. "Are Highly Credible Sources Persuasive?" *Journal of Consumer Research,* Vol. 5, June 1978, pp. 66-69.

Sternthal, Brian, Ruby Roy Dholakia, and Clark Leavitt. "The Persuasive Effect of Source Credibility: Tests of Cognitive Response." *Journal of Consumer Research,* Vol. 4, March 1978, pp. 252-260.

Sternthal, Brian, Lynn W. Phillips, and Ruby Roy Dholakia. "The Persuasive Effect of Source Credibility: A Situational Analysis." *Public Opinion Quarterly,* Vol. 42, 1978, pp. 285-314.

Stewart, David W. "The Moderating Role of Recall, Comprehension, and Brand Differentiation on the Persuasiveness of Television Advertising." *Journal of Advertising Research,* April/May, 1986, pp. 43-47.

Stroebe, Wolfgang, Alice H. Eagly, and Margaret S. Stroebe. "Friendly or Just Polite? The Effect of Self-Esteem on Attribution." *Social Psychology,* Vol. 7, 1977, pp. 265-274.

Swartz, Teresa A. "A Further Examination of the Relationship Between Source Expertise and Source Similarity." *Journal of Advertising,* Vol. 15, 1986, pp. 49-50,

Thibaut, John W., and Henry W. Riecken. "Some Determinants and Consequences of the Perception of Social Causality." *Journal of Personality,* Vol. 24, 1955, pp. 113-133.

Tufte, Edward R. *The Visual Display of Quantitative Information.* Cheshire, CT: Graphics Press, 1983.

Tufte, Edward R. *Envisioning Information.* Cheshire, CT: Graphics Press, 1990.

Walster, Elaine, Ellen Berscheid, and G. William Walster. "New Directions in Equity Research." *Journal of Personality and Social Psychology,* Vol. 25, 1973, pp. 151-176.

Webster, Frederick E., Jr. "On the Applicability of Communication Theory to Industrial Markets." *Journal of Marketing Research,* Vol. 5, November 1968, pp. 426-428.

Whalen, D. Joel. "The Effect of the Attribution of Bias-Expectancy and Receiver Self-Esteem on Source Credibility, Message Comprehension and Persuasion." Unpublished Doctoral Dissertation, Florida State University, 1986.

Whalen, D. Joel, and Robert D. O'Keefe. "The Receiver's Attribution of Open-mindedness to a Spokesperson: The Effect on Message Comprehension." In *Marketing: Meeting the Challenges of the 1990's, New Orleans, LA: Proceedings of the Southern Marketing Association,* edited by J. Joseph Cronin and Melvin T. Stith, pp. 259-263. Atlanta: Southern Marketing Association, November 7, 1987.

Whalen, D. Joel, Robert E. Pitts, and Robert D. O'Keefe. " 'Appealing to Consumer's Greed, Lust, Vanity & Envy' or 'The Things Nice Managers Don't Talk About.' " *Journal of Promotions Management,* Vol. 1, 1991.

Whalen, D. Joel, Robert E. Pitts, and John K. Wong. "Consumers' Evaluative Structures in Two Ethical Situations: A Means-End Approach." *Journal of Business Research,* Vol. 21, 1991, pp. 1-12.

Wicker, Allan W. "An Examination of the 'Other Variables' Explanation of Attitude-Behavior Inconsistency." *Journal of Personality and Social Psychology,* Vol. 19, 1971, pp. 18-30.

Wiest, William M. "A Quantitative Extension of Heider's Theory of Cognitive Balance Applied to Interpersonal Perception and Self-Esteem." *Psychological Monographs, General and Applied,* Vol. 79, 1965, pp. 1-20.

Wood, Wendy, and Alice H. Eagly. "Stages in the Analysis of Persuasive Messages: The Role of Causal Attributions and Message Comprehension." *Journal of Personality and Social Psychology,* Vol. 40, 1981, pp. 246-259.

Zanna, Mark P., James M. Olson, and Russell H. Fazio. "Attitude-Behavior Consistency: An Individual Difference Perspective." *Journal of Personality and Social Psychology,* Vol. 38, 1980, pp. 432-440.

Zeller, Miriam. "Self-Esteem, Reception, and Influenceability." *Journal of Personality and Social Psychology,* Vol. 15, 1970, pp. 87-93.

Index

About the Author

D. Joel Whalen teaches marketing management and communications at Chicago's DePaul University—the largest accredited MBA program in the world, ranked in the Top 10 (1995) by *U.S. News & World Report*. He is an Associate Professor of Marketing and holds a Ph.D. in Marketing Communications (1986) and a Master's in Communication Science from Florida State University (1982). He received his B.S. in Broadcast Journalism at the University of Florida (1972). Whalen created Effective Communication, a popular course taken by all of DePaul's 1,000 first-year graduate students. He wrote the course's textbook, *I See What You Mean*, blending communication and persuasion psychology with his 20 years of business experience.

Whalen leads private communication seminars, teaching businesspeople how to be more successful by being more persuasive. As a successful salesperson, he has consistently set all-time records selling everything from financial services and satellite dishes to advertising. As a young man, he sold water conditioners in his native Florida by walking down dusty country roads, knocking on trailer doors. Later, at the request of the State's Governor (Bob Graham), he designed the program that sold energy conservation to 10 million people. He worked for 20 years in radio and television and became widely known as "Papa Bear"—a top-rated disc jockey in Miami (WSRF-WSHE). He served as campaign media advisor and press secretary to several winning, state-level campaigns and as White House press liaison in Florida. His current research interests include memory and information processing, persuasion psychology, ethics and values, and source credibility.

Whalen has published articles in *Psychology & Marketing, Journal of Business Research, Journal of Business Ethics, Journal of Educational & Psychological Measurement,* the *Design Management Journal,* and the *Journal of Promotions Management,* and in the proceedings of the American Marketing Association, American Marketing Association's Micro-Computers in Marketing Conference; the American Marketing Association Conference on Culture and Sub-Cultural Influences; Southern Marketing Association; and the Decision Science Institute. He has been interviewed by CBS, ABC, and PBS television, *Advertising Age,* the *Atlanta Constitution,* the *Chicago Tribune,* the *Chicago Sun Times,* the *Christian Science Monitor,* the *Financial Times of London, Playboy,* and *Time.*

Whalen has been listed by *Who's Who in America* and was named Advertising Professor of the Year by Chicago's Professional Advertising Clubs. He was twice honored as DePaul's outstanding teacher. Joel Whalen has received five (5) Addy Awards for creative commercials, including an award for one of the first television commercials ever created by a computer.

CPSIA information can be obtained at www.ICGtesting.com
Printed in the USA
LVOW12s2338190913

353252LV00002B/299/A